L.D.R.Wilford

CHEMISTRY

for First Examinations

L. D. R. Wilford

CHEMISTRY

for First Examinations

Blackie

Cover photographs

Both the front cover and back cover photographs have been taken using an optical microscope. The front cover shows pigmentation of polypropylene and the back cover shows a crystalline texture. Both photographs were kindly supplied by ICI Petrochemicals and Plastics Division

ISBN 0 216 91905 3
First published 1987

Published by Blackie and Son Ltd
Bishopbriggs, Glasgow G64 2NZ
7 Leicester Place, London WC2H 7BP

British Library Cataloguing in Publication Data

Wilford, L. D. R.
   Chemistry: for first examinations.
   1. Chemistry
   I. Title
   540   QD33
   ISBN 0-216-91905-3

Filmset by Advanced Filmsetters (Glasgow) Ltd
Printed in Great Britain by Blantyre Printing and Binding Co. Ltd, Glasgow and London

PREFACE

Chemistry is an exciting science subject and this book has been written to show you just how interesting, and straightforward, it really is.

Chemistry must be one of the most colourful subjects and this is why there are so many colour photographs illustrating the text. Many of the photos show how the ideas you have been reading about apply to everyday situations.

> –Do *you* know what acid is found in vinegar?
> –What about lemonade?
> –What *is* an acid anyway?

To help draw your attention to the more important words, scientific terms are printed in bold the first time they are used, and at the end of each chapter you will find a series of questions designed to let you check whether you have fully understood the chapter.

Chemistry for First Examinations will provide you with the information you need to *pass* your chemistry examination. I hope you enjoy using this book.

L. D. R. Wilford
Harrogate

ACKNOWLEDGMENTS

The author and publishers would like to thank the following for permission to reproduce copyright material:

Andrew Lambert who supplied all the photographs with the exception of those listed below.

Public Relations Group, AERE Harwell: Figs 1.12, 2.5, 2.8, 3:10, 3.11(a)
Aerofilms Limited: Fig. 2.1
Ford Motor Company Ltd: Fig. 2.7(a)
David J. McCormick: Figs 2.10, 8.32 (top), 10.26, 12.22
Science Photo Library: Figs 3.1, 4.1, 12.1, 16.1, A9
Cavendish Laboratory, University of Cambridge: Fig. 3.2
The Science Museum, London: Fig. 2.2
ICI Mond Division: Figs 7.15(b), 8.16, 8.19(a) and (b)
Imperial War Museum: Figs 8.12, 15.1, A1, A3
ScotRail: Fig. 8.13
Arnoldo Mondadori Company Ltd: Figs 8.15(a), (b), (c), (d), (e) and (f), 10.1, 10.2
British Alcan Highland Smelters: Fig. 8.17
BP Chemicals: Fig. 8.20
RTZ Services Ltd: Figs 8.22, 8.23, 8.24
British Steel Corporation: Figs 8.25, 8.27
Glasgow Dental Hospital and School: Fig. 8.31
Britoil p.l.c.:   Fig. 8.38, 9.26
Metal Box p.l.c.:   Fig. 8.41
Zinc Development Association: Fig. 8.43
Richard Revels: Fig. 9.1
Ian Corner: Fig. 9.8
Dr G. A. Best: Fig. 9.10
Clyde River Purification Board: Fig. 9.11(b) and (c)
The Director, British Geological Survey (NERC): Crown/NERC copyright reserved   Fig. 9.16
European Space Agency: Fig. 9.27
British Oxygen Company Limited: Fig. 9.28, 12.15, 12.16, 12.17
Camera Press Ltd: Figs 9.32, 12.6
Airship Industries (UK) Ltd: Fig. 9.33
De Beers Ltd: Fig. 10.7, 10.8
National Coal Board: Fig. 10.11, 17.1, 17.7, 17.8, 17.11
Pilkington Brothers p.l.c.:   Fig. 10.27
British Petroleum Company p.l.c.:   Figs 11.3, 11.4, 12.20, 17.9
Mawson Taylor Ltd/Peter McCormick Photography: Fig. 11.21
ICI Petrochemicals and Plastics Division: Figs 11.22, 13.18, 16.2
Amey Roadstone Corporation Ltd: Fig. 11.25
Station Officer Wells, Strathclyde Fire Brigade: Fig. 11.24
Food and Wine from France: Fig. 11.35
The Brewers Society: Fig. 11.36
The Scotch Whisky Association: Fig. 11.37
South American Pictures: Fig. 11.39
Glasgow Royal Infirmary: Figs 11.48, 12.18
Department of Health and Social Security: Fig. 11.51
National Society for Clean Air: Figs 12.7, 12.8, 12.9, 12.10
Doug Scott: Fig. 12.19
Merson Signs: Fig. 12.23
Seaphot/Ken Vaughan: Fig. 12.24
ICI Agricultural Division: Figs 13.6, 13.16, 13.17, 14.26
ICI Fibres Division: Fig. 13.24
Frank Lane Picture Agency/M. J. Thomas: Fig. 13.26
J. Allan Cash Photo Library: Fig. 14.1
The British Sulphur Corporation: Fig. 14.5
Malaysian Rubber Producers Research Association: Fig. 14.6(c)
G-P Inveresk Corporation: Fig. 14.21
North of Scotland Hydro-electric Board: Fig. 17.16
Central Electricity Generating Board: Fig. 17.22
United Kingdom Atomic Energy Authority: Figs A4, A6, A7, A10

Continued on page 262

CONTENTS

PARTICLES

Introduction

Earlier in your study of chemistry you will have found out that 'matter is anything that occupies space and is made up of substances'. These substances belong to what we call the **three states of matter**—they can either be solids, liquids or gases (see Fig. 1.1).

Fig. 1.1   The three states of matter: solid, liquid and gas

Fig. 1.3 Without the expansion gap between the rails, the track would buckle in hot weather

Fig. 1.4 The Coke will take up the shape of the glass

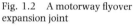

Fig. 1.2 A motorway flyover expansion joint

A **solid** has a definite size and shape (volume) which may be affected by a change in temperature. When a solid is heated it usually increases in size slightly and then decreases on cooling (see Figs 1.2 and 1.3).

A **liquid** has a fixed volume and will take up the shape of any container into which it is poured (see Fig. 1.4). It is also affected by a temperature increase or decrease (see Fig. 1.5). Solids and liquids, unlike gases, are not compressible.

A **gas** has neither a fixed volume nor a fixed shape. It will take up the shape of any container into which it is placed and will spread out evenly within the containing vessel (see Fig. 1.6). Gases are affected quite markedly by a change in temperature. For example, look at how the gas expands readily out of the flask in Fig. 1.7, caused by the warmth of the person's hands. Gases are also affected quite markedly by changes in pressure. For example, the gas cylinder in Fig. 1.8 contains a large volume of gas compressed into a small space.

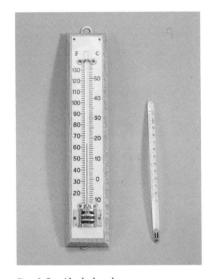

Fig. 1.5 Alcohol and mercury thermometers

Fig. 1.6 The air which keeps this tyre inflated has spread out evenly inside the tyre

Fig. 1.7 The warm hands heat the air in the flask. The air expands and moves down the glass tube to emerge as bubbles in the water

Fig. 1.8 Fortunately gases can be compressed by pressure otherwise the gas in this cylinder would need a much larger container

Evidence for particles

Scientists think that matter is made up of tiny **particles**, so tiny that they cannot be seen even by our most powerful microscopes. This means that even a grain of salt is made up of millions of tiny particles. What evidence have we got that this is the case?

Crystals

Fig. 1.9 shows some large crystals of chrome alum and of copper(II) sulphate. They are very regular in shape. We can perhaps under-stand how these shapes arise by considering a **model**. If we pile polystyrene spheres in a regular way, imagining that each sphere represents a particle within the crystal (see Fig. 1.10), then the shape we get compares very closely with that of part of a chrome alum crystal. From studies like these, as well as others of a more advanced

Fig. 1.9(a)   Chrome alum crystal

Fig. 1.9(b)   Copper(II) sulphate crystal

Fig. 1.10(a)   Imagine that each sphere represents a particle

Fig. 1.10(b)   When piled up the 'particles' form a 'crystal' shape

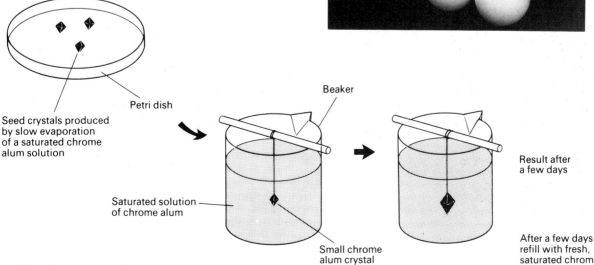

Seed crystals produced by slow evaporation of a saturated chrome alum solution

Petri dish

Beaker

Saturated solution of chrome alum

Small chrome alum crystal

Result after a few days

After a few days refill with fresh, saturated chrome alum solution

Fig. 1.11   Growing a large chrome alum crystal

Fig. 1.12   A modern x-ray crystallography instrument used for studying crystal structure

Fig. 1.13   A model of a sodium chloride (salt) crystal

nature (see Fig. 1.12), scientists have confirmed that not only crystals but all matter is made up of particles.

Generally, in crystals of any one substance it is found that the particles present are always packed in the same way. However, in different crystal substances the particles may be packed in different ways. For example, sodium chloride (salt) has its particles arranged in the way shown in Fig. 1.13.

Gases and liquids

You will be familiar with cooking smells coming from your kitchen and spreading throughout your home. Smells also originate in chemistry laboratories and may spread throughout the school in a similar way. These are examples of **diffusion**. Diffusion is the spreading out of a gas. It takes place in a haphazard or random way (see Fig. 1.15).

This sort of behaviour can be seen quite easily when a little dark red liquid bromine is placed in the bottom of a gas jar and a second gas jar placed on top of the first (see Fig. 1.16). As you can see from Fig. 1.16, after one day the brown/red fumes of gaseous bromine have spread evenly throughout both gas jars.

Fig. 1.14   Cooking smells diffuse outwards from your kitchen!

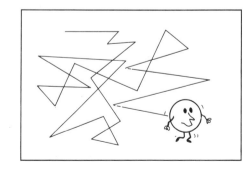

Fig. 1.15   This particle is following a random path

Day 1

Day 2

Fig. 1.16   Bromine is placed in a gas jar and a second gas jar placed on top. After a day the bromine fumes have diffused throughout both jars

Diffusion will also take place in liquids but it is a much slower process because the particles are moving more slowly in liquids than gases. When a solution of copper(II) sulphate is lowered into a beaker of water through a thistle funnel (see Fig. 1.17) the blue solution forms a layer in the bottom of the beaker. Over a period of a few days the blue colour spreads throughout. This is caused by the diffusion of the copper(II) sulphate particles.

In liquids and gases where diffusion is taking place we are dealing with what is called **intimate mixing** (see Fig. 1.18). The particle model appears to give us a reasonable explanation if we consider that there is sufficient space between the particles in a liquid or gas for the particles of the other substances to move into.

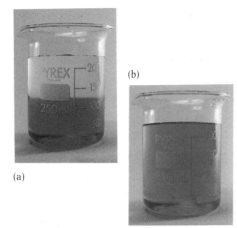
(b)

(a)

Fig. 1.17(a) and (b)   Diffusion of copper(II) sulphate

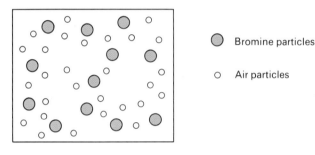

◉ Bromine particles

○ Air particles

Fig. 1.18   Intimate mixing of particles

Do different particles diffuse at different rates?

If a piece of cotton wool soaked in concentrated hydrochloric acid and a piece of cotton wool soaked in concentrated ammonia solution are put in the opposite ends of a dry glass tube, as shown in Fig. 1.19, a white cloud forms after about ten minutes. The white cloud is of a substance called ammonium chloride which forms when ammonia gas reacts with hydrogen chloride gas released from hydrochloric acid (see Fig. 1.20). This white cloud forms in the position shown because the ammonia particles are lighter than the hydrogen chloride particles. Being lighter, the ammonia particles move faster than the hydrogen chloride particles. It is generally found that lighter particles move faster than heavier particles at the same temperature.

Fig. 1.20   White fumes of ammonium chloride form when hydrogen chloride and ammonia particles diffuse and then react together

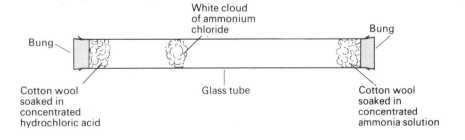

Bung

White cloud of ammonium chloride

Bung

Cotton wool soaked in concentrated hydrochloric acid

Glass tube

Cotton wool soaked in concentrated ammonia solution

Fig. 1.19

Brownian movement

In 1827 Robert Brown, a botanist, used a microscope to observe what happened to pollen grains suspended in water. He noted that the pollen grains were moving about in a very erratic way. It was thirty six years later that another scientist, called Wiener, explained what Brown had observed. Wiener said that the erratic movement of the pollen grains was due to their bombardment by much smaller, but more rapidly moving, water particles. The movement, therefore, of visible particles (pollen grains) caused by smaller but invisible ones (water particles) has been called **Brownian movement**.

You will have seen movement similar to this in a smoke cell (see Fig. 1.21). In the smoke cell the movement of the visible smoke particles is caused by the smaller invisible air particles colliding with them (see Fig. 1.22).

Fig. 1.21   A smoke cell

The three states of matter and particle theory

From the evidence gathered by scientists from experiments similar to those we have just discussed, as well as those including X-ray crystallography (see Fig. 1.12), it is thought that the particles in the three states of matter behave in the following ways.

In *solids* the particles are arranged in a very orderly way, vibrating a little from side to side, about a fixed point (see Fig. 1.23).

In *liquids* the particles are still quite close together but they are now moving around quite quickly in a random way. The particles collide with one another quite often (see Fig. 1.23).

In *gases* the particles are relatively far apart. They are moving at very high speeds—much more rapidly than in a liquid. They collide with each other but less often than in a liquid (see Fig. 1.23).

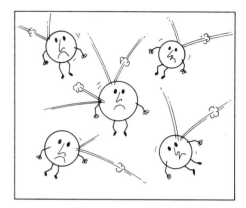

Fig. 1.22   Smoke particles being bombarded by air particles

A summary of the properties of solids, liquids and gases is shown in Table 1.1.

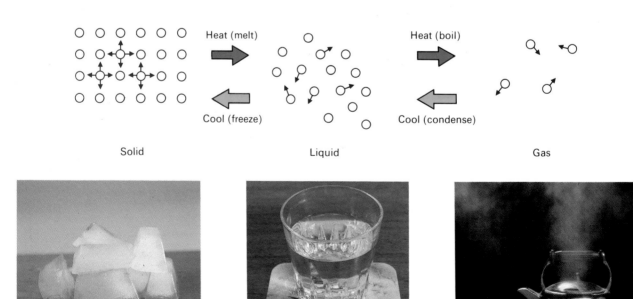

Fig. 1.23   The three states of matter

State / Property	Solid	Liquid	Gas
Shape	Constant	Takes up the shape of the container	Takes up the shape of the whole container
Volume	Constant at a given temperature	Constant at a given temperature	Variable—will spread throughout a given container. However, if the temperature and pressure are fixed the volume of gas is also fixed
Movement of particles	Vibrations only	Move quite quickly with frequent collisions	Very fast moving with fewer collisions
Density	High	Medium	Low
Effect of heat	Expands slightly	Expands slightly—more than solids	Expands much more than liquids or solids
Effect of increased pressure	Pressure has hardly any effect on volume		A large decrease in volume

Table 1.1

Sublimation

Iodine is an example of a substance which changes directly from a solid to a gas and back again without first melting to form a liquid. When a substance undergoes these sorts of changes of state it is said to **sublime**. This process is known as **sublimation**.

Fig. 1.24 shows iodine being heated. It changes directly to a purple vapour from a dark grey solid.

Fig. 1.24 When heated, iodine changes from a dark grey solid to a purple vapour. It sublimes

Physical change

During a physical change no new chemical substance is formed. The changes of state from

$$\text{solid} \longrightarrow \text{liquid} \qquad \text{(melting)}$$

$$\text{and} \qquad \text{liquid} \longrightarrow \text{gas} \qquad \text{(boiling)}$$

and the reverse processes shown in Fig. 1.23 are examples of physical changes. Other examples include sublimation and evaporation.

─────────────────────── QUESTIONS ───────────────────────

1 Explain the following in molecular terms.
  a) A windy day is a good drying day!
  b) When you come home from school and open the front door, you can smell your tea being cooked.
  c) A football is blown up until it is hard on a hot summer afternoon. In the evening the temperature falls and the football now feels softer.
  d) When you take a block of butter out of the 'fridge' it is quite hard. However, after about 15 minutes it is soft enough to spread.

2 Describe what happens to the particles in a piece of metal when it is heated from room temperature to 50°C above its melting point.

3 a) Draw three diagrams to show the arrangement of the particles in:
      i) solids;
     ii) liquids;
    iii) gases.
  b) Write a few sentences to describe the movement of particles in these three states of matter in (a).

4 Explain the meaning of each of the following terms:
  a) diffusion;
  b) intimate mixing;
  c) random movement;
  d) sublime;
  e) physical change.
  In each case include in your answer an example to help with your explanation.

5 Some liquid bromine was placed in the bottom of a gas jar. The gas jar was then covered and left for several hours.

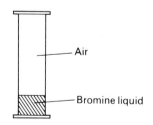

  a) What precautions would you take to ensure this experiment progressed safely?
  b) Describe what you would see after:
      i) a few minutes;
     ii) several hours.
  c) Explain your answer to (b) using your ideas of particles.
  d) What is the name of the physical process that takes place in this experiment?

6

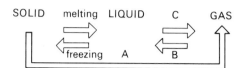

The above diagram shows the three states of matter and how they can be interchanged. Only two changes have been shown.
  a) Name the changes A, B, and C.
  b) Name a substance which will undergo change A.
  c) Name a substance which will undergo changes from solid→liquid→gas between 0°C and 100°C.
  d) Describe what happens to the particles of the solid during change A.

7 a) State what is meant by:
      i) Brownian movement;
     ii) the diffusion of gases.
  b) State how these phenomena provide evidence for the particulate nature of matter. (5)
  (WJEC 1983)

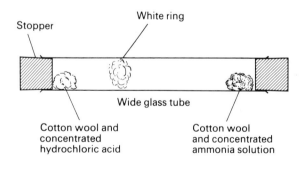

8 The above apparatus was set up. Give explanations for the following observations:
  a) the formation of the white ring;
  b) the position of the ring. (3)
  (WJEC 1984)

9 a) The kinetic theory of matter states that all substances contain particles which are moving. Use this theory to explain the following.
      i) A solid has its own shape, but a liquid takes up the shape of the container. (2)

ii) The pressure exerted by a gas in a sealed container increases with the temperature of the gas. (2)

iii) A gas will move to fill any container. (2)

b) Pollen grains suspended in water are observed using a microscope. Smoke particles in air are also observed.

i) What would you see in both cases? (1)

ii) How would the behaviour of the smoke particles differ from that of the pollen grains? (1)

iii) What causes the particles to behave in the way you have described in (b)(i)? (2)

(NEA 1984)

ATOMS, FORMULAE AND EQUATIONS

Fig. 2.1   Everything around us is made from combinations of 92 basic substances—the elements

The world around us is made up of a very large number of materials. However, if these are examined more closely it can be shown that 92 basic substances exist. Everything else is made up of combinations of some of these substances. These basic or fundamental substances are called the **elements.** In 1803 John Dalton (see Fig. 2.2) suggested that each element was composed of its own particular kind of particle. He called these particles **atoms.**

Elements

An element is a single substance that is made up of only one kind of atom and which cannot be split up into anything simpler by any chemical process. For example, magnesium (see Fig. 2.3) is an element. It is made up of only magnesium atoms. No matter what you do with it, it is not possible to obtain a simpler substance than magnesium from it. You can only make more complicated substances from it such as magnesium carbonate or magnesium oxide.

Fig. 2.2   John Dalton

Fig. 2.3 Magnesium

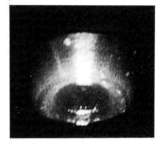

Fig. 2.4 A pie chart of the elements which make up the Earth

Oxygen 49.5%
Silicon 25.7%
Others (over 80 elements) 1.1%
Aluminium 7.4%
Titanium 0.4%
Iron 4.7%
Hydrogen 0.9%
Magnesium 1.9%
Calcium 3.4%
Potassium 2.4%
Sodium 2.6%

As many as 105 elements have been identified. Of these, 15 do not occur in nature and have to be man-made, e.g. plutonium and curium. However, the vast majority of elements occur naturally, usually in combination with other elements. Most of the elements are solid and **metallic** like chromium, copper and lead, whilst some are solid and **non-metallic** like sulphur and carbon. Some like mercury (a metal) and bromine (a non-metal) are liquid, whilst other non-metals such as hydrogen, helium, neon, oxygen and nitrogen are gaseous at room temperature and pressure (see Fig. 2.6).

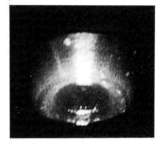

Fig. 2.5 Curium—a man-made element. Curium generates visible light. It was this light that was used to produce the photograph

Fig. 2.6

(a) Chrome-plated bath tap

(b) Mercury

(c) Neon sign

(d) Bromine

(e) Copper kettle

(f) Carbon and sulphur

(g) Lead pipe

Table 2.1 shows physical data for some common metallic and non-metallic elements. You will notice that many metals have high densities, melting points and boiling points, and that most non-metals have low densities, melting points and boiling points. Table 2.2 gives a summary of the different properties of metals and non-metals.

Element	Metal/ non-metal	Density $(g\,cm^{-3})$	Melting point (°C)	Boiling point (°C)
Aluminium	Metal	2.70	660	2350
Copper	Metal	8.93	1085	2580
Gold	Metal	19.28	1064	2850
Iron	Metal	7.87	1540	2760
Lead	Metal	11.34	328	1760
Magnesium	Metal	1.74	650	1100
Silver	Metal	10.50	962	2160
Zinc	Metal	7.14	420	913
Carbon	Non-metal	2.27	3700	Sublimes
Hydrogen	Non-metal	0.09*	−259	−253
Oxygen	Non-metal	1.46†	−219	−183
Sulphur	Non-metal	2.08	115	445

*At −266.8 °C
†At −252.7 °C

Table 2.1   Source—*Tables of Physical and Chemical Constants*, 14th Edition,
G. W. C. Kaye and T. H. Laby, Longman 1973.

Fig. 2.7(a)   Metals can be pressed into different shapes and are said to be malleable

Fig. 2.7(b)   If a material can be drawn into a wire it is said to be ductile

Fig. 2.7(c)   Carbon—a non-metal—is neither malleable nor ductile. It is said to be brittle

Property	Metal	Non-metal
Physical state at room temperature	Usually solid	Usually gas or liquid but can be solid
Malleability	Yes	No—usually brittle or soft when solid
Ductility	Yes	
Appearance (solids only)	Shiny	Dull
Melting point	High	Low
Boiling point	High	Low
Density	High	Low
Conductance (electrical and thermal)	Good	Very poor

Table 2.2

Atoms

Atoms are the smallest particles of which elements are made. They are extremely small. Indeed, if we take hydrogen (the smallest atom known) each atom has a diameter of 0.000 000 01 mm (or 1×10^{-8} mm). About 100 000 000 hydrogen atoms would have to be placed side by side along the edge of your ruler to fill the 1 mm division. Also each atom of hydrogen weighs

0.000 000 000 000 000 000 000 00166 g (or 1.66×10^{-24} g)

and there are approximately

602 000 000 000 000 000 000 000 (6.02×10^{23}) atoms in 1 g

of the element. Since we can only weigh, accurately, objects up to 0.001 g (or 10^{-3} g) in the laboratory, it is not possible for us to weigh a single hydrogen atom, or any other atom for that matter. In fact to find the mass of a single atom a complicated piece of apparatus called a **mass spectrograph** is used (see Fig. 2.8).

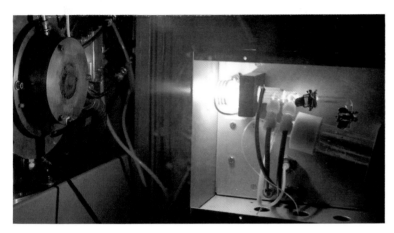

Fig. 2.8 Mass spectrometer

In spite of the extremely small size of atoms, scientists have managed to find out a great deal about them. For example, they have found that atoms consist of an even smaller centre, called a **nucleus**, which is surrounded by clouds of **electrons**. In the next chapter (page 24) we shall look more closely at the discoveries scientists have made about the structure of the atom.

Symbols for the elements

It is convenient to have a simple shorthand system for representing the large number of known elements. In 1818, Jöns Jacob Berzelius introduced a simple set of symbols which could be used to represent the elements. In this system, which is the one used today, the symbol for the element was the first letter of its English or Latin name written as a capital. Where several elements had the same initial letter a second or subsequent letter was added. A list of some elements with their corresponding symbols and physical states is shown in Table 2.3.

The complete list of the elements with their corresponding symbols is shown in the **periodic table** on page 32.

Element	Symbol	Physical state at room temperature and pressure
Aluminium	Al	Solid
Barium	Ba	Solid
Bromine	Br	Liquid
Calcium	Ca	Solid
Carbon	C	Solid
Chlorine	Cl	Gas
Copper (cuprum*)	Cu	Solid
Fluorine	F	Gas
Helium	He	Gas
Hydrogen	H	Gas
Iodine	I	Solid
Iron (ferrum*)	Fe	Solid
Lead (plumbum*)	Pb	Solid
Magnesium	Mg	Solid
Mercury (hydra-gyrum*)	Hg	Liquid
Neon	Ne	Gas
Nitrogen	N	Gas
Oxygen	O	Gas
Phosphorus	P	Solid
Potassium (kalium*)	K	Solid
Silicon	Si	Solid
Silver (argentum*)	Ag	Solid
Sodium (natrium*)	Na	Solid
Sulphur	S	Solid
Tin (stannum*)	Sn	Solid
Zinc	Zn	Solid

Table 2.3 *Latin name

Molecules

Some elements such as nitrogen, hydrogen, oxygen, fluorine and chlorine exist as units which we call **molecules**. Each molecule consists of two atoms joined together chemically as shown in Fig. 2.9. Elements whose molecules contain two identical atoms joined together are said to be **diatomic**.

Some of the non-metal gaseous elements are composed of separate, individual atoms—like the neon gas in some of the signs in Fig. 2.10. When an element exists as separate atoms then it is said to be **monatomic**. Other monatomic, gaseous elements include helium, krypton and xenon.

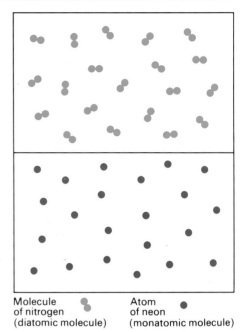

Molecule of nitrogen (diatomic molecule)   Atom of neon (monatomic molecule)

Fig. 2.9   Nitrogen and neon molecules

Fig. 2.10   Neon signs at Piccadilly Circus, London

In chemical shorthand a 'molecule' of neon is written as 'Ne' whilst molecules of helium, krypton and xenon are written as 'He', 'Kr' and 'Xe' respectively. Single molecules of nitrogen, hydrogen, oxygen and fluorine are written as 'N_2', 'H_2', 'O_2' and 'F_2' respectively.

Many **compounds** also exist as molecules. Some examples are shown in Table 2.4. Water consists of molecules with two hydrogen atoms joined chemically to one oxygen atom, carbon dioxide consists of molecules with two oxygen atoms joined chemically to one carbon atom and sulphur dioxide consists of molecules with two oxygen atoms joined chemically to one sulphur atom. These three examples are shown in Fig. 2.11.

Compound	'One molecule'
Water	H_2O
Carbon dioxide	CO_2
Sulphur dioxide	SO_2
Methane (natural gas)	CH_4
Ammonia	NH_3
Hydrogen chloride	HCl
Ethanol (alcohol)	C_2H_5OH

Table 2.4

Fig. 2.11   Molecules of carbon dioxide, water and sulphur dioxide

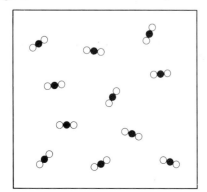

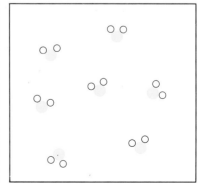

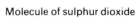

Molecule of carbon dioxide   Molecule of water   Molecule of sulphur dioxide

Compounds

Earlier in your chemistry course you will have seen metals such as copper and magnesium heated in air. Both these metals combine (join) with the oxygen out of the air to produce a new substance. In the case of copper a black ash is produced which coats the copper (see Fig. 2.12(a)). This is copper(II) oxide. In the case of magnesium a white ash, magnesium oxide, is produced (see Fig. 2.12(b)). These new substances are compounds. Compounds are substances which are composed of two or more elements combined together chemically. Magnesium oxide is a compound of magnesium combined chemically with oxygen, whilst copper(II) oxide is a compound of copper combined chemically with oxygen.

There is a shorthand way of describing the formation of these compounds. In the case of magnesium reacting with oxygen:

$$\text{magnesium} + \text{oxygen} \xrightarrow{\text{heat}} \text{magnesium oxide}$$

whilst in the case of copper reacting with oxygen:

$$\text{copper} + \text{oxygen} \xrightarrow{\text{heat}} \text{copper(II) oxide}$$

These are **word equations** and they show that the metals magnesium and copper react with oxygen, when heated, to give the new substances magnesium oxide and copper(II) oxide respectively. Table 2.5 shows a series of common compounds along with their constituent elements.

When the reactions detailed above take place the metal oxide has a greater mass than the original metal. This is because the compounds produced contain the mass of the metal plus the mass of the oxygen. In the case of magnesium oxide—the mass of magnesium metal plus the mass of oxygen from the air.

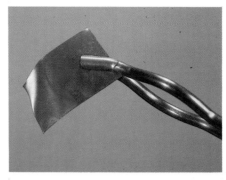
Fig. 2.12(a) Copper after heating in air

Fig. 2.12(b) Magnesium oxide

Common name of the compound	Chemical name of the compound	Elements present
Salt	Sodium chloride	Sodium (Na) Chlorine (Cl)
Sand	Silicon oxide	Silicon (Si) Oxygen (O)
Water	Hydrogen oxide	Hydrogen (H) Oxygen (O)
Sugar	Sucrose	Carbon (C) Hydrogen (H) Oxygen (O)
Rust	Iron(III) oxide	Iron (Fe) Oxygen (O)
Vinegar	Ethanoic acid	Carbon (C) Hydrogen (H) Oxygen (O)
Natural gas	Methane	Carbon (C) Hydrogen (H)

Table 2.5

Fig. 2.13 Some of the common compounds listed in Table 2.5

In the formation of a compound energy is usually released. For example, when magnesium oxide is formed a lot of heat (and light) is produced. It is said to be an **exothermic reaction** (see page 231).

When a new substance is formed during a chemical reaction, we say a **chemical change** is taking place. Both the above reactions are examples of chemical changes—new substances copper(II) oxide and magnesium oxide have been formed.

Mixtures

Mixtures of elements such as iron and sulphur which have been brought into close contact with each other, but which have not chemically combined, may be easily separated. It is found that a magnet will easily separate the iron from the sulphur (see Fig. 2.14). The components of a mixture can be mixed in any proportion and still retain their original properties. Compounds, however, have a definite composition. This means that the proportion by mass of the component elements is fixed. Also, by joining the elements together chemically, the properties of the compounds become quite different from those of the elements they are composed of. This is certainly the case for iron and sulphur.

$$\text{iron} + \text{sulphur} \xrightarrow{\text{heat}} \text{iron(II) sulphide}$$

The compound iron(II) sulphide is formed with the evolution of a lot of heat. It is a highly exothermic reaction. Iron(II) sulphide (as well as magnesium and copper(II) oxides referred to earlier) certainly has different chemical properties from those of its constituent elements (see Table 2.6). The splitting up of these compounds into their constituent elements is a very difficult process.

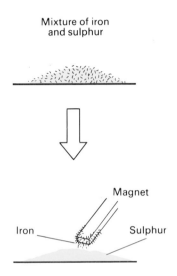

Fig. 2.14   A magnet separates the iron from the sulphur

Substance	Appearance	Effect of a magnet	Effect of dilute hydrochloric acid
Iron	Dark grey powder	Attracted to it	Very little action when cold. When warm a gas is produced with a lot of bubbling (effervescence)
Sulphur	Yellow powder	None	No effect hot or cold
Iron/sulphur mixture	Dirty yellow powder	Iron powder attracted to it	Iron powder reacts as above
Iron sulphide	Dark grey solid	No effect	A foul smelling gas is produced. Some bubbling is seen

Table 2.6   Comparison of a mixture and a compound

Mixtures may contain elements (as in the case of iron and sulphur), compounds (as in sea water, ink, beer and milk) or compounds and elements (as in the air). The air consists of compounds such as water vapour and carbon dioxide gas as well as the important elements oxygen, nitrogen, helium, neon, krypton and xenon (see Fig. 2.15). A summary of the major differences between compounds and mixtures is given in Table 2.7.

Fig. 2.15   Examples of mixtures: solder (tin and lead); the air and sea water

Compound	Mixture
The composition is always the same	The composition can vary
It is a single substance	It contains two or more substances
The properties are very different to those of the component elements	The properties are those of the individual elements
The components can only be separated by chemical reaction	The components may be separated quite easily by physical means
When the new substance is formed it involves chemical change	No chemical change takes place when a mixture is formed

Table 2.7   Major differences between compounds and mixtures

Formulae

The symbols for the elements can be used to determine the 'symbols' for compounds. The 'symbol' of a compound is called a **formula**. For example, the formula for copper(II) oxide is 'CuO', magnesium oxide is 'MgO' and iron(II) sulphide is 'FeS'.

The formula for copper(II) oxide tells us the ratio of the atoms of the elements present:

1 copper atom : 1 oxygen atom

similarly in the cases of magnesium oxide and iron(II) sulphide:

MgO — 1 magnesium atom : 1 oxygen atom
FeS —   1 iron atom : 1 sulphur atom.

Generally, the formula of a compound is a series of symbols and numbers which show the atoms of each element present. Table 2.8 shows the formulae of some other compounds.

Compound	Formula	Atoms present
Water	H_2O	2 hydrogen atoms : 1 oxygen atom
Carbon dioxide	CO_2	1 carbon atom : 2 oxygen atoms
Sulphur dioxide	SO_2	1 sulphur atom : 2 oxygen atoms
Ethanol	C_2H_5OH	2 carbon atoms : 6 hydrogen atoms : 1 oxygen atom
Copper(II) sulphate	$CuSO_4$	1 copper atom : 1 sulphur atom : 4 oxygen atoms
Nitric acid	HNO_3	1 hydrogen atom : 1 nitrogen atom : 3 oxygen atoms

Table 2.8

Table 2.9 shows a list of formulae for some common compounds. In this table you will notice that some of the formulae are more complicated and have brackets in them. For example, calcium hydroxide is $Ca(OH)_2$. The '2' placed after the bracket multiplies all the atoms in the bracket by that number. Therefore this formula represents a ratio of:

1 calcium atom : 2 oxygen atoms : 2 hydrogen atoms.

Compound	Formula
Aluminium oxide	Al_2O_3
Carbon monoxide	CO
Carbon dioxide	CO_2
Copper(II) oxide	CuO
Calcium oxide	CaO
Magnesium oxide	MgO
Sulphur dioxide	SO_2
Sodium hydroxide	$NaOH$
Calcium hydroxide	$Ca(OH)_2$
Aluminium hydroxide	$Al(OH)_3$
Potassium hydroxide	KOH
Nitric acid	HNO_3
Sodium nitrate	$NaNO_3$
Copper(II) nitrate	$Cu(NO_3)_2$
Ammonium nitrate	NH_4NO_3
Sodium sulphate	Na_2SO_4
Iron(III) sulphate	$Fe_2(SO_4)_3$
Aluminium sulphate	$Al_2(SO_4)_3$
Calcium sulphate	$CaSO_4$

Compound	Formula
Ammonium sulphate	$(NH_4)_2SO_4$
Hydrochloric acid	HCl
Potassium chloride	KCl
Sodium chloride	$NaCl$
Aluminium chloride	$AlCl_3$
Ammonium chloride	NH_4Cl
Copper(I) chloride	$CuCl$
Copper(II) chloride	$CuCl_2$
Zinc sulphide	ZnS
Magnesium hydrogencarbonate	$Mg(HCO_3)_2$
Calcium hydrogencarbonate	$Ca(HCO_3)_2$
Silver nitrate	$AgNO_3$
Sulphuric acid	H_2SO_4
Copper(II) sulphate	$CuSO_4$
Iron(II) sulphate	$FeSO_4$
Sodium hydrogencarbonate	$NaHCO_3$
Magnesium carbonate	$MgCO_3$
Sodium carbonate	Na_2CO_3
Calcium carbonate	$CaCO_3$

Table 2.9

Table 2.10 shows the ratio of atoms present in some of the complicated formulae in Table 2.9.

Compound	Formula	Atoms present
Aluminium hydroxide	$Al(OH)_3$	1 aluminium atom : 3 oxygen atoms : 3 hydrogen atoms
Ammonium sulphate	$(NH_4)_2SO_4$	2 nitrogen atoms : 8 hydrogen atoms : 1 sulphur atom : 4 oxygen atoms
Calcium hydrogencarbonate	$Ca(HCO_3)_2$	1 calcium atom : 2 hydrogen atoms : 2 carbon atoms : 6 oxygen atoms
Iron(III) sulphate	$Fe_2(SO_4)_3$	2 iron atoms : 3 sulphur atoms : 12 oxygen atoms

Table 2.10

Why is the formula of calcium hydroxide written as $Ca(OH)_2$ instead of CaO_2H_2? This is because the compound is a hydroxide and possesses 'OH' as a definite grouping of atoms. Table 2.11 contains other examples of compounds containing specific groupings of atoms.

Group of atoms present	Name of grouping	Examples of compounds
NO_3	Nitrate	$NaNO_3$, $Cu(NO_3)_2$
CO_3	Carbonate	Na_2CO_3, K_2CO_3
SO_4	Sulphate	$CaSO_4$, $(NH_4)_2SO_4$
Cl	Chloride	$NaCl$, $CuCl_2$
S	Sulphide	ZnS, FeS
O	Oxide	MgO, CO_2

Table 2.11

The ending '-ate' in the names of compounds indicates that the compound probably contains oxygen. For example:

sodium sulph<u>ate</u>—Na_2SO_4
calcium sulph<u>ate</u>—$CaSO_4$.

The ending '-ide' usually indicates the presence of two elements only. For example:

copper(II) ox<u>ide</u>—CuO
zinc sulph<u>ide</u>—ZnS
sodium chlor<u>ide</u>—$NaCl$.

Valency

We can work out the formulae of the compounds shown in Table 2.9 by using the idea of 'valency'. You will find out more about what valency is and how it is used by thinking about the following examples.

You have seen that water contains 1 atom of oxygen combined with 2 atoms of hydrogen (H_2O), whilst in carbon dioxide 1 atom of carbon is combined with 2 atoms of oxygen (CO_2). If we allow the hydrogen to have a combining power of 1, then oxygen must have a combining power of 2, since 2 hydrogen atoms are required to combine with each oxygen atom to produce water—H_2O. With carbon dioxide, if oxygen has a combining power of 2 then carbon must have a combining power of 4, since it requires to join with 2 oxygen atoms to produce CO_2. This measure of the combining power of an atom of an element is called the **valency** of that atom. Table 2.12 shows a series of elements along with their symbols and valencies.

Valencies are always small whole numbers or zero. The elements with a valency of zero are those which do not normally form compounds (see Chapter 3, page 40). These elements include helium,

Element	Symbol	Valency
Helium	He	0
Neon	Ne	0
Argon	Ar	0
Hydrogen	H	1
Fluorine	F	1
Chlorine	Cl	1
Bromine	Br	1
Lithium	Li	1
Sodium	Na	1
Potassium	K	1
Silver	Ag	1
Oxygen	O	2
Calcium	Ca	2
Barium	Ba	2
Sulphur	S	2, 4 or 6
Copper	Cu	1 or 2
Zinc	Zn	2
Magnesium	Mg	2
Iron	Fe	2 or 3
Lead	Pb	2 or 4
Nitrogen	N	3 or 5
Aluminium	Al	3
Phosphorus	P	3 or 5
Carbon	C	4
Silicon	Si	4

Table 2.12

neon and argon. They are known collectively as the **noble** or **inert gases**. Also in Table 2.9, the compounds of iron are named iron(II) sulphate and iron(III) sulphate showing which valency of iron is being used in the particular compound.

It has been found convenient to give valencies to certain groups of elements. Table 2.13 contains a series of common groups along with their valencies.

Group of Elements	Formula	Valency
Ammonium	NH_4	1
Hydrogen-carbonate	HCO_3	1
Hydroxide	OH	1
Nitrate	NO_3	1
Carbonate	CO_3	2
Sulphate	SO_4	2

Table 2.13

Using valencies

Consider the following examples.

1 What is the formula of the compound formed between aluminium and chlorine?

	Aluminium		Chlorine
Symbols/formulae	Al		Cl
Valencies	3		1
Balance valencies	3	balanced by	1($\times 3$)
Formula		$AlCl_3$	

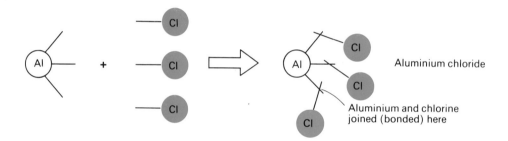

Fig. 2.16

2 What is the formula of the compound formed between sodium and the sulphate group?

	Sodium		Sulphate
Symbols/formulae	Na		SO_4
Valencies	1		2
Balance valencies	1($\times 2$)	balanced by	2
Formula		Na_2SO_4	

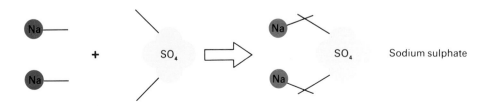

Fig. 2.17

There is a simple rule which may be followed to obtain formulae. For example, using example 1:

$$\text{valency} = 3 \diagdown \diagup 1 = \text{valency}$$
$$\text{Al} \qquad\qquad \text{Cl}$$
$$\text{Al}_1 \diagup \diagdown \text{Cl}_3$$

Formula = $AlCl_3$

Chemical equations

Word equations are a useful way of representing chemical reactions. However, a better method is to use the symbols and formulae of the substances reacting (the reactants). In this way we can produce what is called a **chemical equation**. When writing chemical equations it is important to remember that the same atoms must be present at the end of the chemical reaction as were in the starting materials. They will be rearranged to make new substances but the *number of atoms will be unchanged*.

The word equation we wrote earlier in this chapter for the reaction of iron when heated with sulphur is:

$$\text{iron} + \text{sulphur} \xrightarrow{\text{heat}} \text{iron sulphide}$$

When we replace the words with symbols and formulae we obtain:

$$\text{Fe} + \text{S} \xrightarrow{\text{heat}} \text{FeS}$$

In this style of equation we can show the physical states of the reactants and products:

$$\underset{\text{(solid)}}{\text{Fe}} + \underset{\text{(solid)}}{\text{S}} \xrightarrow{\text{heat}} \underset{\text{(solid)}}{\text{FeS}}$$

We can replace the word 'solid' by the letter 's', i.e.

$$\text{Fe}_{(s)} + \text{S}_{(s)} \xrightarrow{\text{heat}} \text{FeS}_{(s)}$$

We must now balance the equation so that the number of atoms shown on the left-hand side equals the number of atoms shown on the right-hand side. As you can see from the above equation it is already a **balanced chemical equation**.

Now consider the more complicated case of magnesium burning in oxygen to produce magnesium oxide. The word equation we wrote earlier in the chapter for this reaction is:

$$\text{magnesium} + \text{oxygen} \xrightarrow{\text{heat}} \text{magnesium oxide}$$

When we replace the words with symbols and formulae it is important to remember that the oxygen involved in this reaction is from the air. It will be reacting as oxygen molecules and must therefore be shown as 'O_2'.

$$\text{Mg} + O_2 \xrightarrow{\text{heat}} \text{MgO}$$

$$\underset{\text{(solid)}}{\text{Mg}} + \underset{\text{(gas)}}{O_2} \xrightarrow{\text{heat}} \underset{\text{(solid)}}{\text{MgO}}$$

We can replace the words 'solid' and 'gas' by the letters 's' and 'g' respectively.

$$\text{Mg}_{(s)} + O_{2(g)} \xrightarrow{\text{heat}} \text{MgO}_{(s)}$$

We must now balance the equation. There are two atoms of oxygen on the left (O_2) whilst there is only one on the right in the formula of MgO. We *cannot* change the formula of magnesium oxide, since this would change the ratio of the atoms present in that compound. Therefore, to produce the necessary two oxygen atoms on the right-hand side we will need 2MgO (this means $2 \times$ MgO).

$$Mg_{(s)} + O_{2(g)} \xrightarrow{\text{heat}} 2MgO_{(s)}$$

We have balanced the number of oxygen atoms on the left-hand and right-hand sides. However, as you can see, this will give us two atoms of magnesium on the right-hand side whilst there is only one on the left-hand side. We need, therefore, 2Mg.

$$2Mg_{(s)} + O_{2(g)} \xrightarrow{\text{heat}} 2MgO_{(s)}$$

This is now the balanced chemical equation for the reaction between magnesium and oxygen. This may be interpreted in the following way—two magnesium atoms react with one molecule of oxygen gas, when heated, to produce two units of magnesium oxide.

Throughout the rest of this book you will come across chemical equations which may be more complicated than those in this chapter; however, they will all be balanced in a similar way.

--- QUESTIONS ---

1 Write down the ratio of atoms represented by the formulae of the following compounds:
   a) magnesium carbonate;
   b) aluminium oxide;
   c) calcium hydrogencarbonate;
   d) copper nitrate;
   e) ammonium nitrate.

2 Using the valencies on pages 19 and 20 work out the formula and name of the compound formed when:
   a) zinc combines with chlorine;
   b) potassium combines with chlorine;
   c) silicon combines with oxygen;
   d) potassium combines with the sulphate group;
   e) silver combines with oxygen;
   f) calcium combines with the carbonate group;
   g) lead combines with the hydroxide group.

3 Balance the following equations:
   a) $Al + Br_2 \longrightarrow AlBr_3$
   b) $Mg + CO_2 \longrightarrow MgO + C$
   c) $Ca + H_2O \longrightarrow Ca(OH)_2 + H_2$
   d) $Zn + O_2 \longrightarrow ZnO$
   e) $ZnO + HNO_3 \longrightarrow Zn(NO_3)_2 + H_2O$
   f) $NaHCO_3 \longrightarrow Na_2CO_3 + H_2O + CO_2$

4 Air, potassium, water, argon, dilute sulphuric acid, carbon dioxide, phosphorus, diamond, brass, zinc, sea water, sodium chloride.
   Which of the above substances are:
   a) metallic elements;
   b) non-metallic elements;
   c) compounds;
   d) mixtures?

5 Helium, oil, air, mercury, water, copper, carbon monoxide, salt, solder.
   Which of the above is:
   a) a liquid compound;
   b) a solid compound;
   c) a solid element;
   d) a gaseous mixture?

6 A mixture of iron filings and sulphur was heated. A red glow was seen to spread through the mixture and a dark grey solid was formed.
   a) What did the red glow indicate?
   b) Name the dark grey solid.
   c) The dark grey solid is a compound. Explain the difference between the mixture of iron and sulphur and the compound formed from them.
   d) Write a word equation and a balanced chemical equation for the reaction between iron and sulphur.

7 Which of the following are: (i) chemical changes; and (ii) physical changes?
   a) adding sugar to a cup of tea;
   b) digestion of a meal;
   c) expansion and contraction of telephone wires;
   d) melting of ice cubes;
   e) burning a candle;
   f) switching on an electric fire.

3

STRUCTURE OF THE ATOM AND THE PERIODIC TABLE

Fig. 3.1 A field ion micrograph of atoms of iridium

In Chapter 2 you learned that all the elements are made up of very tiny particles called atoms. When John Dalton developed his atomic theory he stated that atoms of any one element were identical and that each atom was indivisible. However, in the last one hundred years it has been proved by scientists such as Moseley, Thomson, Rutherford and Chadwick that the atom is in fact made up of even smaller particles.

Electrons, protons and neutrons

It has been found that the atoms of elements are made up of *three* 'sub-atomic' particles. These particles are found in distinct and separate regions within the atom. All of these particles are extremely light. They are so light that their masses cannot be measured in grams—**atomic mass units** (a.m.u.) are used instead.

Two of these particles possess equal and opposite electric charges, whilst the third has no charge. A summary of each type of particle, its charge and mass is shown in Table 3.1.

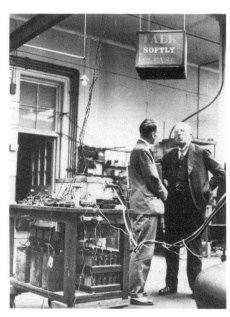

Fig. 3.2 Lord Rutherford in his laboratory

The two heavier particles, the **neutrons** and **protons** make up what is called the **nucleus**. The much smaller **electrons** are found in shells around the nucleus (see Fig. 3.3). About 1837 electrons are needed to equal the mass of one neutron or proton. The nucleus is therefore the heavier part of the atom.

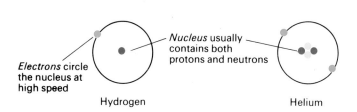

Fig. 3.3   An atom of hydrogen has 1 proton and 1 electron whilst that of helium has 2 protons, 2 neutrons and 2 electrons

Sub-atomic particle	Symbol	Mass of particle (a.m.u.*)	Charge
proton	p	1	+1
neutron	n	1	0
electron	e^-	$\dfrac{1}{1837}$	−1

Table 3.1   *a.m.u. = atomic mass units

The diagrams in Fig. 3.3 represent the atoms of the elements hydrogen and helium. In the case of hydrogen, the element possesses one proton only in its nucleus and since all atoms are electrically neutral (they have no overall electric charge), it must have the same number of electrons as protons. In the case of helium, it possesses two neutrons and two protons in the nucleus. The electrical charge of the protons is balanced by two electrons.

Atomic number and mass number

The number of protons in the nucleus is called the **atomic number** and is given the symbol **Z**. Hence, in the examples in Fig. 3.3, the hydrogen atom has an atomic number of 1 since it has one proton in the nucleus, whilst the atomic number of helium is 2 since it has two protons in the nucleus. Each element has its own atomic number and no two elements have the same atomic number.

atomic number (Z) = number of protons

(The atomic number also equals the number of electrons in a neutral atom.)

The total number of particles found in the nucleus is called the **mass number** and is given the symbol **A**.

mass number (A) = number of protons (Z) + number of neutrons

If we take the example in Fig. 3.3 again, the helium atom has a mass number of 4 since it has two protons and two neutrons in its nucleus, whilst because the hydrogen atom has no neutrons in its nucleus it has a mass number of 1.

The mass number and atomic number of an element are usually written in the following shorthand way:

$$\begin{matrix}\text{mass number (A)} \\ \text{atomic number (Z)}\end{matrix} \boxed{\text{ symbol }} \quad \text{e.g. } {}_{1}^{1}\text{H}, {}_{2}^{4}\text{He}.$$

Using the above relationship if we know A and Z we can calculate the number of neutrons present since:

number of neutrons = mass number − atomic number
                                    (A)   (Z)

Element	Symbol	Atomic number (Z)	Number of electrons	Number of neutrons	Mass number (A)	^A_ZSymbol
Hydrogen	H	1	1	0	1	$^1_1$H
Helium	He	2	2	2	4	$^4_2$He
Carbon	C	6	6	6	12	$^{12}_6$C
Nitrogen	N	7	7	7	14	$^{14}_7$N
Oxygen	O	8	8	8	16	$^{16}_8$O
Fluorine	F	9	9	10	19	$^{19}_9$F
Neon	Ne	10	10	10	20	$^{20}_{10}$Ne
Sodium	Na	11	11	12	23	$^{23}_{11}$Na
Magnesium	Mg	12	12	12	24	$^{24}_{12}$Mg
Sulphur	S	16	16	16	32	$^{32}_{16}$S
Potassium	K	19	19	20	39	$^{39}_{19}$K
Calcium	Ca	20	20	20	40	$^{40}_{20}$Ca

Table 3.2

For example, the number of neutrons in one atom of $^{23}_{11}$Na is:

$$23 - 11 = 12$$
$$\text{(A)} \quad \text{(Z)}$$

and the number of neutrons in one atom of $^{235}_{92}$U is:

$$235 - 92 = 143.$$
$$\text{(A)} \quad \text{(Z)}$$

Table 3.2 shows the number of protons, neutrons and electrons in some common atoms.

Isotopes

All the atoms of a particular element contain the same number of protons. However, the number of neutrons may differ. Atoms of the same element which have different numbers of neutrons are called **isotopes**.

The isotopes of chlorine are shown in Fig. 3.4. Chemically, the two isotopes of chlorine always behave the same way. Generally, isotopes of any one element always have the same chemical properties. The only effect of the extra neutrons is to alter the mass of the atom and properties that depend on it such as density. Some other examples of atoms with isotopes are shown in Table 3.3.

Some of the isotopes of certain atoms are unstable because of the extra number of neutrons and are said to be **radioactive**. The best known element which has a radioactive isotope is uranium. Its two major isotopes are: $^{235}_{92}$U and $^{238}_{92}$U. Radioactivity is discussed in more detail in Appendix 1.

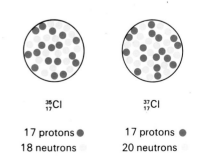

$^{35}_{17}$Cl $^{37}_{17}$Cl

17 protons ●   17 protons ●
18 neutrons   20 neutrons

Fig. 3.4   The nuclei of two isotopes of chlorine

Relative atomic mass

Atoms are too small to be weighed individually. It was decided, therefore, to fix a scale for atomic masses by comparing the masses of atoms to a standard. The standard chosen initially in the 19th century was the lightest element—hydrogen. This was taken to weigh 1 unit. However, since oxygen combines with more substances than hydrogen an atomic mass scale related to oxygen was produced. With the discovery of isotopes further changes were needed since, as you saw in the previous section, oxygen was found to possess more than one isotope. In 1961 the situation was clarified when the International Union of Pure and Applied Chemists recommended that the standard used for comparison, for all atoms, should be the $^{12}_{6}C$ atom. An atom of $^{12}_{6}C$ (or carbon-12) was taken to weigh exactly 12 units.

When measuring the **relative atomic mass** (or **R.A.M.**) of an element you have to take account of the abundance of its isotopes. The R.A.M. of an element can therefore be defined as the average mass of its isotopes compared to the mass of one atom of $^{12}_{6}C$.

$$R.A.M. = \frac{\text{average mass of isotopes of element}}{\frac{1}{12} \times \text{mass of 1 atom of } ^{12}_{6}C}$$

For example, in the case of chlorine which has two isotopes:

	$^{35}_{17}Cl$	$^{37}_{17}Cl$
Abundancies	75%	25%
Ratio of atoms	3 :	1

Hence the 'average mass' of a chlorine atom is:

$$\frac{(3 \times 35) + (1 \times 37)}{4} = 35.5$$

The R.A.M. for chlorine is 35.5.

Taking account of the proportion of isotopes present in an element it is possible to calculate its R.A.M. very accurately. Table 3.4 shows the R.A.M.s for some common elements. You will notice that the values given in this table are whole numbers (except for chlorine). This is because the majority of elements have R.A.M. values which are very close to whole numbers and it is convenient for us to round them off.

Element	$^{A}_{Z}$symbol	Particles present
Hydrogen	$^{1}_{1}H$	1p, 1e$^-$
Deuterium	$^{2}_{1}H$	1p, 1e$^-$, 1n
Tritium	$^{3}_{1}H$	1p, 1e$^-$, 2n
Oxygen	$^{16}_{8}O$	8p, 8e$^-$, 8n
	$^{17}_{8}O$	8p, 8e$^-$, 9n
	$^{18}_{8}O$	8p, 8e$^-$, 10n

Table 3.3

Element	Symbol	R.A.M.
Hydrogen	H	1
Helium	He	4
Carbon	C	12
Nitrogen	N	14
Oxygen	O	16
Fluorine	F	19
Neon	Ne	20
Sodium	Na	23
Magnesium	Mg	24
Sulphur	S	32
Chlorine	Cl	35.5
Potassium	K	39
Calcium	Ca	40
Iron	Fe	56
Copper	Cu	64
Zinc	Zu	65
Silver	Ag	108
Iodine	I	127
Lead	Pb	207

Table 3.4

Relative formula mass

If you add the R.A.M.s of the atoms shown in the formula of a substance then you obtain what is called its **relative formula mass**. If you are dealing with substances made up of molecules then it is also known as the **relative molecular mass** or R.M.M.

Examples

1 Calculate the relative formula mass of carbon dioxide.

Formula	CO_2	
Atoms present	$(1 \times C)$	$(2 \times O)$
R.A.M.s	(1×12)	(2×16)

Relative formula mass $= 12 + 32 = 44$.

2 Calculate the relative formula mass of sodium chloride.

$$\begin{array}{lll}
\text{Formula} & \text{NaCl} & \\
\text{Atoms present} & (1 \times \text{Na}) & (1 \times \text{Cl}) \\
\text{R.A.M.s} & (1 \times 23) & (1 \times 35.5)
\end{array}$$

Relative formula mass $= 23 + 35.5 = 58.5$.

3 Calculate the relative formula mass of ammonium sulphate.

$$\begin{array}{lllll}
\text{Formula} & & (\text{NH}_4)_2\text{SO}_4 & & \\
\text{Atoms present} & (2 \times \text{N}) & (8 \times \text{H}) & (1 \times \text{S}) & (4 \times \text{O}) \\
\text{R.A.M.s} & (2 \times 14) & (8 \times 1) & (1 \times 32) & (4 \times 16)
\end{array}$$

Relative formula mass $= 28 + 8 + 32 + 64 = 132$.

Percentage composition

R.A.M.s and relative formula masses can be used to determine the percentage composition of a substance. This is best explained with examples.

1 Calculate the percentage composition of methane gas by mass.
   (a) First find the relative formula mass of CH_4.

$$\begin{array}{lll}
\text{Formula} & \text{CH}_4 & \\
\text{Atoms present} & (1 \times \text{C}) & (4 \times \text{H}) \\
\text{R.A.M.s} & (1 \times 12) & (4 \times 1)
\end{array}$$

Relative formula mass $= 12 + 4 = 16$.

(b) Next calculate the percentage composition of the constituent elements.

$$\text{Percentage of carbon present} = \frac{\text{mass of carbon}}{\text{relative formula mass}} \times 100$$

$$= \frac{12}{16} \times 100$$

$$= \frac{3}{4} \times 100 = 75\%$$

$$\text{Percentage of hydrogen present} = \frac{\text{mass of hydrogen}}{\text{relative formula mass}} \times 100$$

$$= \frac{4}{16} \times 100$$

$$= \frac{1}{4} \times 100 = 25\%$$

2 Calculate the percentage of nitrogen in the fertilizer ammonium sulphate—$(NH_4)_2SO_4$. From the previous section we know that the relative formula mass is 132.

$$\text{Atoms of nitrogen present} = 2 \times N$$
$$\text{Mass of nitrogen present} = 2 \times 14 = 28$$

$$\text{Percentage of nitrogen} = \frac{\text{mass of nitrogen present}}{\text{relative formula mass}} \times 100$$

$$= \frac{28}{132} = 21.2\%$$

The law of constant composition

This states that all pure samples of a compound contain the same elements in the same proportion by mass. This means that in the case of our example, methane, regardless of where or how it is made, will contain only carbon and hydrogen atoms in the ratio of 1:4, and three times as much carbon by mass as hydrogen. Its percentage composition will be constant at 75% carbon and 25% hydrogen.

Arrangement of electrons

The structure of the atom is sometimes likened to our solar system (see Fig. 3.5) with the electrons orbiting the nucleus very much like the planets orbit the Sun—only a lot faster. The electrons move very rapidly around the nucleus in distinct orbits often called 'shells' or 'energy levels'. Each of the electron shells can only hold a certain number of electrons:

1st electron shell—up to 2 electrons
2nd electron shell—up to 8 electrons
3rd electron shell—up to 8 electrons

and so on.

Fig. 3.5   In the solar system, planets orbit the Sun like electrons orbit a nucleus

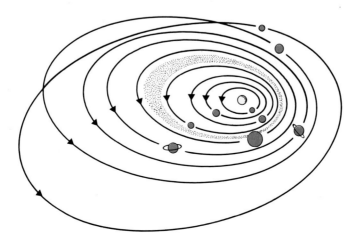

There are 105 elements and Table 3.5 shows the way the electrons are arranged in the first twenty of these elements. The way the electrons are arranged is called the **electronic structure** or **electronic configuration**. Fig. 3.6 shows how these electrons are arranged in the electron shells of some of the atoms.

Element	Symbol	Number of protons (atomic number) (Z)	Number of electrons	Electron structure
Hydrogen	H	1	1	1
Helium	He	2	2	2
Lithium	Li	3	3	2,1
Beryllium	Be	4	4	2,2
Boron	B	5	5	2,3
Carbon	C	6	6	2,4
Nitrogen	N	7	7	2,5
Oxygen	O	8	8	2,6
Fluorine	F	9	9	2,7
Neon	Ne	10	10	2,8
Sodium	Na	11	11	2,8,1
Magnesium	Mg	12	12	2,8,2
Aluminium	Al	13	13	2,8,3
Silicon	Si	14	14	2,8,4
Phosphorus	P	15	15	2,8,5
Sulphur	S	16	16	2,8,6
Chlorine	Cl	17	17	2,8,7
Argon	Ar	18	18	2,8,8
Potassium	K	19	19	2,8,8,1
Calcium	Ca	20	20	2,8,8,2

Table 3.5

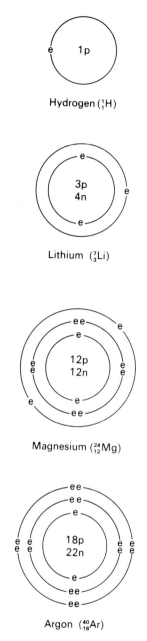

Fig. 3.6 Electron arrangement (in 'shells') for some atoms

The periodic table

You have already seen that there are 105 elements many of which you may know little or nothing about (Fig. 2.5). These elements can be grouped according to their physical properties. If we do this then we find that we have a series of metals, such as sodium, magnesium, zinc, copper and lead (see Fig. 3.7(b)) in one group, and a series of non-metals such as carbon, sulphur, oxygen, bromine and chlorine in another (see Fig. 3.7(a)). However, it is convenient to organize the elements in a more structured way. Over the past 150 years many scientists, including Döbereiner, Newlands, Meyer and perhaps most important of all, Mendeleev, have tried to do this. The modern method of arranging the elements is shown in the table in Fig. 3.9. This table is known as the **periodic table** of the elements and was produced following the work of Rutherford and Moseley. They realized that the elements should be arranged by atomic number (the number of protons in the nucleus). In the modern periodic table the

Fig. 3.8   Dmitri Mendeleev. It is his table of elements that we use today—the periodic table

Fig. 3.7(a)   The non-metals carbon, sulphur, bromine and iodine

Fig. 3.7(b)   The metals magnesium, sodium, copper, zinc and lead

	Alkali metals GROUP 1 (I)	Alkaline earth metals GROUP 2 (II)											GROUP 3 (III)	GROUP 4 (IV)	GROUP 5 (V)	GROUP 6 (VI)	Halogens GROUP 7 (VII)	Noble gases GROUP 0
1st PERIOD				1 H 1 Hydrogen														4 He 2 Helium
2nd PERIOD	7 Li 3 Lithium	9 Be 4 Beryllium											11 B 5 Boron	12 C 6 Carbon	14 N 7 Nitrogen	16 O 8 Oxygen	19 F 9 Fluorine	20 Ne 10 Neon
3rd PERIOD	23 Na 11 Sodium	24 Mg 12 Magnesium	← Transition metals →										27 Al 13 Aluminium	28 Si 14 Silicon	31 P 15 Phosphorus	32 S 16 Sulphur	35·5 Cl 17 Chlorine	40 Ar 18 Argon
4th PERIOD	39 K 19 Potassium	40 Ca 20 Calcium	45 Sc 21 Scandium	48 Ti 22 Titanium	5 V 23 Vanadium	52 Cr 24 Chromium	55 Mn 25 Manganese	56 Fe 26 Iron	59 Co 27 Cobalt	59 Ni 28 Nickel	64 Cu 29 Copper	85 Zn 30 Zinc	70 Ga 31 Gallium	73 Ge 32 Germanium	75 As 33 Arsenic	79 Se 34 Selenium	80 Br 35 Bromine	84 Kr 36 Krypton
5th PERIOD	85 Rb 37 Rubidium	88 Sr 38 Strontium	89 Y 39 Yttrium	91 Zr 40 Zirconium	93 Nb 41 Niobium	96 Mo 42 Molybdenum	98 Tc 43 Technetium	101 Ru 44 Ruthenium	103 Rh 45 Rhodium	106 Pd 46 Palladium	108 Ag 47 Silver	112 Cd 48 Cadmium	115 In 49 Indium	119 Sn 50 Tin	122 Sb 51 Antimony	128 Te 52 Tellurium	127 I 53 Iodine	131 Xe 54 Xenon
6th PERIOD	133 Cs 55 Caesium	137 Ba 56 Barium	↑	178·5 Hf 72 Hafnium	181 Ta 73 Tantalum	184 W 74 Tungsten	186 Re 75 Rhenium	190 Os 76 Osmium	192 Ir 77 Iridium	195 Pt 78 Platinum	197 Au 79 Gold	201 Hg 80 Mercury	204 Tl 81 Thallium	207 Pb 82 Lead	209 Bi 83 Bismuth	210 Po 84 Polonium	210 At 85 Astatine	222 Rn 86 Radon
7th PERIOD	223 Fr 87 Francium	226 Ra 88 Radium	↑															

Non-metals / Metals

139 La 57 Lanthanum	140 Ce 58 Cerium	141 Pr 59 Praseo-dymium	144 Nd 80 Neodimium	147 Pm 81 Promethium	150 Sm 82 Samarium	152 Eu 63 Europium	157 Gd 84 Gadolinium	159 Tb 65 Terbium	162 Dy 66 Dysprosium	165 Ho 67 Holmium	167 Er 68 Erbium	169 Tm 69 Thulium	173 Yb 70 Ytterbium	175 Lu 71 Litetium
227 Ac 89 Actinium	232 Th 80 Thorium	231 Pa 91 Protoactinium	238 U 92 Uranium	237 Np 93 Neptunium	242 Pu 94 Plutonium	243 Am 95 Americium	247 Cm 96 Curium	249 Bk 97 Berkelium	251 Cf 98 Californium	254 Es 99 Einsteinium	253 Fm 100 Fermium	256 Md 101 Mendelevium	254 No 102 Nobelium	257 Lw 103 Lawrencium

Artificial elements

Fig. 3.9 The periodic table

elements are arranged in order of increasing atomic number. The elements having similar chemical properties are found in the same columns. These columns are called **groups** (or sometimes families). There are eight groups of elements, the first column is group 1, the second column is group 2, and so on. The last group in the periodic table is called group 0.

Groups 1 and 2 contain metals. Group 1 contains:

> lithium (Li)
> sodium (Na)
> potassium (K)
> rubidium (Rb)
> caesium (Cs)
> francium (Fr).

Group 2 contains:

> beryllium (Be)
> magnesium (Mg)
> calcium (Ca)
> strontium (Sr)
> barium (Ba)
> radium (Ra).

Elements to the right of the periodic table are non-metals. For example, group 7 contains the non-metals:

> fluorine (F)
> chlorine (Cl)
> bromine (Br)
> iodine (I)
> astatine (At).

There is a series of elements known as **metalloids** which lie on a dividing line that can be drawn between the metals and non-metals in the periodic table. These metalloid elements behave like non-metals in some ways and like metals in others.

Horizontally, the rows of elements are called **periods**. These are numbered 1 to 7 going down the periodic table. For example, period 3 contains the elements:

> sodium (Na), magnesium (Mg), aluminium (Al), silicon (Si), phosphorus (P), sulphur (S), chlorine (Cl), argon (Ar).

Between groups 2 and 3 are the elements sometimes known as the **transition elements** or heavy metals (see Fig. 3.12).

Fig. 3.10   The metalloid silicon

Fig. 3.11(a)   Silicon is used extensively in the microelectronics industry. This 'wafer' contains hundreds of 'chips'. Each chip will be made into a microprocessor (see Fig. 3.11(b))

Fig. 3.11(b)   Microprocessors are used in computers, washing machines and even pop-up toasters

Fig. 3.12   Some transition elements

Electron structure and the periodic table

Table 3.6(a) shows the electron structure for the first three elements in group 1. In each case you will notice that the outer shell contains just one electron. Table 3.6(b) shows the electron structure for the first three elements in group 2. Again you will notice that the outer shell contains just two electrons. Table 3.7 shows the electron structures for the first two members of group 7. You will notice that the outer shell contains just seven electrons. From these observations it will be clear that the number of electrons in the outer shell is the same as the group number except in the case of group 0 where the elements have two or eight electrons in the outer shell.

Element	Symbol	Atomic number (Z)	Electron structure
Lithium	Li	3	2,1
Sodium	Na	11	2,8,1
Potassium	K	19	2,8,8,1

Table 3.6(a)   Electron structure of first three elements in group 1

Element	Symbol	Atomic number (Z)	Electron structure
Beryllium	Be	4	2,2
Magnesium	Mg	12	2,8,2
Calcium	Ca	20	2,8,8,2

Table 3.6(b)   Electron structure of first three elements in group 2

Element	Symbol	Atomic number (Z)	Electron structure
Fluorine	F	9	2,7
Chlorine	Cl	17	2,8,7

Table 3.7   Electron structure of first two elements in group 7

Chemical families—group 1 (the alkali metals)

The most familiar elements in this group are lithium, sodium and potassium. These are all very reactive metals and they have to be stored in oil to stop them coming into contact with water and air (see Fig. 3.13). There are three other members in this group—rubidium, caesium, and francium—but these metals are too reactive to use in your laboratory.

At first sight they do not look much like metals (see Fig. 3.14(a)). However, they are all very soft metals and when they are freshly cut with a knife they all have a typically shiny metallic surface (see

Fig. 3.13   Potassium is stored in oil to prevent it reacting with air

Element	Symbol	Atomic number (Z)	Appearance	Hardness	Melting point (°C)	Boiling point (°C)	Density (g cm⁻³)
Lithium	Li	3	Grey metal	Soft	181	1317	0.54
Sodium	Na	11	Grey metal	Soft	98	900	0.97
Potassium	K	19	Grey metal	Very soft	63	777	0.86

Table 3.8

Fig. 3.14(a)　Sodium

Fig. 3.14(b)　Freshly cut sodium

Fig. 3.14(b)). Table 3.8 shows some of the physical properties of these group 1 metals. They are all good conductors of electricity. They have low densities as well as low melting and boiling points. (These are all lower than you might expect for metals.)

Reaction of group 1 metals with water

When small pieces of these reactive metals are placed in water they react immediately. All three float on water and as they react the colourless gas hydrogen is given off. In all three cases the reactions evolve enough heat to cause the metals to melt. When potassium reacts with cold water the hydrogen produced usually bursts into flame (ignited by the exothermic reaction) and burns with a pink colour (see Fig. 3.15). In each case there is an alkaline solution left at the end of the reaction (see Fig. 3.16). Because of this the elements of group 1 are known as the **alkali metals**. Of the three, potassium is the most reactive towards water followed by sodium and then lithium.

These three reactions are very similar and may be represented by the general word equation:

$$\text{metal} + \text{water} \longrightarrow \text{metal hydroxide} + \text{hydrogen gas}$$
$$\text{(alkali)}$$

The equations for the reaction of sodium and potassium with water are:

$$\text{sodium} + \text{water} \longrightarrow \text{sodium hydroxide} + \text{hydrogen gas}$$

$$2Na_{(s)} + 2H_2O_{(l)} \longrightarrow 2NaOH_{(aq)} + H_{2(g)}$$

$$\text{potassium} + \text{water} \longrightarrow \text{potassium hydroxide} + \text{hydrogen gas}$$

$$2K_{(s)} + 2H_2O_{(l)} \longrightarrow 2KOH_{(aq)} + H_{2(g)}$$

'l' and 'aq' mean 'liquid' and 'aqueous (in water) solution' respectively.

Fig. 3.15　Potassium reacts vigorously with cold water

Fig. 3.16　An alkaline solution is left after potassium reacts with water

Reaction of group 1 metals with oxygen

When heated in oxygen, or air, the alkali metals burn to form solid white oxides. The colour of the flame is characteristic of the metal, for instance, lithium burns with a red flame, sodium with a yellow-orange flame and potassium with a lilac (pink) flame (see Fig. 3.17). The order of reactivity towards oxygen is the same as that found with water, that is, lithium is least reactive and potassium is most reactive.

The word equation to represent the chemical reaction which has taken place is:

$$\text{metal} + \text{oxygen} \longrightarrow \text{metal oxide}$$

The word and chemical equations for the reaction of lithium with oxygen are:

$$\text{lithium} + \text{oxygen} \longrightarrow \text{lithium oxide}$$

$$4Li_{(s)} + O_{2(g)} \longrightarrow 2Li_2O_{(s)}$$

Fig. 3.17   Burning potassium in air/oxygen

Reaction of group 1 metals with chlorine

Fig. 3.18 shows what happens when a piece of burning alkali metal is plunged into a gas jar of chlorine. The metal continues to burn forming a lot of white smoke. This white smoke is made up of small particles of the metal chloride (a salt—see Chapter 7, page 80). For example:

$$\text{sodium} + \text{chlorine} \longrightarrow \text{sodium chloride}$$

$$2Na_{(s)} + Cl_{2(g)} \longrightarrow 2NaCl_{(s)}$$

Again, lithium and potassium react in a similar way with chlorine, but as in the previous reactions, potassium is the most reactive towards chlorine whilst lithium is the least reactive of these alkali metals.

As you can see from these reactions above, these metals behave in a similar manner so they are placed in the same group. Also you will note that the reactivity of these elements *increases* upon going down the group.

Fig. 3.19   Reactivity increases going down group 1

Fig. 3.18   Sodium burning in chlorine gas

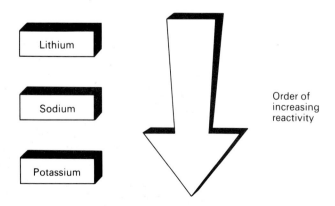

Chemical families—group 2 (the alkaline earth metals)

You will be most familiar with the metals magnesium and calcium. These metals are harder than those of group 1 and, when pure and clean, they are silvery-grey coloured. However, they tarnish quickly when left in air due to the formation of a metal oxide layer (see Fig. 3.20). Some of the physical properties of magnesium and calcium are shown in Table 3.9. You will notice that these properties are more like those you might have expected for metals.

Fig. 3.20   Tarnished magnesium

Element	Symbol	Atomic number (Z)	Appearance	Hardness	Melting point (°C)	Boiling point (°C)	Density (g cm^{-3})
Magnesium	Mg	12	Silvery grey metal	Hard	650	1110	1.74
Calcium	Ca	20	Silvery grey metal	Hard	840	1490	1.53

Table 3.9

Reaction of group 2 metals with water

Although these metal elements do react with water they do so less vigorously than the elements of group 1. Before reacting magnesium with water it is necessary to remove the oxide layer by cleaning the magnesium with emery paper. When a piece of clean magnesium is placed in cold water a few bubbles of hydrogen appear on the surface of the metal. This gas can be collected over a period of hours using the method shown in Fig. 3.21(a).

magnesium + water $\longrightarrow$ magnesium oxide + hydrogen

$$Mg_{(s)} \quad + H_2O_{(l)} \longrightarrow \quad MgO_{(s)} \quad + \quad H_{2(g)}$$

The magnesium oxide has a slight solubility in water, producing magnesium hydroxide:

magnesium oxide + water $\longrightarrow$ magnesium hydroxide

$$MgO_{(s)} \quad + H_2O_{(l)} \longrightarrow \quad Mg(OH)_{2(aq)}$$

A clean piece of calcium will react in a similar way, but it is a much more vigorous reaction:

calcium + water $\longrightarrow$ calcium oxide + hydrogen

$$Ca_{(s)} \quad + H_2O_{(l)} \longrightarrow \quad CaO_{(s)} \quad + \quad H_{2(g)}$$

calcium oxide + water $\longrightarrow$ calcium hydroxide

$$CaO_{(s)} \quad + H_2O_{(l)} \longrightarrow \quad Ca(OH)_{2(aq)}$$

Calcium is more reactive than magnesium with water.

Fig. 3.21(a)   Hydrogen will collect in the up-turned test tube

Reaction of group 2 metals with oxygen

When heated in oxygen, or air, magnesium burns with a brilliant white flame producing clouds of white smoke of magnesium oxide (see Fig. 3.21(b)). Calcium, when cleaned thoroughly with emery paper and heated strongly, burns very vigorously with a brick

Fig. 3.21(b)   Magnesium burns with a brilliant white flame. Do not look at it directly

red flame and also produces clouds of white smoke of calcium oxide. Calcium is more reactive towards oxygen than magnesium.

The word equation to represent the chemical reaction which takes place is:

$$metal + oxygen \longrightarrow metal\ oxide$$

The equations for the reactions of magnesium and calcium with oxygen are:

$$magnesium + oxygen \longrightarrow magnesium\ oxide$$

$$2Mg_{(s)} + O_{2(g)} \longrightarrow 2MgO_{(s)}$$

$$calcium + oxygen \longrightarrow calcium\ oxide$$

$$2Ca_{(s)} + O_{2(g)} \longrightarrow 2CaO_{(s)}$$

Note that the group 2 metal oxides are less soluble in water than those of group 1.

Chemical families—group 7 (the halogens)

You will see by studying Figs 3.22–4 and Table 3.10 that all the members of this group have a different appearance.

Fluorine is too reactive to handle in the school laboratory. Astatine, not shown in the table, is another group 7 element. It is also never handled in the school laboratory because it is radioactive and too unstable.

Fig. 3.22   Chlorine

Fig. 3.23   Bromine

Fig. 3.24   Iodine

Element	Symbol	Atomic number (Z)	Appearance	Melting point (°C)	Boiling point (°C)	Density (g cm^{-3})
Fluorine	F	9	Pale yellow gas	−220	−188	1.11*
Chlorine	Cl	17	Pale green gas	−101	−34	1.56*
Bromine	Br	35	Red-brown liquid	−7	59	3.12
Iodine	I	53	Dark grey solid	114	184	4.94

Table 3.10   *at −35 °C.

Reaction of group 7 elements with water

When chlorine, bromine and iodine are each added to water it is found that chlorine is the most soluble followed by bromine and iodine. (In fact, it is found that iodine is only very slightly soluble in cold water.)

When chlorine dissolves in water it forms a greenish solution called chlorine water. If universal indicator paper is placed in this solution it turns red showing the solution is acidic.

water + chlorine $\longrightarrow$ hypochlorous acid + hydrochloric acid

$$H_2O_{(l)} + Cl_{2(g)} \longrightarrow HOCl_{(aq)} + HCl_{(aq)}$$

The red colour of the indicator paper is quickly lost since the hypochlorous acid (chloric(I) acid) is a good bleaching agent (see Fig. 3.25). For further details of this reaction see Chapter 15, page 210.

Bromine solution, better known as bromine water, is orange. Bromine reacts with water in a similar way to chlorine. It gives a very weakly acidic solution which also acts as a bleach (but not as strong as chlorine water). Iodine which is almost insoluble in water is only very slightly acidic and has little bleaching action.

The halogens have a low solubility in water. However, it is found that they dissolve quite readily in trichloroethane or tetrachloromethane to give solutions which have the characteristic colours shown in Fig. 3.26.

Reaction of halogens with sodium metal

You have seen earlier in this chapter (page 36) that a piece of burning sodium will continue to burn in chlorine gas producing a lot of white smoke—sodium chloride. Sodium will also react with bromine and iodine, but less vigorously. White fumes of sodium bromide and sodium iodide are produced respectively.

sodium + bromine $\longrightarrow$ sodium bromide

$$2Na_{(s)} + Br_{2(g)} \longrightarrow 2NaBr_{(s)}$$

sodium + iodine $\longrightarrow$ sodium iodide

$$2Na_{(s)} + I_{2(s)} \longrightarrow 2NaI_{(s)}$$

All these substances are salts formed by the direct reaction of a group 7 element with a metal and this is how the group gets its name—halogen means 'salt former'.

The order of reactivity of the halogens is (in descending order): chlorine, bromine, iodine.

Displacement reactions of halogens

The observed order of reactivity can be confirmed by a '**displacement reaction**'. It is found that a more reactive halogen will displace a less reactive halogen from one of its compounds. For example, if chlorine is bubbled into a solution of potassium bromide then the less reactive halogen, bromine, is displaced by the more reactive halogen, chlorine. As you can see from Fig. 3.27 the colourless solution turns orange as the 'free' bromine is produced by displacement.

potassium bromide + chlorine $\longrightarrow$ potassium chloride + bromine

$$2KBr_{(aq)} + Cl_{2(g)} \longrightarrow 2KCl_{(aq)} + Br_{2(aq)}$$

Fig. 3.25   The bleaching action of hypochlorous acid quickly removes the red colour that the universal indicator paper turns initially

Fig. 3.26   Halogens will dissolve in trichloroethane to give their characteristic colours

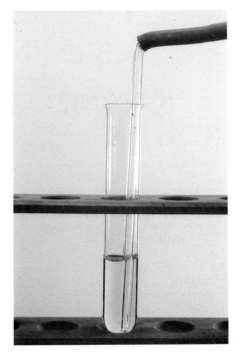

Fig. 3.27   Bromine being displaced by the more reactive chlorine

If iodine were added to potassium bromide solution then no reaction would take place since bromine is more reactive than iodine (see Fig. 3.28).

Chemical families—group 0 (inert gases)

The inert (or noble) gases are a most unusual chemical family. Most elements have a variety of chemical reactions but until just over 20 years ago these gases were thought to be entirely unreactive. However, since 1962 a number of compounds, such as xenon tetrafluoride, have been produced. No compounds of helium, neon or argon are yet known. Many compounds of the inert gases are easily decomposed.

Why are the inert gases so unreactive? Table 3.11 gives some information about three inert gases. You will notice that the outer shell of each atom contains the maximum allowed number of electrons. Since the inert gases are very unreactive, this arrangement of electrons must be particularly stable and hence difficult to change. This idea is important and forms the basis of the theory of how atoms join (**bond**) to one another.

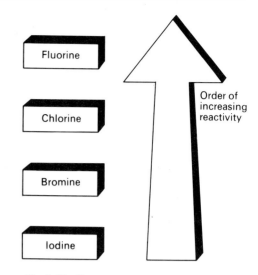

Fig. 3.28   Reactivity increases going up group 7

Element	Symbol	Atomic number (Z)	Electronic structure
Helium	He	2	2
Neon	Ne	10	2,8
Argon	Ar	18	2,8,8

Table 3.11

Chemical families—the transition elements

You will be familiar with many of these metals because of their everyday use (see Fig. 3.29). How are they different from the metals of group 1 and 2? Table 3.12 shows the physical properties of three transition elements. You will see from this table that they have much higher densities. They are also harder and stronger and less reactive.

Element	Symbol	Appearance	Melting point (°C)	Boiling point (°C)	Density (g cm^{-3})
Iron	Fe	Grey shiny metal	1540	2760	7.87
Nickel	Ni	Bright grey, shining metal	1455	2150	8.90
Copper	Cu	Pink/orange shining metal	1085	2580	8.93

Table 3.12

(a) Copper pipes

(b) Garage door galvanized with zinc

Fig. 3.29   Everyday uses of some transition elements

(c)   Nickel alloy coins

Reactivity and electron structure

You have seen that the elements within a group behave, chemically, in a similar way. It has been found that the chemical properties of an element are related to the number of electrons in the outer shell.

Table 3.6(a) shows the electron structure for the first three elements of group 1. You will notice that in each case the outer shell contains just one electron. When these elements react they lose this outer electron. By doing this they obtain a full outer shell like an inert gas which, as we have already seen, is very stable. For example, when the element sodium reacts it loses its outer electron and forms a **positive (+) ion** (a charged particle). See Fig. 3.30. The sodium ion has the same arrangement of electrons as the inert gas neon. This sort of behaviour is seen with all the alkali metals. The smaller the atom is, the closer the outer electron is to the nucleus, and the more difficult it is to remove. This is because there is a strong attractive force on it (**electrostatic attraction**) from the positive nucleus. As you go down the group, the size of the atoms increases and the outer electron gets further away from the nucleus and hence becomes easier to remove. This means that as you go down group 1 the reactivity will increase.

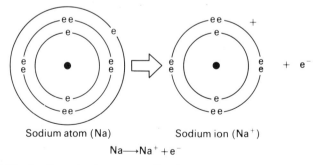

Sodium atom (Na)   Sodium ion (Na$^+$)

$$Na \longrightarrow Na^+ + e^-$$

Fig. 3.30   A sodium atom becomes a sodium ion

Table 3.6(b) shows the electron structure for the first three elements of group 2. In each case the outer shell contains two electrons. When they react they lose these two electrons and so obtain the arrangement of electrons of the nearest inert gas. For example, when the element magnesium reacts it forms the positive ion, Mg^{2+} (see Fig. 3.31). As a result the magnesium ion has the same arrangement of electrons as the inert gas neon. A magnesium atom is smaller than a sodium atom so that the negative electrons in the outer shell are closer to the positive nucleus than the single electron in the sodium atom. Therefore, these electrons are held more strongly. In addition, to form a Mg^{2+} ion from a magnesium atom, two electrons must be removed and the removal of the second electron requires additional energy. As a result, group 2 elements form ions less easily than the corresponding group 1 elements and they are less reactive.

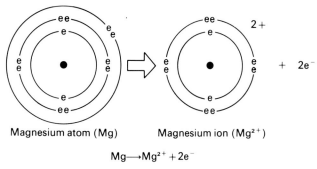

Magnesium atom (Mg)   Magnesium ion (Mg^{2+})

$$Mg \longrightarrow Mg^{2+} + 2e^-$$

Fig. 3.31   A magnesium atom becomes a magnesium ion

As you go down the elements in either group 1 or group 2, the atoms get bigger, the outer electron(s) are further away from the nucleus and these electrons are more easily removed. The reactivity of the elements in these groups therefore increases as you go down the group.

Table 3.7 shows the electron structures for the first two elements of group 7. In each case the outer shell contains 7 electrons. When the elements react they gain one electron per atom to obtain a full outer shell, (an inert gas arrangement of electrons). For example, when the element fluorine reacts it gains a single electron and forms a **negative** ($-$) **ion** (see Fig. 3.32). As a result the fluoride ion has obtained the same arrangement of electrons as the inert gas neon. The most reactive member of this group will be fluorine. This is because the electron is going into the outer shell of the smallest element in group 7. The attractive force on it will be the greatest of all the halogens since the outer shell of fluorine is closest to the nucleus. As you go down the group the outermost, extra electron is further from the nucleus. It will therefore be held less securely. The reactivity of elements in group 7 will therefore decrease down the group.

Fig. 3.32   A fluorine atom becomes a fluoride ion

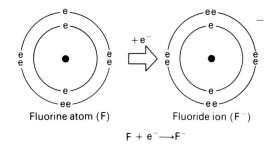

Fluorine atom (F)   Fluoride ion (F^-)

$$F + e^- \longrightarrow F^-$$

Changes across a period

The elements sodium, magnesium, aluminium, silicon, phosphorus, sulphur, chlorine and argon make up period 3 of the periodic table. As you go from left to right across this period there is a gradual trend from metallic sodium through the metalloid silicon to non-metallic argon. There are also changes in reactivity. The reactivity of the elements decreases from sodium to silicon and then increases again from silicon to chlorine. On the other hand, the next element argon is very unreactive. Going across a period there are also changes in the structure of the elements as well as the type of oxide they form. For example, metallic sodium contains ions (Na^+) (see Chapter 4, page 54), whilst chlorine exists as simple molecules (Cl_2). Also metal oxides, such as sodium oxide, form basic (or alkaline) solutions whilst the oxides of the non-metals, like sulphur (sulphur dioxide), form acidic solutions (see Chapter 7).

──────────────────────── QUESTIONS ────────────────────────

1 Calculate the relative formula mass of:
   a) iron(III) oxide, Fe_2O_3;
   b) sodium carbonate, Na_2CO_3;
   c) magnesium hydroxide, $Mg(OH)_2$;
   d) lead nitrate, $Pb(NO_3)_2$;
   e) sodium hydroxide, NaOH.

Relative atomic masses (R.A.M.s)
H = 1
C = 12
N = 14
O = 16
S = 32
Na = 23
Mg = 24
Fe = 56
Pb = 207

Table 1

2 Calculate the percentage composition by mass of:
   a) sulphur dioxide, SO_2;
   b) carbon monoxide, CO;
   c) ammonia, NH_3;
   d) urea, $CO(NH_2)_2$;
   e) ethanol, C_2H_5OH.

3 Calculate the percentage of nitrogen in the fertilizer ammonium nitrate(NH_4NO_3).

4 Calculate the percentage of carbon in benzene(C_6H_6).

5 An atom X has an atomic number of 11 and a relative atomic mass of 23.
   a) How many electrons are there?
   b) How many protons are there?
   c) How many neutrons are there?
   d) How many electrons will there be in the outer shell (energy level)?
   e) Write down the symbol for the ion it will form.
   f) Which group of the periodic table would X be in?
   g) i) How would you expect X to react with water?
      ii) Write a word equation and a balanced chemical equation for this reaction.

6 The atomic number of caesium(Cs) is 55. It is in group 1 of the periodic table.
   a) How many electrons would you expect a caesium atom to contain in its outer shell (energy level)?

b) Write down the formula of the chloride and sulphate of caesium.
c) How would you expect caesium to react with water? Write a word equation and balanced chemical equation for this reaction.
d) How would you expect caesium to react with chlorine? Write a word equation and balanced chemical equation for this reaction.

7 Find the element tin(Sn) in the periodic table.
   a) Which group of the periodic table is this element in?
   b) How many electrons will it have in its outer shell (energy level)?
   c) Is tin a metal or a non-metal?
   d) What is the formula of the chloride of tin?
   e) Give two uses of tin.
   f) Name and give the symbols of the other elements in this group.

8 a) Three members of a group in the periodic table are:

   $^{35}_{17}Cl$ $^{80}_{35}Br$ $^{127}_{53}I$

   i) Write down the electronic structure of an atom of chlorine.
   ii) To which group of the periodic table do these elements belong?
   iii) What is the number of protons in an atom of iodine?
   iv) What is the number of neutrons in a bromine atom?
   v) State the order of reactivity of these elements, putting the most reactive element first.
   vi) Account for the order of reactivity you have quoted in (v).

   b) When burning sodium is plunged into a gas jar of chlorine clouds of white smoke are produced.
   i) What does the white smoke consist of?
   ii) Write a word equation and balanced chemical equation for this reaction.
   iii) Describe the reaction which takes place when burning sodium is plunged into a gas jar containing bromine vapour.

9 Study the part of the periodic table shown below (Table 2). The letters T–Z are not symbols, they indicate the positions of certain elements.

1	2								3	4	5	6	7	0
T											U			V
	W												X	
Y						Z								

Table 2

Choose the letter of an element which:
a) is a halogen;
b) is the most reactive metal;
c) is a transition element;
d) is a noble gas;
e) will lose two electrons when reacting;
f) has a total of seven electrons per atom;
g) has three protons in the nucleus of each of its atoms.

10 Use the information in Table 3 to answer the questions below about the elements A, B, C, D, and E.

Element	Atomic number	Mass number	Electron structure
A	3	7	2,1
B	18	40	2,8,8
C	8	16	2,6
D	12	24	2,8,2
E	19	39	2,8,8,1

Table 3

a) Which element has 22 neutrons in each atom?
b) Is the bonding between C and E ionic or covalent?
c) Which element is a noble gas?
d) Which two elements form ions with the same electronic structure as neon?
e) Which two elements are in the same group of the periodic table?   (6)
(Cambridge 1984)

11 Using a periodic table, arrange the elements calcium, chromium, fluorine, iodine, magnesium, and manganese into three pairs such that each member of a pair has similar reactions.   (3)
(Cambridge 1984)

12 The element gallium is in group III of the periodic table and exists as two isotopes $^{69}_{31}Ga$ and $^{71}_{31}Ga$.
a) Complete the Table 4.   (3)

	$^{69}_{31}Ga$	$^{71}_{31}Ga$
Number of protons		
Number of neutrons		
Number of electrons		

Table 4

b) State the number of electrons in the outer energy level of a gallium atom.   (1)
c) Write the formula of an ion of gallium   (1)
d) Write the formula for gallium chloride and gallium sulphate.   (2)
e) A sample of gallium contains 60% of atoms of $^{69}_{31}Ga$ and 40% of atoms of $^{71}_{31}Ga$. Which one of the following is the relative atomic mass of this sample of gallium?

   69.2,   69.8,   70.2,   70.8   (1)

(NEA 1984)

13 A period from the periodic table is shown below. The number given with each symbol is the atomic number of the element.

Na   Mg   Al   Si   P   S   Cl   Ar
11   12   13   14   15   16   17   18

a) Name the noble gas included in the period.   (1)
b) Name one solid non-metal in the period.   (1)
c) i) Write the formula of the simplest oxide formed between sodium and oxygen (atomic number 8).   (1)
   ii) Will the oxide be a solid, liquid or gas?   (1)
   iii) Name an indicator which you could use to test a solution of this oxide.   (1)
   iv) What colour is this indicator in a solution of this oxide?   (1)
   v) What is the colour of the same indicator when in a solution of an oxide of sulphur?   (1)
d) Which element in *this* period will be in the same group as the element of atomic number 9?   (1)
(JMB/WMEB 1978)

14 a) When a small piece of sodium is dropped into water in a large beaker, a strongly exothermic reaction, producing hydrogen and sodium hydroxide, takes place.
   i) What evidence of an exothermic reaction is *observed*? (1)
   ii) How could you show, in this reaction, that hydrogen was being formed? (2)
   iii) How could you show that sodium hydroxide was formed? (2)
   b) Give two *other* observations which you could make during this experiment. (2)
   c) Write an equation for the reaction of sodium with water. (1)
   (JMB 1984)

15 a) The table below (Table 5) shows some properties of the second, third and fourth elements in group VII of the periodic table. Use the information to predict the properties of the fifth element *astatine* and write these properties in the blank spaces provided. (6)
   b) For which one of the above elements are the molecules most widely spaced at room temperature and normal atmospheric pressure? (1)

c) In which two of the above elements are the molecules least free to move about at room temperature and atmospheric pressure? (1)
(AEB 1981)

16 The electronic arrangements of the elements A–H are listed below.

A 2,1   E 2,8,1
B 2,7   F 2,5
C 2,8,5   G 2,8,7
D 2,2   H 2,8,2

Use the letters A to H to answer the following questions.
a) List the elements which would be members of group I in the periodic table. (1)
b) List the elements which would be members of group VII of the table (the halogens). (1)
c) List, in order of increasing atomic number, the elements which belong to the third period. (1)
d) List in order of increasing atomic number all the non-metallic elements. (1)
(AEB 1981)

	Chlorine	Bromine	Iodine	Astatine
Colour	Yellow-green	Dark red-brown	Very dark purple, almost black	
State at room temperature	Gas	Liquid	Solid	
Effect on moist indicator paper	Bleaches	Bleaches	Bleaches	
Reaction with iron	Reacts violently to form iron(III) chloride	Fast reaction to form iron(III) bromide	Slow reaction to form iron(III) iodide	
Reaction with potassium iodide solution	Forms iodine and potassium chloride	Forms iodine and potassium bromide	No apparent reaction	

Table 5

BONDING

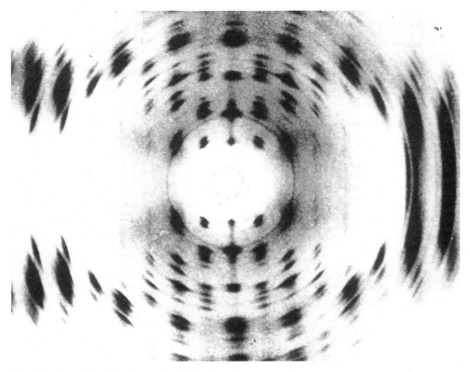

Fig. 4.1 X-ray diffraction image of a DNA molecule

In Chapter 2 we looked at a variety of compounds. These compounds, such as magnesium oxide, were formed by a chemical reaction between elements. In the new substance the elements became joined (bonded) together. In the first part of this chapter we are going to look at the ways in which atoms can join (bond) together.

Effect of electricity on chemicals

Consider Fig. 4.2 which shows solid lead(II) bromide ($PbBr_2$) in a crucible with two carbon rods in contact with it. When the electricity is allowed to flow, the bulb does not light. This is because solid lead(II) bromide is behaving as an **insulator**—it will not allow electricity to pass through it. However, if this compound is heated until it is molten, the bulb will light. The lead(II) bromide is now behaving as a **conductor** of electricity. When this happens an orange-red gas is seen around the positive carbon **electrode**. Also, lead metal is produced at the negative carbon electrode. An electrode is a point where the electric current enters and leaves the molten material. The names given to the two electrodes are:

> **anode**—the positive electrode
> **cathode**—the negative electrode.

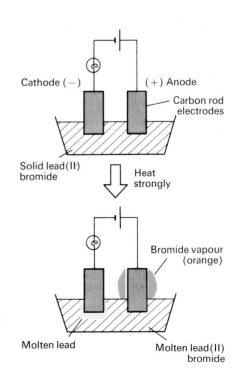

Fig. 4.2 The electrolysis of molten lead bromide

The break up (decomposition) of the compound lead(II) bromide into its constituent elements by the passage of an electric current is called **electrolysis**:

$$\text{molten lead(II) bromide} \longrightarrow \text{bromine} + \text{lead}$$

$$PbBr_{2(l)} \longrightarrow Br_{2(g)} + Pb_{(l)}$$

For lead metal to be formed at (we usually say 'deposited on') the cathode, the particles of lead must be attracted towards that electrode (see Fig. 4.3). Since unlike charges attract, the particles of lead in molten lead(II) bromide must be positively charged. In fact they are Pb^{2+} ions. To produce *neutral* lead metal atoms, these lead ions must collect two negative particles (electrons) at the cathode:

$$\text{lead ion} + \text{electrons} \longrightarrow \text{lead atom}$$

$$Pb^{2+} + 2e^- \longrightarrow Pb$$

This process of gaining electrons is called **reduction** (see Chapter 9, page 128).

For bromine to be deposited at the anode, the bromine particles must be negatively-charged ions. To form bromine molecules each ion must first of all lose its extra negative charge at the anode and so form a neutral bromine atom:

$$\text{bromide ion} \longrightarrow \text{bromine atom} + \text{electron}$$

$$Br^- \longrightarrow Br + e^-$$

and then two bromine atoms combine to form bromine molecules:

$$\text{two bromine atoms} \longrightarrow \text{bromine molecule}$$

$$2Br \longrightarrow Br_2$$

Lead(II) bromide is an **electrolyte**. An electrolyte is a substance that conducts electricity when in the molten state (or in solution) and is decomposed by the electricity.

If molten sodium chloride (another electrolyte) were used in a similar experiment then electrolysis would also take place. The bulb would light. Sodium ions would gain electrons at the cathode and molten sodium metal would be deposited. At the anode, chloride ions would lose electrons and green chlorine gas would be formed.

At the cathode

$$\text{sodium ion} + \text{electron} \longrightarrow \text{sodium atom}$$

$$Na^+ + e^- \longrightarrow Na$$

At the anode

$$\text{chloride ion} \longrightarrow \text{chlorine atom} + \text{electron}$$

$$Cl^- \longrightarrow Cl + e^-$$

$$\text{two chlorine atoms} \longrightarrow \text{chlorine molecule}$$

$$2Cl \longrightarrow Cl_2$$

If this experiment were repeated with substances like molten paraffin wax or the liquid ethanol (alcohol) (see Fig. 4.4) then nothing would happen. These compounds are **insulators**.

There appear, therefore, to be two distinct types of substance. There are those, such as sodium chloride, which are made up of charged particles (ions). The ions in these substances are held together by what we call an **ionic** (or **electrovalent**) bond. There are

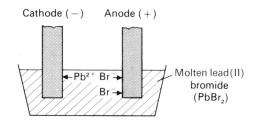

Fig. 4.3 The lead ions (Pb^{2+}) are attracted to the cathode ($-$) and the bromide ions (Br^-) are attracted to the anode ($+$)

Fig. 4.4(a) Paraffin wax will not conduct electricity—it is an insulator

Fig. 4.4(b) Ethanol is another insulator

also those substances which do not contain ions. The particles in these substances are held together by what we call **covalent bonds**.

Ionic (or electrovalent) bonding

Ionic bonds are usually found in compounds that contain metals combined with non-metals. When this type of bond is formed electrons are transferred from the metal atoms to the non-metal atoms during the chemical reaction. In doing this the atoms will become more stable by getting full outer shells.

Fig. 4.5   Compounds with electrovalent bonding

Sodium chloride

When sodium is burned in chlorine gas, sodium chloride (salt), a white crystalline solid, is formed:

sodium + chlorine $\longrightarrow$ sodium chloride
(metal)   (gas)   (crystalline solid)

$$2Na_{(s)} + Cl_{2(g)} \longrightarrow 2NaCl_{(s)}$$

Sodium has just one electron in its outer shell ($_{11}$Na 2,8,1). It needs to lose this electron to have a full outer shell. Chlorine has seven electrons in its outer shell ($_{17}$Cl 2,8,7). It needs just one more electron to fill its outer shell. When these two elements react the outer electron of each sodium atom is transferred to the outer shell of a chlorine atom (see Fig. 4.7). In this way both the atoms become 'like' noble or inert gases (they have full outer shells). Because the sodium atom has lost its outer electron it is no longer electrically neutral. It has become a sodium ion. It has one electron less than the number of protons in the nucleus. Chlorine now has one electron more than the number of protons in its nucleus. It has become a chloride ion.

Fig. 4.6   Ionic bonding. The metal atom transfers an electron to the non-metal atom

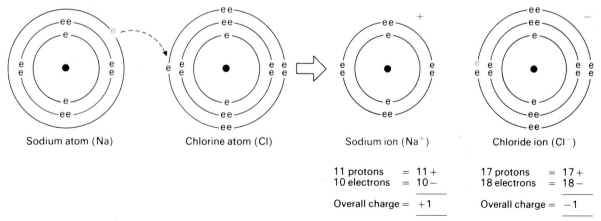

Sodium atom (Na)	Chlorine atom (Cl)	Sodium ion (Na$^+$)	Chloride ion (Cl$^-$)

		11 protons = 11 +	17 protons = 17 +
		10 electrons = 10 −	18 electrons = 18 −
		Overall charge = +1	Overall charge = −1

Fig. 4.7   Sodium and chlorine atoms become ions

Ions are atoms which have either gained or lost electrons and so become negatively or positively charged. In the above reaction to produce sodium chloride, the sodium atom has lost one electron and so it now has an overall charge of +1 (Na$^+$). The chlorine atom has gained an electron and its overall charge has now become −1 (Cl$^-$) (see Fig. 4.7).

Usually only the outer electrons are important in bonding so we can simplify the diagrams by missing out the inner shells. The reaction of sodium with chlorine to form sodium chloride may be shown as in the diagram in Fig. 4.8.

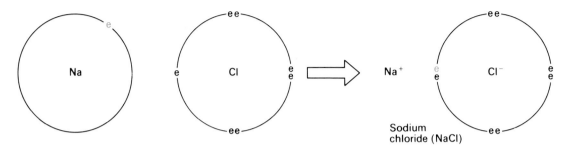

Fig. 4.8   The bonding in sodium chloride

The charges on the sodium ion and chloride ion are equal and opposite. They balance each other and the resulting formula for sodium chloride is NaCl. Particles which have the opposite charges attract each other and because of this the Na^+ ion and the Cl^- ion are attracted, or pulled, to one another. They are said to be **bonded** together. It is because ions are involved that this type of bonding is called ionic bonding. The alternative name—electrovalent bonding— is derived from the fact that there are electric charges on the atoms involved in the bonding.

Magnesium oxide

You will have seen magnesium burn in oxygen on many occasions. It burns with a bright white flame producing clouds of white smoke. A white ash of magnesium oxide is left behind.

$$magnesium + oxygen \longrightarrow magnesium\ oxide$$

$$2Mg_{(s)} \quad + \quad O_{2(g)} \quad \longrightarrow \quad 2MgO_{(s)}$$

The electron structures of the elements are:

$$_{12}Mg \quad 2,8,2 \qquad _{8}O \quad 2,6$$

When these two elements react the two outer electrons of the magnesium atom are transferred to the oxygen atom (see Fig. 4.9). In this way both atoms become ions with the electronic structure of the inert gas neon. In magnesium oxide the Mg^{2+} ions and O^{2-} ions are equal and oppositely charged and are attracted to one another. The formula of magnesium oxide is MgO.

Fig. 4.9   The bonding in magnesium oxide

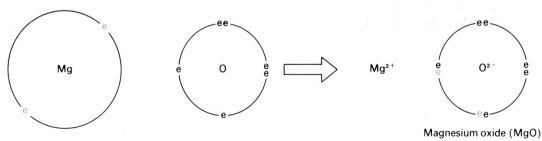

Magnesium oxide (MgO)

Calcium chloride

When chlorine gas is passed over heated calcium metal, a white smoke is produced. This substance is calcium chloride.

calcium + chlorine $\longrightarrow$ calcium chloride

$$Ca_{(s)} \quad + \quad Cl_{2(g)} \quad \longrightarrow \quad CaCl_{2(s)}$$

The electron structures of the elements are:

$$_{20}Ca \quad 2,8,8,2 \qquad _{17}Cl \quad 2,8,7$$

When these two elements react, the calcium atoms give each of two chlorine atoms one electron (see Fig. 4.10). In this case a compound is formed containing two chloride ions to each calcium ion. Its formula is $CaCl_2$.

Fig. 4.10

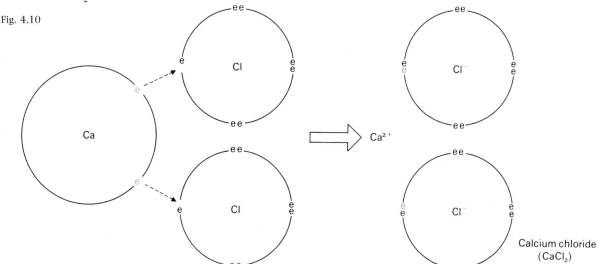

Calcium chloride ($CaCl_2$)

Covalent bonding

This type of bonding is commonly found in non-metals and in the compounds they form with each other. Covalent bonds are formed between elements by the sharing of electrons. By sharing electrons each of the atoms involved obtains a complete outer shell (an inert gas structure). The simplest example we can look at is hydrogen.

The hydrogen molecule

The hydrogen atom has one electron. To obtain a full outer shell, and hence have an inert gas structure, it must have two electrons. To obtain two electrons two hydrogen atoms approach close enough so that their outer shells overlap (see Fig. 4.12). A molecule of hydrogen is formed with two hydrogen atoms sharing a pair of electrons. This shared pair of electrons is known as a **single covalent bond**.

(a)

(b)

Fig. 4.11   Models of: (a) bromine and (b) chlorine molecules. Both molecules are bonded by a covalent bond

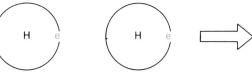

Fig. 4.12   2 hydrogen atoms

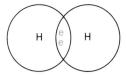

Hydrogen molecule (H_2)

51

Chemists use a further way of showing the bonding in this molecule. They represent the single covalent bond by a single line (see Fig. 4.13).

The methane molecule

Methane (the main constituent of natural gas) is a gas whose molecules contain the elements carbon and hydrogen. Each molecule of methane contains one carbon atom joined to four hydrogen atoms. The electron structures of the two elements are:

$$_6C \quad 2,4 \qquad _1H \quad 1$$

The carbon atom needs four more electrons to have a full outer shell whilst each hydrogen atom needs only one. The atoms in the molecule share electrons as shown in Fig. 4.14, in order to fill their outer shells. In methane there are four single covalent bonds.

Since the inner electrons of carbon are not involved in the bonding the diagrams in Fig. 4.14 can be made simpler (see Fig. 4.15).

Fig. 4.13(a) A model of the hydrogen molecule

H—H

Fig. 4.13(b) A single covalent bond in hydrogen

Fig. 4.14 Bonding in the methane molecule

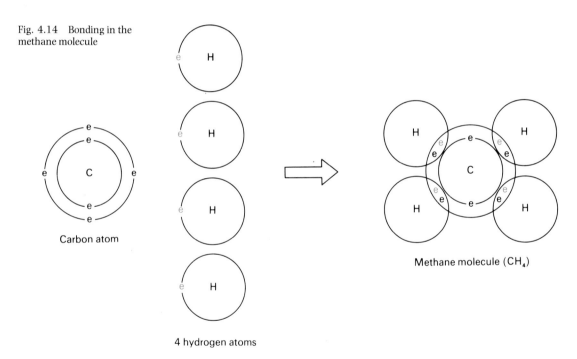

Carbon atom

4 hydrogen atoms

Methane molecule (CH₄)

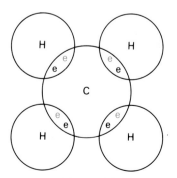

Fig. 4.15(a) Simplified diagram of a methane molecule

Fig. 4.15(b) Four single covalent bonds in the methane molecule

Fig. 4.15(c) A model of the methane molecule

The ammonia molecule

Ammonia is a gas which contains the elements nitrogen and hydrogen. The molecule of ammonia contains one nitrogen and three hydrogen atoms. The electron structures of the two elements are:

$$_7N \quad 2,5 \qquad _1H \quad 1$$

The nitrogen atom needs three more electrons to obtain a full outer shell whilst each hydrogen atom requires only one. The nitrogen and hydrogen atoms share electrons forming three single covalent bonds as shown in Fig. 4.16.

Fig. 4.17(a)   A model of the ammonia molecule

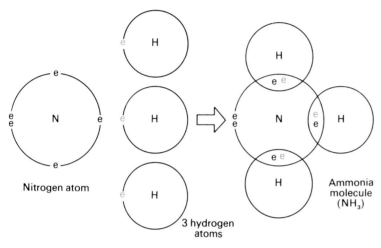

Fig. 4.16   Bonding in the ammonia molecule

Fig. 4.17(b)   Three single covalent bonds in the ammonia molecule

Other covalent molecules

Some molecules have more than one covalent bond between the atoms. A **double covalent bond** involves the sharing of two pairs of electrons. The simplest example of a molecule which contains this type of bond is oxygen (O_2). The electron structure of each oxygen atom is 2,6. Each of these atoms requires two more electrons to obtain the inert gas structure of neon. To get these extra electrons each atom shares two of its electrons as shown in Fig. 4.18. This double bond can be drawn in a simplified way as shown in Fig. 4.19.

Fig. 4.19(a)   A model of the oxygen molecule

$$O{=}O$$

Fig. 4.19(b)   The double covalent bond in an oxygen molecule

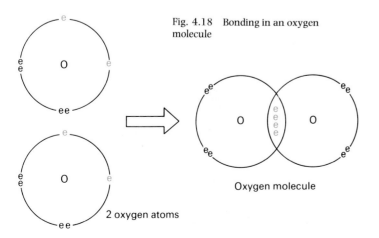

Fig. 4.18   Bonding in an oxygen molecule

Another example of a substance which contains a double bond is the gas ethene (used to make the plastic polythene—see Chapter 11, page 152). A simplified diagram is shown in Fig. 4.21. The electron structures of the two elements present in this compound are:

$_6C$ 2,4 $_1H$ 1.

Each carbon atom needs four more electrons to have a full outer shell whilst each hydrogen atom needs only one. The atoms in this molecule share electrons as shown in Fig. 4.21, so producing four single and one double covalent bonds.

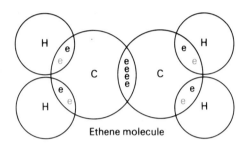

Ethene molecule

Fig. 4.21   Bonding in the ethene molecule

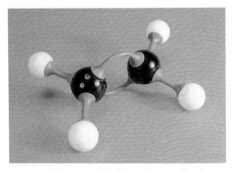

Fig. 4.20(a)   A model of the ethene molecule

Fig. 4.20(b)   The single and double covalent bonds in the ethene molecule

Bonds in metals

Another way in which atoms obtain a more stable electron structure can be found in metals. In metals each atom is vibrating in a fixed position. However, the electrons in the outer shell of the metal atoms are given to a 'pool' and are able to move throughout the whole metal structure (see Fig. 4.22). When the metal atoms lose these outer electrons they become positive ions. Metals are therefore held together by a similar force to that found in ionically-bonded substances such as sodium chloride. The bonding in metals is therefore often strong.

Positive ions

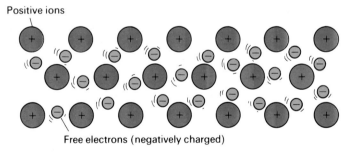

Free electrons (negatively charged)

Fig. 4.22   In metals, the outer-shell electrons can move throughout the structure

—————————————————————QUESTIONS—————————————————————

1 Atoms of three elements A, B and C have 8, 9 and 11 electrons respectively. Atoms of neon have 10 electrons.
  a) Determine the most likely formula of the compound formed by the combination of:
    i) elements A and C;
    ii) elements B and C;
    iii) atoms of element A with each other.
  b) In each of the cases (i)–(iii) name the type of bond formed.
  c) State which one of the compounds formed you would expect to be an electrolyte and give its formula.

2 The diagram below shows a suitable apparatus for carrying out the electrolysis of lead(II) iodide.

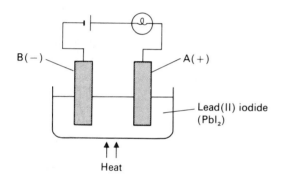

  a) What is the name of:
    i) electrode A;
    ii) electrode B?
  b) Name a suitable material for use as electrodes.
  c) Name the substances produced at electrodes A and B.
  d) Write equations for the reactions that take place at electrodes A and B.
  e) Explain why the lead(II) iodide had to be heated.
  f) Lead iodide is an *electrolyte*. What do you understand by this term?

3 Explain the meaning of each of the following terms:
  a) insulator;
  b) conductor;
  c) electrode;
  d) electrolysis.
  In each case use an example to help with your explanation.

4 Draw diagrams to show the bonding in each of the following ionic compounds:
  a) calcium oxide, CaO;
  b) magnesium chloride, $MgCl_2$;

  c) Lithium fluoride, LiF;
  d) potassium chloride, KCl.

5 Four elements are listed below. The atomic number of each element is given in brackets.

Fluorine(9) Neon(10) Sodium(11) Magnesium(12)
    F   Ne   Na   Mg

  a) Name the element which has 8 electrons in its outer energy level. (1)
  b) i) How many protons does a magnesium ion(Mg^{2+}) contain? (1)
    ii) How many electrons does a magnesium ion(Mg^{2+}) contain? (1)
  c) Name and explain by means of a diagram, the type of chemical bonding linking atoms of fluorine in the molecule F_2.
    (Type of bonding—1)
    (Diagram (showing all outer energy level electrons)—2)
  d) Complete the following by inserting one word in each space.
    Solid sodium fluoride contains particles called _____ but because they are not free to move the solid is a non-conductor of electricity. If the solid is _____ the sodium fluoride becomes a good conductor. (2)
  (JMB/WMEB 1980)

6 a) The element chlorine exists as two isotopes. Complete the following table (Table 1) about these two different kinds of chlorine atoms. (2)

	Isotope 1	Isotope 2
Atomic number	17	
Mass number	35	
Number of electrons		
Number of protons		17
Number of neutrons		20

Table 1

  b) In a chlorine molecule the two chlorine atoms are joined by a covalent bond. Draw a simple diagram showing this covalent bonding by indicating the arrangement of the outer electrons in the chlorine atoms. (2)
  c) Magnesium chloride is an ionic compound. Complete Table 2 which describes the ions in this compound. (3)

	Chloride ion	Magnesium ion
Symbol for ion		Mg^{2+}
Number of protons	17	
Number of electrons		10

Table 2

d) The atomic numbers of three elements L, M, N are 12, 15 and 17 respectively. Write the formula for the simplest compound formed between:
   i) L and N;
   ii) L and M;
   iii) M and N. (3)
(JMB/WMEB 1981)

7 The atomic numbers of the following elements are: hydrogen (1), carbon (6), oxygen (8), aluminium (13), chlorine (17), calcium (20).
   a) Write the electronic arrangement of one *atom* of the following elements, by indicating the number of electrons in each successive shell (e.g. nitrogen: 2,5):
      i) carbon;
      ii) aluminium;
      iii) chlorine;
      iv) calcium. (4)
   b) Write the electronic arrangement for one *ion* of the following elements:
      i) aluminium;
      ii) chlorine;
      iii) calcium. (3)

c) Give a diagram for a molecule of each of the following compounds, showing the outermost electron shells only:
   i) methane, CH_4;
   ii) tetrachloromethane, CCl_4;
   iii) oxygen, O_2;
   iv) hydrogen chloride, HCl;
   v) water, H_2O. (10)
(AEB 1981)

8 a) Atoms of the non-metal fluorine each have nine electrons.
   i) Write down or draw the arrangement of the electrons in a single fluorine atom.
   ii) Show how an atom of fluorine will form an ion.
   b) Sodium fluoride and magnesium fluoride are both ionic solids. Write down the formulae of the ions they contain.
(OLE 1983)

9 a) Complete Table 3. (5)
   b) There are two isotopes of hydrogen, ^1H and ^2H. Each of these isotopes forms water when burned in oxygen. Complete Table 4.
   (Relative atomic mass of oxygen = 16.)
   One of these forms of water is used as a coolant in nuclear power stations. This may result in it becoming radioactive. What problem does this cause? (3)
   c) Draw a diagram which shows the electron arrangement in a molecule of silicon tetrachloride, $SiCl_4$. Only the outer energy level electrons need be shown for each atom. (3)
(NEA 1985)

Particle	Mass number	Atomic number	Number of protons	Number of neutrons	Number of electrons
Boron atom, B	11		5		
Magnesium ion, Mg^{2+}	24	12			
Oxide ion, O^{2-}	16	8			

Table 3

Isotope	Mass number	Number of protons	Number of neutrons	Relative molecular mass of water formed
^1H	1			
^2H	2			

Table 4

STRUCTURE

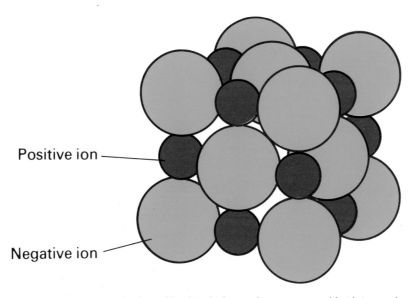

Positive ion

Negative ion

Fig. 5.1   The structure of sodium chloride—the large spheres represent chloride ions and the small spheres represent sodium ions

In Chapter 4 you learned that atoms can bond together in a number of ways. They can form ions as in ionic compounds. They can share electrons as in covalent elements and compounds. They can give electrons to a 'pool' as in metals. In all these cases usually only the outer shell electrons are involved. These different bonding schemes give rise to several different types of structure.

Metallic structure

The ions in a piece of a pure metal are all of the same size. At room temperature they are closely packed together in a regular pattern to form a **crystal structure** or **crystal lattice**. The way in which the ions are arranged in the structure is usually very simple as shown in Fig. 5.3. Layers like this can be stacked one on top of the other. In doing

Fig. 5.2(a)   Crystal structure in a broken magnet

Fig. 5.2(b)   Zinc crystals on galvanized steel

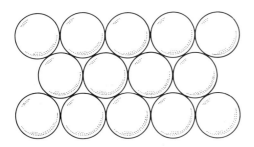

A second and third layer of spheres are then added

Fig. 5.3   Arrangement of ions in the crystal lattice of a metal

so three possible arrangements of the ions are produced, as shown in Fig. 5.4.

Face-centred cubic structure (e.g. copper or aluminium)

Close-packed hexagonal structure (e.g. zinc or magnesium)

Body-centred cubic structure (e.g. sodium, iron or chromium)

Fig. 5.4

Metals like copper and aluminium have a **face-centred cubic structure** whilst metals such as zinc or magnesium have a **close-packed hexagonal structure**. The **body-centred cubic structure** which is less efficient in its use of space is shown by sodium, iron and chromium.

Fig. 5.5   Uses of some metals

(a)   Brass coffee pot

(b)   Bronze statue

(c)   Aluminium alloy wheel

(d)   Steel bridge

(e)   Aircraft bodies are largely aluminium

Ionic structures

As soon as we begin to think about the structure of crystals of ionic compounds we encounter some problems. A major one is that not all the ions are of the same size. The other problem is that since they are ions they all have electrical charges, which either attract or repel each other. In a crystal of sodium chloride there are two different sorts of ion. There are sodium ions each with a positive electrical charge and there are chloride ions each with a negative electrical charge. Ions with similar charges *repel* each other and ions with opposite charges *attract* each other. In a crystal of sodium chloride the ions are arranged so that those with similar charges are as far from each other as is possible. The ions with opposite charges are as near to each other as they can be. The crystal structure of sodium chloride is shown in Fig. 5.1. The oppositely charged ions are very strongly attracted to one another. All the ions are therefore very tightly held in this structure.

Covalent structures

Usually when a substance contains only non-metals then it consists of molecules. These may be divided into two groups.

1 Small molecules

Such molecules often have between two and a hundred atoms per molecule. They may be simple elements such as hydrogen (H_2) or oxygen (O_2) or more complex compounds such as methane (CH_4) or ethanol (C_2H_5OH)—see Fig. 5.6. The atoms in these molecules are held together by strong covalent bonds. Some simple molecules such as iodine (I_2) form crystals at room temperature. In this type of crystal the molecules are attracted to each other by weak forces called **van der Waals' forces**. The way in which the molecules are arranged in the crystal of iodine are shown in Fig. 5.7.

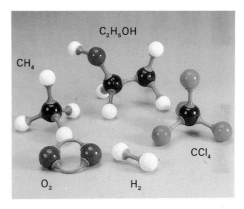

Fig. 5.6   Molecular models of: CH_4, O_2, C_2H_5OH, H_2 and CCl_4

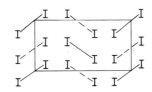

I——I Molecules in plane of the page .
I– – –I Molecules below and above
the plane of the page

Fig. 5.7   Structure of iodine

2 Giant molecules

Giant molecules have many millions of atoms per molecule joined together by strong covalent bonds. Silicon(IV) oxide is a giant molecule and part of its structure is shown in Fig. 5.8. Diamond and graphite, both forms of carbon, are further examples of giant molecules. We shall be looking at these examples in more detail in Chapter 10 (page 134).

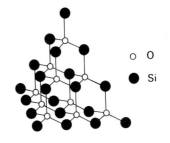

o O

● Si

Fig. 5.8   Silicon dioxide structure

The effect of structure and bonding on properties

The different types of bonding and structure you have just studied give rise to a difference in properties. Some properties related to the different bonding and structure types are shown in Table 5.1.

Property Structure	Melting point (°C)	Boiling point (°C)	Density ($g\,cm^{-3}$)	Electrical conductivity	Solubility in water
Simple molecules, e.g. methane	Low—melts at $-183\,°C$	Low—boils at $-161\,°C$	Low—$0.424\,g\,cm^{-3}$	No	Variable solubility
Giant molecules, e.g. silicon(IV) oxide	High—melts at $1610\,°C$	High—boils at $2230\,°C$	Medium—$2.65\,g\,cm^{-3}$	No*	Insoluble
Ionic, e.g. sodium chloride	High—melts at $801\,°C$	High—boils at $1413\,°C$	Medium—$2.17\,g\,cm^{-3}$	Yes, when molten or dissolved in water	Yes
Metallic, e.g. iron	High—melts at $1540\,°C$	High—boils at $2760\,°C$	High—$7.87\,g\,cm^{-3}$	Yes	Insoluble

Table 5.1   *Except graphite (see Chapter 10)

Melting points

From Table 5.1 you will see that substances which consist of small molecules have much lower melting points than those substances which are composed of giant molecules. In order for a solid to melt some or all of the bonds have to be loosened or broken. The particles move away from each other and eventually they move so far apart that any structure that existed, collapses, and a liquid is formed. There are only weak forces of attraction between the small molecules (van der Waals' forces) and so it is much easier to melt a substance which has small molecules in its structure. On the other hand, to separate the particles in a giant structure, such as silicon(IV) oxide, requires much more energy. This is because the SiO_2 units in this structure are held together by strong covalent bonds. The melting points of substances like this, as well as diamond and graphite, are therefore much higher than those for structures based on small molecules.

Metals and ionic substances have very strong forces of attraction between their particles. A lot of (heat) energy is needed, therefore, to separate the particles and melt the substance.

Density

As well as depending on how heavy the atoms are, the density of a substance also depends on the amount of 'empty' space between its particles. If there is 'a lot of empty space' between the particles, as in the case of silicon(IV) oxide (see Fig. 5.8), the density will be quite low (see Table 5.1). Substances, such as methane, which are gases at room temperature and consequently have large spaces between the molecules, have very low densities (see Table 5.1). Many common metals on the other hand have a closely packed structure as well as heavy atoms and hence they have a high density (see Table 5.1).

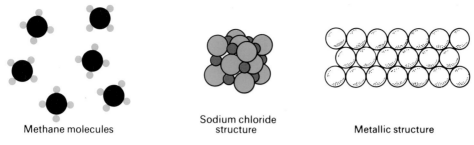

Fig. 5.9   Comparison of three kinds of structure

Electrical conductivity

If charged particles can move, then electricity can flow. When ionic substances are molten, or dissolved in water, the ions are free to move (see Fig. 5.10). The 'pooled' electrons of metals are also free to move within the metal and so electricity will be conducted.

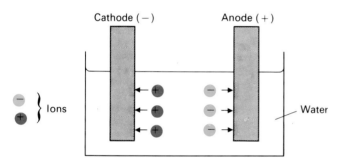

Fig. 5.10   Positive ions are attracted to the cathode and negative ions to the anode

Solubility in water

Water molecules bombard the surface of the ionic crystals. The water molecules separate the ions and bond to them. The ions are therefore kept apart (see Fig. 5.11). Water is an unusual solvent and can interact with and dissolve some covalent molecules better than others.

Fig. 5.11   When an ionic substance dissolves in water the water molecules separate the ions and bond to them

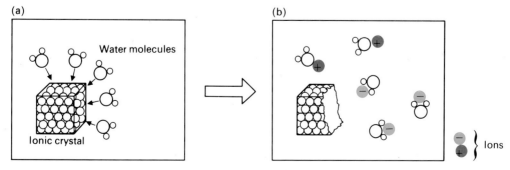

————————————————————QUESTIONS————————————————————

1 Describe what happens if an ionic crystal such as sodium chloride is:
a) added to water;
b) heated to a very high temperature.

2 a) Draw a simple diagram to show how the ions are arranged in a crystal of sodium chloride.
b) Explain why the melting points of sodium chloride and of iodine are so different.
c) Draw a simple diagram to show how the molecules are arranged in a crystal of iodine.

3 Explain the following:
a) Metals generally have high densities.
b) Ionic compounds when molten or dissolved in water will conduct electricity, however, they will not conduct when in the solid state.
c) The structure of ionic substances affects their melting points.

4 Study the data given in Table 1.
a) Which of the substances is:
   i) nitrogen;
   ii) potassium chloride;
   iii) carbon (as diamond)?
b) Name the weak forces of attraction which exist between molecules such as nitrogen.
c) Name the type of bonding found in the three substances mentioned in (a).

5 Sodium and chlorine react together to form a compound which has a giant ionic structure.
a) Explain how the ions are held together in this ionic structure.   (1)
b) What is the shape of a crystal of sodium chloride?   (1)
c) Draw diagrams to show the electronic arrangement of a sodium *ion* and a chloride *ion*, given that the atomic number of sodium is 11 and that of chlorine is 17.   (4)
(AEB 1984)

6 a) Name an ionic and a covalent compound and explain how each structure is formed from its elements.   (6)
b) Show how each type of bonding influences the properties of the compound in terms of physical appearance, melting point, solubility in water and electrical conductivity.   (9)
(SUJB 1982)

Substance	Melting point (°C)	Boiling point (°C)	Density (g cm⁻³)	Electrical conductivity	Solubility in water
A	3750	4200	3.51	No	Insoluble
B	−210	−196	0.37	No	Insoluble
C	772	1407	1.98	Yes when molten or in solution	Soluble

Table 1

7 Table 2 provides some information about certain chemicals.

Substance	Melting point (°C)	Boiling point (°C)	Electrical conductivity		
			of solid	of liquid	in water
A	1540	3000	Good	Good	Insoluble
B	−114	−85	Poor	Poor	Good
C	712	1418	Poor	Good	Good
D	−68	57	Poor	Poor	Good
E	−25	144	Poor	Poor	Insoluble
F	−39	357	Good	Good	Insoluble
G	1700	2776	Poor	Poor	Insoluble
H	2045	3000	Poor	Good	Insoluble

Table 2

Answer the following questions by writing one of the letters A to H. Each letter may be used once, more than once or not at all.

From the substances shown indicate:

a) the substance with the lowest melting point; (1)
b) one substance which is a liquid at room temperature; (1)
c) the substance which is a gas at room temperature; (1)
d) one substance which could be a metal; (1)
e) one substance which is likely to be an ionic solid at room temperature; (1)
f) one substance which, at room temperature, is likely to consist of molecules containing covalent bonds; (1)
g) the substance which, at room temperature, is likely to have a covalently bonded macromolecular structure; (1)
h) one substance which is likely to consist of molecules containing covalent bonds, and which when added to water produces ions in solution; (1)
i) the substance which is likely to be an ionic solid at room temperature, and which is insoluble in water. (1)

ELECTROLYSIS OF SOLUTIONS

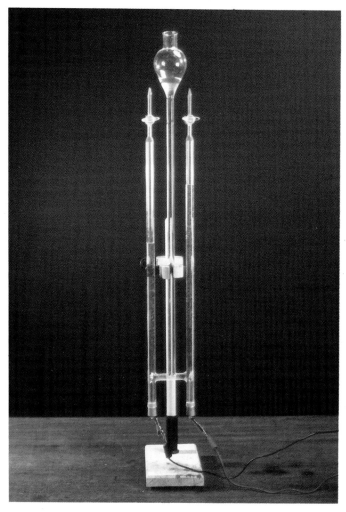

Fig. 6.1   The Hofmann voltameter

Ionic substances usually dissolve in water. In this chapter we are going to examine what happens when we try to electrolyse solutions formed from ionic compounds.

Electrolysis of water

Water is a very stable substance. However, it can be made to decompose if an electric current is passed through it. The apparatus normally used to show this is called a **Hofmann voltameter** (see Figs 6.1 and 6.2).

Deionized (pure) water is poured into the apparatus. When the electric current is switched on nothing happens to the water because it is such a poor conductor of electricity. However, if a small amount of dilute sulphuric acid or sodium hydroxide solution is added an electric current flows quite well. Gases are evolved at the two electrodes and collected as shown in Fig. 6.2. About twice as much gas is liberated at the cathode as at the anode. The gas collected at the cathode burns with a 'pop' showing it to be hydrogen. For hydrogen to be collected in this way, positively charged hydrogen ions must have been attracted to the cathode.

hydrogen ion + electron ⟶ hydrogen atom

$$H^+ \quad + \quad e^- \quad \longrightarrow \quad H$$

two hydrogen atoms ⟶ hydrogen molecule

$$2H \quad \longrightarrow \quad H_{2(g)}$$

If during this process a water molecule loses a hydrogen atom as an ion (H^+) then the remaining portion must be OH^-.

water − hydrogen ion ⟶ hydroxide ion

$$H_2O \quad - \quad H^+ \quad \longrightarrow \quad OH^-$$

OH^- is known as the **hydroxide ion**. During the electrolysis these hydroxide ions are attracted to the anode. The gas collected at the anode relights a glowing splint, showing it to be oxygen.

hydroxide ion ⟶ hydroxide group + electron

$$OH^- \quad \longrightarrow \quad OH \quad + \quad e^-$$

or $\quad 4OH^- \quad \longrightarrow \quad 4OH \quad + \quad 4e^-$

These four hydroxide groups now rearrange to produce oxygen and water:

four hydroxide groups ⟶ water + oxygen

$$4OH \quad \longrightarrow 2H_2O_{(l)} + \quad O_{2(g)}$$

During the electrolysis process electrons deposited at the anode are passed through to the cathode.

In the Hofmann voltameter shown in Fig. 6.2 platinum electrodes are used. However, if carbon electrodes are used a mixture of gases is produced at the cathode. As well as oxygen the mixture contains carbon monoxide and carbon dioxide. These other gases are formed by the reaction of some oxygen with the carbon electrodes.

Electrolysis of sodium chloride solution

When sodium chloride (NaCl) is dissolved in water the sodium and chloride ions become free to move. A suitable cell for carrying out the electrolysis of this solution is shown in Fig. 6.3. When a concentrated solution of sodium chloride is electrolysed in this cell the gases chlorine and hydrogen are obtained. Sodium might have been expected to be produced at the cathode. Why does this not happen?

Four ions are present in solution:

From water		*From sodium chloride*	
H^+ and	OH^-	Na^+ and	Cl^-
(hydrogen ion)	(hydroxide ion)	(sodium ion)	(chloride ion)

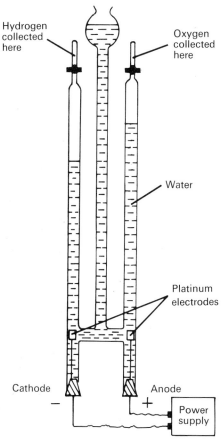

Fig. 6.2 Electrolysis of water using the Hofmann voltameter

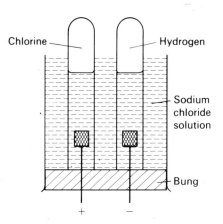

Fig. 6.3 The electrolysis of sodium chloride solution

H$^+$ and Na$^+$ ions are attracted to the cathode (see Fig. 6.4). The H$^+$ ions accept electrons more easily than the Na$^+$ ions and so hydrogen gas (H$_2$) is produced at the cathode (see Fig. 6.5).

$$H^+ + e^- \longrightarrow H$$

$$2H \longrightarrow H_{2(g)}$$

Fig. 6.4   A closer look at the electrolysis of sodium chloride solution

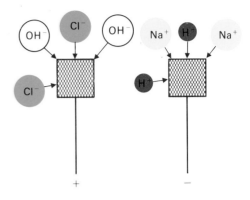

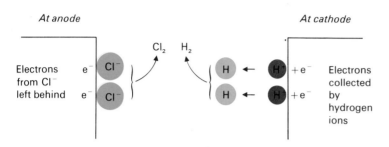

At anode   *At cathode*

Electrons from Cl$^-$ left behind

Cl$_2$ H$_2$

Electrons collected by hydrogen ions

Fig. 6.5   Chlorine gas is collected at the anode, hydrogen gas is collected at the cathode

Because sodium is more reactive than hydrogen it loses electrons more easily. Generally it is found that during the electrolysis of aqueous solutions, very reactive metals, like sodium, are not formed at the cathode. You will recall from Chapter 3 that these reactive metals react with water liberating hydrogen.

OH$^-$ and Cl$^-$ are attracted to the anode (see Fig. 6.4). The Cl$^-$ ions release (give up) electrons more readily than the OH$^-$ ions and so chlorine gas is produced at the anode.

$$Cl^- \longrightarrow Cl + e^-$$

$$2Cl \longrightarrow Cl_{2(g)}$$

Electrolysis of copper(II) sulphate solution

Copper(II) sulphate solution (CuSO$_{4(aq)}$) may be electrolysed in a cell similar to that shown in Fig. 6.3. When the solution is electrolysed oxygen gas and copper metal are formed at the anode and cathode respectively. Can we account for these observations?

Four ions are present in the solution:

From water	*From copper(II) sulphate*	
H$^+$ and OH$^-$	Cu^{2+} and	SO$_4^{2-}$
	(copper ion)	(sulphate ion)

H$^+$ and Cu^{2+} ions are attracted to the cathode. Cu^{2+} ions accept electrons more readily than the H$^+$ ions. Copper metal is therefore deposited at the cathode (see Fig. 6.6).

$$\text{copper ion} + \text{electrons} \longrightarrow \text{copper atom}$$

$$Cu^{2+} + 2e^- \longrightarrow Cu_{(s)}$$

OH$^-$ and SO$_4^{2-}$ ions are attracted to the anode. The OH$^-$ ions release electrons more easily than the SO$_4^{2-}$ ions. Oxygen gas and water are therefore produced at the anode (see Fig. 6.6).

$$\text{hydroxide ions} \longrightarrow \text{oxygen} + \text{water} + \text{electrons}$$

$$4OH^- \longrightarrow O_{2(g)} + 2H_2O_{(l)} + 4e^-$$

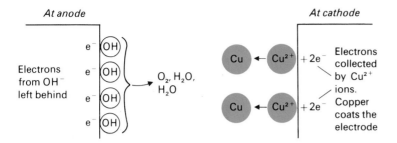

Fig. 6.6 Oxygen is collected at the anode, copper is produced at the cathode

A different result is obtained if copper electrodes are used. The same ions as above are present in the solution of copper(II) sulphate. As above, OH^- and SO_4^{2-} ions are attracted to the anode. However, neither gives up electrons. Instead the following occurs. Copper atoms from the anode itself lose electrons and become copper ions (see Fig. 6.7).

copper atom $\longrightarrow$ copper ion + electrons

$$Cu \longrightarrow Cu^{2+} + 2e^-$$

The electrons which are formed at the anode travel around the external circuit to the cathode. Here the electrons are passed onto the Cu^{2+} ions in solution and copper is deposited.

copper ion + electrons $\longrightarrow$ copper atom

$$Cu^{2+} + 2e^- \longrightarrow Cu_{(s)}$$

The mass of the copper cathode increases whilst that of the copper anode decreases (see Fig. 6.8). The colour of the copper(II) sulphate solution remains the same since Cu^{2+} ions from the anode are replacing those deposited at the cathode.

Table 6.1 summarizes the results of a series of electrolysis experiments.

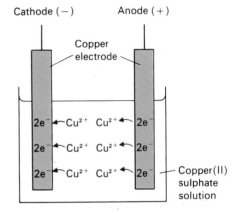

Fig. 6.7 The electrolysis of copper(II) sulphate solution using copper electrodes

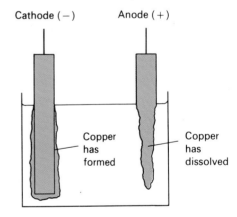

Fig. 6.8(a) During electrolysis copper lost from the anode transfers to the cathode

Solution	Material of electrodes	Substance formed at the anode (+)	Substance formed at the cathode (−)
Dilute sulphuric acid or dilute sodium hydroxide	Platinum*	Oxygen	Hydrogen
Copper(II) sulphate	Platinum*	Oxygen	Copper
	Copper	None	Copper
Concentrated sodium chloride	Platinum*	Chlorine	Hydrogen

Table 6.1

*Platinum (an inert electrode) may be replaced by carbon. The only difference to occur is that where oxygen is produced some carbon dioxide and carbon monoxide will also be formed.

Fig. 6.8(b) Copper electrodes before and after electrolysis

Uses of electrolysis

Electrolysis is used for our benefit in a number of ways.

Copper purification

In the previous section you saw that when copper(II) sulphate solution is electrolysed using copper electrodes copper is lost from the anode and gained at the cathode. This process is used in purifying copper (see Fig. 6.9). Impure copper is used as the anode whilst the cathode is pure copper. The electrolyte used is copper(II) sulphate solution acidified with a little dilute sulphuric acid. When the current flows, copper is dissolved from the impure anode and transferred to the pure cathode. The impurities from the anode are left behind (see Fig. 6.9). In a typical plant 1500 of these electrolysis cells will run for about 14 days. In this time the pure copper cathode will increase in mass from about 5 kg to over 100 kg.

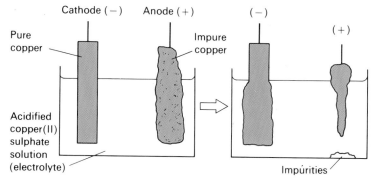

Fig. 6.9   Industrial purification of copper

Electroplating

It is sometimes useful to coat one metal with a thin coating of another metal. If this coating is carried out by electrolysis then the process is known as **electroplating**. For example, steel car bumpers are chromium plated in a cell like the one in Fig. 6.11. This is done not only to prevent corrosion but also to make them more attractive. Steel is also electroplated with tin before being made up into 'tins' for food.

Fig. 6.10(a)   This kettle is electroplated with chrome

Fig. 6.10(b)   Electroplated silver

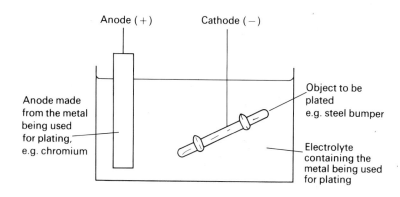

Fig. 6.11   The electroplating process

The manufacture of sodium hydroxide (NaOH)

Sodium hydroxide is a very important compound. It is used in the manufacture of soaps, many sodium salts, some organic chemicals as well as paper and many other items. It is made by the electrolysis of saturated brine (concentrated sodium chloride solution). A diagram of a typical cell used is shown in Fig. 6.12. It is called a **diaphragm cell**.

The cell contains titanium anodes and steel cathodes separated by a porous diaphragm made of asbestos. The saturated brine is added to the anode compartment. The ions present in this concentrated sodium chloride solution are:

From water	*From sodium chloride*
H^+ and OH^-	Na^+ and Cl^-

When the current flows in the cell 50% of the chloride ions (Cl^-) are attracted to the anode. Here each Cl^- loses an electron and chlorine atoms then molecules of chlorine gas are produced.

chloride ion $\longrightarrow$ chlorine atom + electron

$$Cl^- \longrightarrow Cl + e^-$$

two chlorine atoms $\longrightarrow$ a chlorine molecule

$$2Cl \longrightarrow Cl_{2(g)}$$

This gas then rises to the surface (see Fig. 6.13) and is piped away.

Fig. 6.12   The diaphragm cell

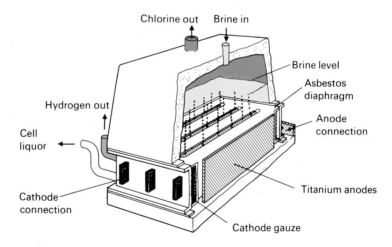

Fig. 6.13   How the diaphragm cell works

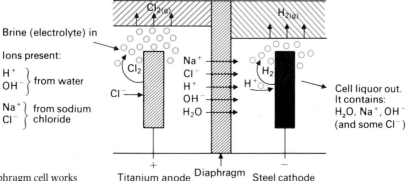

The hydrogen ions (H$^+$) are attracted to the cathode (equivalent to the chloride ions attracted to the anode). These ions gain an electron and the resulting hydrogen atoms combine to give hydrogen gas. The gas rises to the surface and is piped away.

hydrogen ion + electron $\longrightarrow$ hydrogen atom

$$H^+ \quad + \quad e^- \quad \longrightarrow \quad H$$

two hydrogen atoms $\longrightarrow$ a hydrogen molecule

$$2H \quad \longrightarrow \quad H_{2(g)}$$

The brine level in the anode compartment is kept higher than the level of liquid in the cathode compartment. This is done to encourage the depleted brine to seep through the asbestos diaphragm as shown in Fig. 6.13. The sodium (Na$^+$) and hydroxide (OH$^-$) ions build up in the cathode compartment together with some unused chloride ions (Cl$^-$). This cell 'liquor' is concentrated by evaporation. During the evaporation sodium chloride (NaCl) crystallizes out. The final concentrated liquid contains 50% by mass of sodium hydroxide (NaOH) with only a trace of sodium chloride (1%).

Chlorine is the most important by-product of this process. It is used in the manufacture of plastics and solvents but it also has many other applications (see Fig. 6.14). It will be discussed in more detail in Chapter 15.

Extraction of metals

Some reactive metals are extracted from their ores by electrolysis. For example, aluminium is extracted by electrolysis of its ore dissolved in a molten substance called **cryolite**. Many millions of tonnes of this metal are used worldwide every day (see Fig. 6.15). The details of the production of aluminium, as well as the very reactive metal sodium will be discussed in Chapter 8.

(a) PVC window

(b) PVC handbag

Fig. 6.15(a) The Red Arrows' jets are made mostly of aluminium

Fig. 6.15(b) Aluminium milk bottle tops

(c) Dry cleaning

Fig. 6.14 Some uses of chlorine compounds

———————————————————————QUESTIONS————————————————————

1

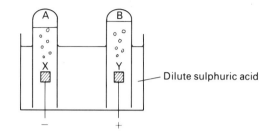

Dilute sulphuric acid

This is a diagram of an experiment in which electricity was passed through a mixture of distilled water containing a little dilute sulphuric acid.
a) Name the gas that collects at A.
b) Name the gas that collects at B.
c) If $100\,cm^3$ of gas collects in A how much would there be in B?
d) Name the metal usually used for X and Y.
e) X is called the _____.
f) Y is called the _____.
g) Write down the formulae of the three ions present in the solution.
h) Write down the equations for the reactions that take place at both X and Y (or describe the changes that take place if you cannot write the equations).

2 The apparatus shown in the diagram below was used to investigate the gases produced when a concentrated solution of potassium chloride was electrolysed.

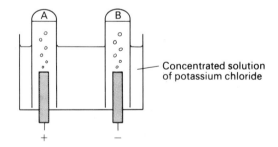

Concentrated solution of potassium chloride

a) Name a non-metal suitable for use as electrodes.
b) Name the gas collected in A and the gas collected in B.
c) Describe how you would test the gases collected.
d) The volume of gas collected in B was slightly less than that collected in A. The teacher said the volumes should have been equal but gave a simple explanation of the 'missing' gas in B. What was the explanation?
(Assume that the apparatus was working perfectly.)

e) Write down the equations which describe the production of the gases at the electrodes in A and B.
f) i) If the concentrated solution of potassium chloride was now replaced by dilute sodium hydroxide what gases would be produced at A and B?
  ii) In what ratio would you expect these gases to be produced?

3 Table 1 shows the results of testing a number of substances (solids and liquids) to see if they conducted an electric current. The electrodes were platinum.

Substance	Physical state	Conductivity	Products	
A	Solid	No	—	—
B	Liquid	Yes	Hydrogen	Chlorine
C	Liquid	Yes	Silvery metal	Brown vapour
D	Liquid	No	—	—
E	Liquid	Yes	Hydrogen	Oxygen
F	Liquid	Yes	—	—
G	Solid	Yes	—	—
H	Liquid	Yes	Red metal	Oxygen

Table 1

a) Which of the substances A–H is(are) an electrolyte(s).
b) Give the letters of those substances which may be metals.
c) Give the letter of the substance which may be sodium chloride.
d) Which substance could be mercury?
e) Give the name of a substance which might be C.
f) One of the substances tested was polythene. Which substance was this?
g) Give the letter of a substance which could be sugar solution.
h) Name a substance which might be H.
i) Name a substance which might be E.
j) What volume of hydrogen would you expect to collect during the test on E if $20\,cm^3$ of oxygen were collected?

4 Sodium hydroxide is manufactured electrolytically from sodium chloride.
  a) Name:
    i) the electrolyte;
    ii) the material of the electrodes;
    iii) the material of the diaphragm.
  b) Write equations for the reactions which take place at the anode and cathode.
  c) Give two large-scale uses of sodium hydroxide.
  d) i) Name the important gaseous byproduct of the manufacture.
    ii) Give two large-scale uses of this gas.

5 Copper is purified using an electrolysis cell of the type shown in the diagram below.

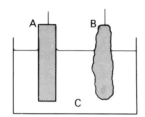

  a) Name the material of the electrodes A and B and the electrolyte C.
  b) Electrode A is the _____.
     Electrode B is the _____.
  c) Draw a labelled diagram to show the changes which take place as the purification process proceeds.
  d) Write equations for the reactions which take place at the anode and cathode. (If you cannot do this then describe the changes which take place at the electrodes.)
  e) Which electrode will have increased in mass during the purification process?
  f) Why is it necessary to add a little dilute sulphuric acid to the electrolyte?
  g) Give two uses of pure copper metal.

6 Electroplating is an important industrial process.
  a) Explain what electroplating is.
  b) Why are certain metals electroplated?
  c) Give two examples of the use of electroplating.

7 Complete Table 2 which is about the electrolysis of three compounds either molten or in solution, using inert electrodes.   (5)

Electrolyte	Product at cathode (−ve electrode)	Product at anode (+ve electrode)
Concentrated sodium chloride solution		
	Magnesium	Bromine
Copper(II) sulphate solution		

Table 2

(JMB/WMEB 1982)

8 The apparatus for the electrolyses of copper(II) sulphate solution, and of water acidified with dilute sulphuric acid, in separate voltameters, each with platinum electrodes, is shown in the diagram.

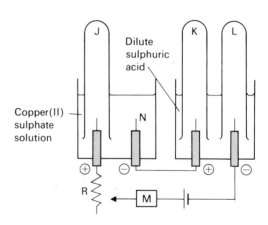

  a) Give the ions present, with their charges, in each voltameter.
  b) Name the gases which will collect in J, K and L.
  c) What ought to be the ratio by volume of the gas in L to the gas in K?
  d) Why is the ratio usually greater than expected?
  e) What will be formed at electrode N?
  f) What are R and meter M and what are their functions?
  g) Which other piece of apparatus would you need to find the quantity of electricity being passed in the circuit?
  h) Further changes will take place in the copper voltameter if the electrolysis is continued for some time. Describe them.
  i) Why is it necessary to add dilute acid to the water voltameter?   (15)

9 a) Complete Table 3 which is about the electrolysis of four chemicals using inert electrodes.   (5)

Electrolyte	Product at cathode (−ve electrode)	Product at anode (+ve electrode)
Molten sodium chloride		Chlorine
Molten calcium bromide	Calcium	
Sodium chloride solution		Chlorine
Copper(II) sulphate solution		

Table 3

b) State what is meant by the terms:
   i) 'electrolysis';
   ii) 'inert electrodes'.   (2)
c) Explain why the blue colour of the copper(II) sulphate solution becomes paler during electrolysis.   (1)
d) Explain why solid sodium chloride is a non-conductor of electricity, whereas molten sodium chloride and sodium chloride solution are good conductors of electricity.   (2)
(NEA 1985)

ACIDS, BASES AND SALTS

Fig. 7.1   These foods all contain acids

What have the following substances got in common with one another: sour milk, soda water, lemonade, vinegar, fruit juice, vitamin C tablets?

Answer—they each contain an **acid** of one sort or other. What properties do these substances have which make you think they contain acids?

The word acid means 'sour'. All acids possess this property in addition to often being corrosive and soluble in water. They also affect **indicators** (see Table 7.1). Indicators are substances which change colour when they are mixed with acids or alkalis. Acids are

Indicator	Colour in acid solution
Blue litmus	Red
Phenolphthalein	Colourless
Methyl orange	Pink
Universal indicator	Red

Table 7.1

Fig. 7.2   Vinegar contains ethanoic acid

Fig. 7.3 The effect of acid on the indicators in Table 7.1

Fig. 7.4 The hole in this lab coat was caused by an acid

neutralized by **bases** (see p. 79), carbonates and some metals. These are the properties we use not only to recognize the presence of 'everyday' acids but also the more common laboratory acids. Some common acids which you come across every day, either in the laboratory or in your home, are listed in Table 7.3.

Acids are:
1 'sour'
2 soluble in water
3 often corrosive
4 change the colour of indicators
5 neutralized by bases
6 react with some metals to release hydrogen
7 react with carbonates to form carbon dioxide

Table 7.2

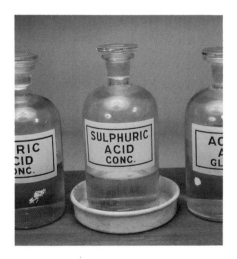

Fig. 7.5(a) Sulphuric acid—a 'laboratory' acid

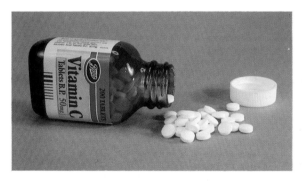

Fig. 7·5(b) Vitamin C (ascorbic acid)—an 'everyday' acid

Acid	Formula	Occurrence
Nitric acid	HNO_3	Found in laboratory
Hydrochloric acid	HCl	Produced by the stomach
Sulphuric acid	H_2SO_4	Found in laboratory
Ethanoic acid	CH_3COOH	Found in vinegar
Citric acid	$C_6H_8O_7$	Found in lemon juice
Tartaric acid	$C_3H_6O_6$	Found in grape juice
Carbonic acid	H_2CO_3	Found in lemonade

Table 7.3

Why are acids acidic?

The properties of acids depend upon the fact that when they are placed in water, they release hydrogen ions (H^+). It is the presence of these ions in solutions of acids which gives rise to the properties which we associate with acids. Hydrogen ions are only formed in any quantity in the presence of water. Anhydrous acids (see Fig. 7.5) do not, in general, show the properties we have listed.

The hydrogen atom consists of a single proton and a single electron and when the electron is removed, a hydrogen ion (H^+) is formed.

$$\text{hydrogen atom} \longrightarrow \text{hydrogen ion} + \text{electron}$$

$$H \longrightarrow H^+ + e^-$$

The reaction between an acid and water molecules involves the formation of an H^+ ion surrounded by water molecules—the hydrated hydrogen ion, which is represented as $H^+(aq)$ (see Fig. 7.6).

$$\underset{\substack{\text{(from} \\ \text{acid)}}}{H^+} + \text{water} \longrightarrow \underset{\substack{\text{(hydrated} \\ \text{hydrogen ion)}}}{H^+(aq)}$$

The presence of $H^+(aq)$ in solutions of acids can be shown by the fact that the solutions conduct electricity. When electricity is passed through such solutions, hydrogen gas is always given off at the cathode (see Fig. 7.7).

Some reactions of acids

Even though there are many different kinds of acid, there are some reactions which are common to all the acids you will use.

1 Dilute acids react with reactive metals to form a salt (see page 81) and hydrogen gas. For example, magnesium reacts with dilute hydrochloric acid:

$$\text{magnesium} + \underset{\text{hydrochloric acid}}{\text{dilute}} \longrightarrow \underset{\text{chloride}}{\text{magnesium}} + \text{hydrogen}$$

$$Mg_{(s)} + 2HCl_{(aq)} \longrightarrow MgCl_{2(aq)} + H_{2(g)}$$

2 Dilute acids react with metal carbonates to form a salt, carbon dioxide and water. For example, lead(II) carbonate reacts with dilute nitric acid:

$$\underset{\text{carbonate}}{\text{lead(II)}} + \underset{\text{nitric acid}}{\text{dilute}} \longrightarrow \underset{\text{nitrate}}{\text{lead(II)}} + \underset{\text{dioxide}}{\text{carbon}} + \text{water}$$

$$PbCO_{3(s)} + 2HNO_{3(aq)} \longrightarrow Pb(NO_3)_{2(aq)} + CO_{2(g)} + H_2O_{(l)}$$

3 Dilute acids react with metal oxides, when warmed (usually), to form a salt and water. For example, copper(II) oxide reacts with dilute sulphuric acid:

$$\underset{\text{oxide}}{\text{copper(II)}} + \underset{\text{sulphuric acid}}{\text{dilute}} \longrightarrow \underset{\text{sulphate}}{\text{copper(II)}} + \text{water}$$

$$CuO_{(s)} + H_2SO_{4(aq)} \longrightarrow CuSO_{4(aq)} + H_2O_{(l)}$$

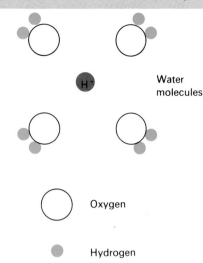

Fig. 7.6 The H^+ ion is surrounded by water molecules—the hydrated hydrogen ion

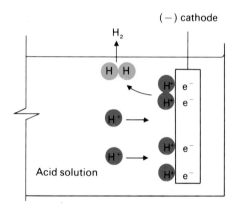

Fig. 7.7 Hydrogen is given off at the cathode when acid solutions are electrolysed

4 Dilute acids react with alkalis to form a salt and water. For example, sodium hydroxide reacts with dilute hydrochloric acid:

$$\text{sodium} \atop \text{hydroxide} + {\text{dilute} \atop \text{hydrochloric acid}} \longrightarrow {\text{sodium} \atop \text{chloride}} + \text{water}$$

$$NaOH_{(aq)} + HCl_{(aq)} \longrightarrow NaCl_{(aq)} + H_2O_{(l)}$$

Some definitions of acids

The accepted 'definition' of an acid has changed as our knowledge about acids has increased. Different definitions are useful in different circumstances. The common definitions are:

1 an acid is a substance which reacts with a base to form a salt and water only;

2 an acid is a substance which releases hydrogen ions when dissolved in water.

Strengths of acids

An acid can be described as either strong or weak. (Do not confuse these descriptions with 'concentrated' and 'dilute'—these terms tell us about the proportion of water and acid in a solution.) The strength or weakness of an acid depends on whether or not the solution formed when the acid dissolves in water contains a high or low concentration (amount) of hydrogen ions (H^+ (aq)).

If the acid completely breaks up into ions (ionizes) when dissolved in water it is described as 'strong'. For example:

Fig. 7.8 A strong acid has a high concentration of H^+ ions in solution

$$\text{sulphuric acid} \xrightarrow{\text{water}} \text{sulphate ions} + \text{hydrogen ions}$$

$$H_2SO_{4(l)} \xrightarrow{\text{water}} SO_{4(aq)}^{2-} + 2H_{(aq)}^+$$

Hydrochloric acid and nitric acid behave similarly. If the acid does not completely ionize when dissolved in water then there will be a lower concentration of $H_{(aq)}^+$ (some molecules remain as molecules in solution) and it will be called a 'weak acid'. For example:

$$\text{ethanoic acid} \underset{\text{water}}{\rightleftharpoons} \text{ethanoate ions} + \text{hydrogen ions}$$

$$CH_3COOH_{(l)} \underset{\text{water}}{\rightleftharpoons} CH_3COO_{(aq)}^- + H_{(aq)}^+$$

The double arrow $\rightleftharpoons$ means the reaction is reversible. This weak acid is found in vinegar.

Two other examples of weak acids which you can come across every day are carbonic acid and sulphurous acid.

1 Carbonic acid is formed when carbon dioxide dissolves in water:

$$\text{water} + \text{carbon dioxide} \rightleftharpoons \text{carbonic acid}$$

$$H_2O_{(l)} + CO_{2(g)} \rightleftharpoons H_2CO_3$$

This weak acid is present in lemonade and Coca-Cola.

2 Sulphurous acid is formed when sulphur dioxide dissolves in water:

$$\text{water} + \text{sulphur dioxide} \rightleftharpoons \text{sulphurous acid}$$

$$H_2O_{(l)} + SO_{2(g)} \rightleftharpoons H_2SO_{3(aq)}$$

This weak acid causes acid rain (see Chapter 14, page 201).

Fig. 7.9 Carbonic acid causes lemonade to fizz

pH scale

We record the strength of an acid in solution as a number described as **pH**. The term 'pH' is derived from the German for 'power of hydrogen'. The pH scale ranges from 0–14 and the pH value of a substance is related directly to the concentration of H^+ ions in solution.

An acidic solution would have a pH below 7 whilst an alkaline solution would have a pH above 7. A pH of 7 indicates a neutral solution, that is, one which is neither acid nor alkaline. Phenolphthalein, litmus, or any other common indicator, will tell us whether or not a solution is acidic (or alkaline) (see Fig. 7.10), but they cannot tell us how 'acid' (or alkaline) the solution is. However, there is mixture of indicators called **universal indicator** which can distinguish degrees of acidity and alkalinity. Universal indicator changes colour at different pH values as shown in Fig. 7.11.

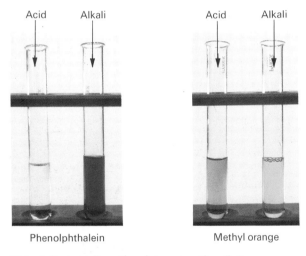

Fig. 7.10   Indicators tell you if a substance is acid or alkaline

The pH values of some common substances such as toothpaste and orange juice are located on the pH scale in Fig. 7.12. The more accurate measurement of pH values requires a pH meter (see Fig. 7.13).

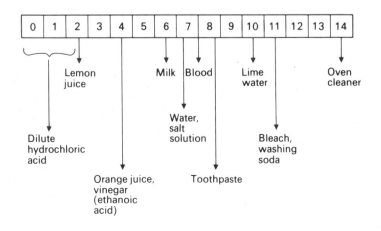

Fig. 7.12   pH values of some common substances

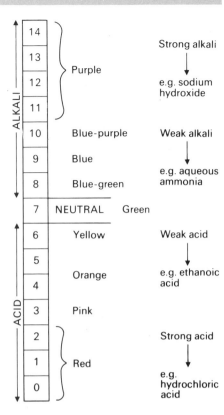

Fig. 7.11(a)   Universal indicator changes colour at the different pH values shown

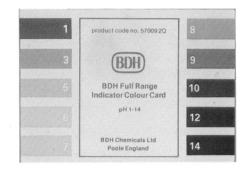

Fig. 7.11(b)   An indicator colour chart

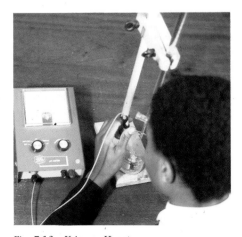

Fig. 7.13   Using a pH meter

Bases

The terms 'base' and 'alkali' are often confused. The main (or parent) term is 'base'. A **base** is a substance which reacts with an acid to produce a salt and water only. When this type of reaction takes place, we say the acid has been **neutralized**. In general, most metal oxides and metal hydroxides (as well as ammonia solution) are bases. However, unlike the acids which we discussed in previous sections, many of these bases are insoluble in water. Some examples of bases are shown in Table 7.4.

Insoluble bases	Soluble bases (alkalis)
Copper(II) oxide (CuO)	Sodium hydroxide (NaOH)
Iron(III) oxide (Fe_2O_3)	Potassium hydroxide (KOH)
Copper(II) hydroxide ($Cu(OH)_2$)	Calcium hydroxide ($Ca(OH)_2$)
Lead(II) oxide (PbO)	Ammonia solution (NH_3(aq))

Table 7.4

If a base is soluble in water, the solution is called an **alkali**. An alkali contains hydroxide ions ($OH^-_{(aq)}$) in solution. (Some common alkalis are shown in Table 7.4.) Alkalis are substances which have a soapy 'feel'. They react with the natural oils in the skin and produce soap which gives the characteristic slippery 'feel'. As previously mentioned on page 77, alkalis will neutralize acids. Just like acids, alkalis are classified as strong or weak. The strength or weakness is related to the concentration of $OH^-_{(aq)}$ ions. Strongly alkaline solutions have a pH over 11 whilst weakly alkaline solutions have a pH between 7 and 11.

Fig. 7.14   Some common alkaline substances

Strengths of alkalis

If an alkali completely ionizes when dissolved in water then a large concentration of OH^- (aq) is produced and a strongly alkaline solution results, for example:

potassium hydroxide $\xrightarrow{\text{water}}$ potassium ions + hydroxide ions

$$KOH_{(s)} \xrightarrow{\text{water}} K^+_{(aq)} + OH^-_{(aq)}$$

However, if only a small proportion of an alkali ionizes, it is a weak alkali. For example:

magnesium hydroxide $\xrightleftharpoons{\text{water}}$ magnesium ions + hydroxide ions

$$Mg(OH)_{2(s)} \xrightleftharpoons{\text{water}} Mg^{2+}_{(aq)} + 2OH^-_{(aq)}$$

Some neutral substances

Some substances do not affect indicators. Their solutions are neither acid or alkaline. They are **neutral**. Common salt (sodium chloride), sodium nitrate and cane sugar give neutral solutions when dissolved in water.

Fig. 7.15(a)   Salt gives a neutral solution when dissolved in water

Salts

On page 77 you learned how an acid can be neutralized by an alkali. During the reaction between dilute hydrochloric acid and dilute sodium hydroxide, sodium chloride and water were produced. Sodium chloride is one of a range of compounds called **normal salts**. All acids contain hydrogen atoms. For example:

hydrochloric acid (HCl); nitric acid (HNO_3); sulphuric acid (H_2SO_4). A normal salt may be defined as a compound formed when all the replaceable hydrogen atoms of an acid are replaced by metal atoms or by the ammonium ion (NH_4^+). Some other examples of normal salts along with the acids they are made from are shown in Table 7.5.

Fig. 7.15(b) Rock salt is spread on icy roads in winter to lower the melting point of the ice

Acid	Type of normal salt	Example
Nitric acid (HNO_3)	Nitrates	Sodium nitrate ($NaNO_3$)
Sulphuric acid (H_2SO_4)	Sulphates	Sodium sulphate (Na_2SO_4)
Hydrochloric acid (HCl)	Chlorides	Sodium chloride (NaCl)
Carbonic acid (H_2CO_3)	Carbonates	Sodium carbonate (Na_2CO_3)
Ethanoic acid (CH_3COOH)	Ethanoates	Sodium ethanoate (CH_3COONa)

Table 7.5

With acids such as sulphuric acid which has two replaceable hydrogen atoms per molecule, it is possible to replace only *one* of these with a metal atom. We then produce what is called an **acid salt**. An acid salt may be defined as one in which only some of the replaceable hydrogen of an acid has been replaced by a metal. Some examples of such salts are shown in Table 7.6.

Acid	Name of acid salt	Example
Sulphuric acid (H_2SO_4)	Hydrogen sulphates	Sodium hydrogen-sulphate ($NaHSO_4$)
Carbonic acid (H_2CO_3)	Hydrogen carbonates	Sodium hydrogen-carbonate ($NaHCO_3$)

Table 7.6

Methods of preparing salts

For the purposes of preparation, salts can usefully be classified as: those which are *soluble* in water, and those which are *insoluble* in water. The following normal salts are soluble in cold water:

1 All common sodium, potassium and ammonium salts, and all nitrates.
2 All chlorides except those of silver, mercury and lead (though lead is soluble in hot water).
3 All sulphates except those of barium, lead and calcium.

The following salts are insoluble in water:

1 Most carbonates other than those of ammonium, sodium and potassium.
2 Most sulphides other than those of ammonium, sodium and potassium.

General methods of preparing soluble salts

We have already mentioned these methods under general reactions of acids (see page 76). More details are given here. There are four general methods.

1 Acid and alkali

To form the normal salt of a very reactive metal such as sodium, we do not start from the metal. It would be dangerous to add the metal directly to the acid. In this case we tackle the problem indirectly and use an alkali. Because both reactants are in solution a special technique is required. An indicator is used to show when the alkali has been completely neutralized by the acid. Acid is slowly added to a measured volume of alkali using a burette (see Fig. 7.16) until the indicator (often phenolphthalein) changes colour. The same volume of acid and alkali are then mixed without the indicator and the solution is then evaporated to obtain the salt by crystallization (see Fig. 7.17). For example:

$$\text{dilute hydrochloric acid} + \text{dilute sodium hydroxide} \longrightarrow \text{sodium chloride} + \text{water}$$

$$HCl_{(aq)} + NaOH_{(aq)} \longrightarrow NaCl_{(aq)} + H_2O_{(l)}$$

Fig. 7.16   Acid is added to the alkali until it changes colour

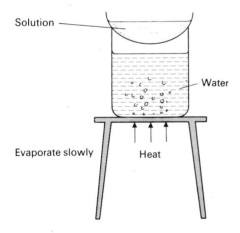

Fig. 7.17(a)   Method for evaporating the solution

Solution

Water

Evaporate slowly   Heat

Fig. 7.17(b)   What the evaporating basin should look like when you are finished

2 Acid and metal

For less reactive metals, direct reaction between metal and acid is suitable. This method is commonly used for the metals magnesium, zinc and iron. A typical procedure is as follows. Magnesium ribbon is added to dilute sulphuric acid until an excess of magnesium remains.

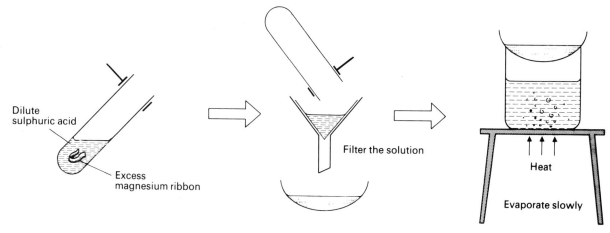

Fig. 7.18   The preparation of crystals of magnesium sulphate

The excess magnesium is removed by filtration and the magnesium sulphate solution is evaporated slowly. The hot concentrated solution so produced is tested by dipping a cold glass rod into it. If crystals form on the end of the rod the solution is ready to crystallize and so is left to cool. The crystals produced on cooling are filtered and dried in air. For example:

magnesium + $\begin{array}{c}\text{dilute} \\ \text{sulphuric acid}\end{array}$ $\longrightarrow$ $\begin{array}{c}\text{magnesium} \\ \text{sulphate}\end{array}$ + hydrogen

$$Mg_{(s)} + H_2SO_{4(aq)} \longrightarrow MgSO_{4(aq)} + H_{2(g)}$$

3   Acid and base (insoluble metal oxide)

To prepare the normal salt of an unreactive metal such as copper and lead, it is *not* usually possible to use direct reaction of such a metal with an acid. In these cases the acid is neutralized using the metal oxide. The method is generally the same as that in (2), though some warming of the reactants may be necessary. For example:

$\begin{array}{c}\text{copper(II)} \\ \text{oxide}\end{array}$ + $\begin{array}{c}\text{dilute} \\ \text{sulphuric} \\ \text{acid}\end{array}$ $\longrightarrow$ $\begin{array}{c}\text{copper(II)} \\ \text{sulphate}\end{array}$ + water

$$CuO_{(s)} + H_2SO_{4(aq)} \longrightarrow CuSO_{4(aq)} + H_2O_{(l)}$$

4   Acid and carbonate

This method may be used to make the normal salt of many metals. The reaction takes place at room temperature and procedures are essentially those carried out in (2). For example:

$\begin{array}{c}\text{lead (II)} \\ \text{carbonate}\end{array}$ + $\begin{array}{c}\text{dilute} \\ \text{nitric acid}\end{array}$ $\longrightarrow$ $\begin{array}{c}\text{lead(II)} \\ \text{nitrate}\end{array}$ + $\begin{array}{c}\text{carbon} \\ \text{dioxide}\end{array}$ + water

$$PbCO_{3(s)} + HNO_{3(aq)} \longrightarrow Pb(NO_3)_{2(aq)} + CO_{2(g)} + H_2O_{(l)}$$

Summary

Soluble normal salts may be prepared by the neutralization of an acid in the following ways.
1 Reaction of a dilute acid with an alkali.
2 Reaction of a dilute acid with a metal.
3 Reaction of a dilute acid with a base.
4 Reaction of a dilute acid with a carbonate.

Preparation of an acid salt

Normal salt:

$$\text{sodium hydroxide} + \text{dilute sulphuric acid} \longrightarrow \text{sodium sulphate} + \text{water}$$

$$2NaOH_{(aq)} + H_2SO_{4(aq)} \longrightarrow Na_2SO_{4(aq)} + 2H_2O_{(l)}$$

Acid salt:

$$\text{sodium hydroxide} + \text{dilute sulphuric acid} \longrightarrow \text{sodium hydrogen-sulphate} + \text{water}$$

$$NaOH_{(aq)} + H_2SO_{4(aq)} \longrightarrow NaHSO_{4(aq)} + H_2O_{(l)}$$

The preparation of the acid salt requires twice the volume of acid as in the preparation of the normal salt. Therefore, if $25\,cm^3$ of dilute sulphuric acid were required to form the normal salt from a given volume of alkali, then $50\,cm^3$ of the acid would be required to produce the acid salt sodium hydrogensulphate from the same volume of alkali.

Method of preparing insoluble salts

None of the previously mentioned methods can be used to prepare an insoluble salt such as lead sulphate. In this case, solutions of two soluble salts are taken and mixed (see Fig. 7.19). To produce lead(II) sulphate, lead(II) nitrate and sodium sulphate might be used. The precipitate of lead(II) sulphate may be filtered off, washed with distilled water and dried.

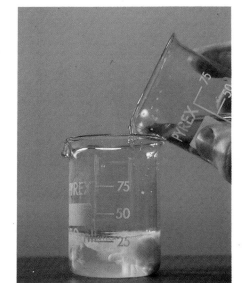

Fig. 7.19 When lead nitrate is added to sodium sulphate a white precipitate of lead sulphate forms

$$\text{lead(II) nitrate} + \text{sodium sulphate} \longrightarrow \text{lead(II) sulphate} + \text{sodium nitrate}$$

$$Pb(NO_3)_{2(aq)} + Na_2SO_{4(aq)} \longrightarrow PbSO_{4(s)} + 2NaNO_{3(aq)}$$

This method may be summarized as:

$$\text{soluble salt} + \text{soluble salt} \longrightarrow \text{insoluble salt} + \text{soluble salt}$$

$$\text{(XA)} \qquad \text{(YB)} \qquad \text{(XB)} + \text{(YA)}$$

This method is sometimes known as **double decomposition**.

Some useful salts

Some of the uses of a series of salts are shown in Table 7.7.

Salt	Used in:
Ammonium chloride	battery cells
Ammonium sulphate	fertilizer
Calcium carbonate	making iron
Calcium chloride	drying agents and extraction of sodium
Calcium sulphate	plaster casts for broken limbs and 'plaster' to plaster walls
Magnesium sulphate	medicine
Potassium nitrate	fertilizer and gunpowder
Silver bromide	photography
Sodium carbonate	softening water, making glass, bath salts and modern soap powders
Sodium chloride	flavouring foods, making hydrochloric acid, solvay process for manufacturing washing soda and hospital saline
Sodium stearate	soap
Tin(II) fluoride	toothpaste
Zinc sulphide	TV screens

Table 7.7

Water of crystallization

Many normal salts produce crystals which contain water incorporated into their structures. This water is referred to as **water of crystallization**. The salts which contain this type of combined water are called **hydrates**. Examples of such hydrates are given in Table 7.8 and Fig. 7.20.

Salt	Formula
Cobalt(II) chloride hexahydrate	$CoCl_2 . 6H_2O$
Copper(II) sulphate pentahydrate	$CuSO_4 . 5H_2O$
Sodium sulphate decahydrate	$Na_2SO_4 . 10H_2O$
Sodium hydrogen-sulphate monohydrate	$NaHSO_4 . H_2O$
Iron(II) sulphate heptahydrate	$FeSO_4 . 7H_2O$
Magnesium sulphate heptahydrate	$MgSO_4 . 7H_2O$
Sodium carbonate decahydrate	$Na_2CO_3 . 10H_2O$

Table 7.8

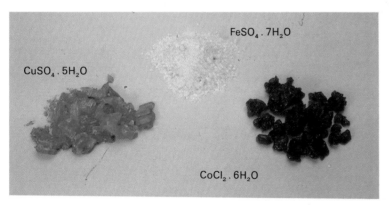

Fig. 7.20 Three examples of hydrates

By heating, it is possible to drive away this water of crystallization. For example, if crystals of copper(II) sulphate pentahydrate ($CuSO_4 . 5H_2O$) are heated they lose their water of crystallization. A white powder remains—anhydrous copper(II) sulphate (see Fig. 7.21).

hydrated   anhydrous
copper(II) $\xrightarrow{\text{heat}}$ copper(II) + water
sulphate   sulphate

$$CuSO_4 . 5H_2O_{(s)} \xrightarrow{\text{heat}} CuSO_{4(s)} + 5H_2O_{(g)}$$
(blue)   (white)

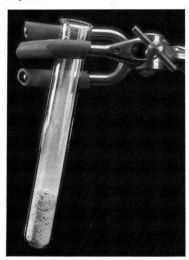

Fig. 7.21(a)   Anhydrous copper(II) sulphate

White anhydrous copper(II) sulphate turns blue when water is added to it. During the process a lot of heat is given out (i.e. the reaction is very exothermic):

$$CuSO_{4(s)} + 5H_2O_{(l)} \longrightarrow CuSO_4 . 5H_2O + \text{heat}$$
(white)   (blue)

As this colour change only happens when water is added to anhydrous copper(II) sulphate the reaction may be used to test for the presence of water.

The shape of the crystal of a hydrate is very much dependent on the presence of water of crystallization. If it is removed then the shape is lost (Fig. 7.21).

Some crystals such as those of sodium chloride, sodium nitrate and copper carbonate are anhydrous.

When colourless crystals of sodium carbonate decahydrate ($Na_2CO_3 . 10H_2O$)—washing soda—are left out in the air they become coated with a white powder (see Fig. 7.22). This white powder is the monohydrate formed by the process:

$$Na_2CO_3 . 10H_2O_{(s)} \longrightarrow Na_2CO_3 . H_2O_{(s)} + 9H_2O_{(g)}$$

When a hydrate loses its water of crystallization to the atmosphere in this manner it is said to **effloresce** (and the process is called **efflorescence**). Sodium sulphate decahydrate ($Na_2SO_4 . 10H_2O$) will also effloresce.

With some substances, not necessarily salt hydrates, the reverse of this process occurs. For example, if solid sodium hydroxide is left in the air it absorbs water vapour and eventually forms a very concentrated solution of sodium hydroxide (see Fig. 7.23). This process is called **deliquescence** (substances which behave like this are said to **deliquesce**). Anhydrous calcium chloride will also deliquesce.

Some substances, if left out in the air, absorb water vapour but do not form solutions or change their state. For example, concentrated sulphuric acid absorbs moisture from the air and becomes diluted whilst still remaining a liquid. Substances that do this are said to be **hygroscopic**.

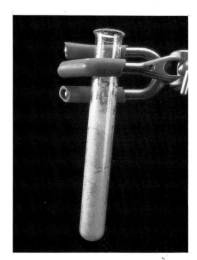

Fig. 7.21(b)   If water is added to anhydrous copper(II) sulphate it turns blue

Fig. 7.22   When sodium carbonate decahydrate crystals are left out in the air they become coated with a white powder

Pellet of solid sodium hydroxide

Exposure to air for a few hours

Pool of concentrated sodium hydroxide solution

Fig. 7.23   Deliquescence

————————————————————————QUESTIONS————————————————————————

1 a) A girl has *three* unlabelled bottles of colour-less liquids and she is told they are an acid, an alkali and water. Copy out and complete Table 1 to show how each substance would react.

Liquid	Reaction with red litmus	Reaction with blue litmus
Acid		
Water		
Alkali		

Table 1

b) $20 \, cm^3$ of the alkali are put into a flask and some litmus solution added. After $10 \, cm^3$ of acid have been added, the litmus has not changed colour. Explain why.
c) Describe two changes you would see in the litmus as more acid was added in small quantities and explain what these changes show.

2 a) Name an element found in all acids.
b) Describe two tests you would carry out on a liquid to decide whether it was an acid or not. In each case describe the test and the result you would expect.
c) If some acid were spilt on your clothes which of the following substances would you put on the cloth to prevent further damage: sodium hydroxide solution; sodium hydroxide solid; concentrated ammonia solution; sodium hydrogencarbonate?
d) Explain your choice of substance.
e) An acid and an alkali are often used to form a salt:

$$acid + alkali \longrightarrow salt + water$$

Which acid and alkali would you use to make potassium nitrate?
f) Name the piece of apparatus you would use to measure out the volume of acid needed to just neutralize the alkali.
g) How could you tell that just the correct volume of acid has been added to neutralize the alkali?
h) How would you obtain crystals of the salt from the neutral solution?

3 a) Describe what you would observe when a piece of magnesium is placed in dilute sulphuric acid.
b) Describe a test you would carry out to identify the gas produced in this reaction.
c) Write a word equation and a balanced chemical equation for this reaction.

4 a) i) What is a normal salt?
      ii) Give two examples of normal salts.
   b) i) What is an acid salt?
      ii) Give two examples of acid salts.

5 a) Explain what you understand by the terms:
      i) strong acid;
      ii) concentrated acid.
   b) Give an example of:
      i) a strong acid;
      ii) a weak acid.
   c) i) Name the reagent you would use to react with sodium hydroxide to prepare a specimen of sodium chloride by neutralization.
      ii) Write a word equation and a balanced chemical equation for this reaction.

6 a) Describe what you would observe when excess copper(II) carbonate is added to dilute sulphuric acid.
b) Describe a test you would carry out to identify the gas produced in this reaction.
c) Complete the following equations:

copper(II) carbonate + dilute sulphuric acid $\longrightarrow$ _____ + _____ + _____

$$CuCO_{3(s)} + H_2SO_{4(aq)} \longrightarrow CuSO_4 + \underline{\hspace{1cm}} + \underline{\hspace{1cm}}$$

7 A class is asked to make some lead(II) sulphate which is an insoluble salt.
a) The first pupil puts pieces of lead into dilute sulphuric acid. Why is this method unsuitable?
b) The second pupil adds lead(II) oxide to dilute sulphuric acid. Why is this method unsuitable?
c) i) The third pupil uses a successful method, starting with lead(II) nitrate solution. Which one of the following solutions did the pupil use: sodium chloride; zinc nitrate; copper(II) sulphate; potassium carbonate?
   ii) Describe a method for making a pure specimen of the lead(II) sulphate.
   iii) Complete the following equation for the reaction:

$$Pb(NO_3)_{2(aq)} + \underline{\hspace{1cm}} \longrightarrow \underline{\hspace{1cm}} + \underline{\hspace{1cm}}$$

8 Sodium sulphate crystals exist as the *decahydrate* $Na_2SO_4 . 10H_2O$. It is a salt *hydrate*. If it is heated quite strongly the *water of crystallization* is driven off and the *anhydrous* salt remains.

a) Explain the meaning of the terms in italic in the passage.
b) Draw a diagram of an apparatus which would be suitable for heating the hydrated salt in and for collecting a sample of the water given off.
c) Describe one chemical test you could carry out to show that the liquid given off was water.
d) Describe one other test you could carry out to show that the liquid obtained was pure water.

9 The following question is about the preparation of copper(II) sulphate crystals.

$$CuO_{(s)} + H_2SO_{4(aq)} \longrightarrow CuSO_{4(aq)} + H_2O_{(l)}$$

reagent 1   reagent 2

a) i) Name the two reagents used to prepare the copper(II) sulphate in the above reaction.
ii) Give the meaning of the symbols (s), (l), (aq).
b) Reagent 1 is added *in excess* to reagent 2 and the solution is warmed. After a few minutes the solution is *filtered*. At this stage *some* of the water *is removed* from the *filtrate* and the copper(II) sulphate is allowed to crystallize. In (i)–(iii) explain the following:
i) Why is reagent 1 used *in excess*?
ii) Why is the solution *filtered*?
iii) Why is only *some* of the water removed?
iv) Name the process by which the water is removed.
v) What is a *filtrate*?
c) Describe what would happen to the crystals of copper(II) sulphate if all the water were removed.

10 Complete Table 2 which is about the methods of making salts. (3)

Method of preparation	Name of salt prepared	Two substances used in preparation
Neutralization	Potassium sulphate	_____ and _____
Acid + metal	_____	_____ and dilute hydrochloric acid
Precipitation	Lead sulphate	_____ and _____

Table 2

(JMB/WMEB 1982)

11 Dilute aqueous solutions of a number of compounds were found to have pH values of 1, 4, 7, 8, 12. Using these pH values, only, answer the following questions.

a) One of the solutions was neutral. What was its pH? (1)
b) Two of the solutions were acidic. Give the two possible pH values. (1)
c) If one of these acids was vinegar, which pH would be the most likely one for the vinegar? (1)
d) Give the pH of the solution which would be most suitable to use to neutralize some concentrated acid which had been spilt on the floor. (1)
(AEB 1982)

12 a) Describe how you would prepare pure dry crystals of sodium chloride starting with solutions of hydrochloric acid and sodium hydroxide of approximately equal molar concentrations. (7)
b) Name a metallic chloride which is insoluble in cold water. Indicate how you would prepare a pure, dry sample of it using dilute hydrochloric acid as one of your starting materials. (4)
c) Sodium chloride is an ionic compound. Give *four* properties which are typical of such a compound. (4)
(SUJB 1984)

13 Study the following scheme.

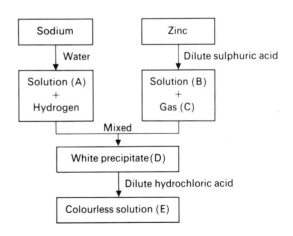

a) Give the name or formula of:

    solution   (A);
    solution   (B);
    gas   (C);
    precipitate (D);
    solution   (E). (5)

b) Describe a test to identify hydrogen. (2)
c) Describe what is observed when sodium reacts with water. (2)
(NEA 1985)

METALS AND THE REACTIVITY SERIES

Fig. 8.1 Metals have many uses

Most of the elements known to man are metals. As you learned in Chapter 2, metals have characteristic physical properties. Even though the metal elements have some common properties they are different in other ways. For example, if iron is left unprotected from the air it will rust very quickly (see Fig. 8.2). Gold, however, remains totally unchanged after many hundreds of years. Iron is said to be quite a reactive metal, whilst gold is a very unreactive metal. In this chapter we are going to take a closer look at the reactivity of metals and the ways in which they react with different substances.

Fig. 8.2 Iron rusts quickly if left unprotected

Reactions with water

Table 8.1 summarizes the reactions which take place when small, clean pieces of metals are placed in cold water or heated in steam. On the basis of the results shown in Table 8.1 we can write an order of

88

Metal	Symbol	Reaction with water	Equation
Copper	Cu	No reaction	
Lead	Pb	No observable reaction*	
Iron	Fe	No reaction with cold water.* When steam is passed over the strongly heated metal powder some hydrogen gas is produced	iron + steam $\rightleftharpoons$ iron(III) oxide + hydrogen $2Fe_{(s)} + 3H_2O_{(g)} \rightleftharpoons \quad Fe_2O_{3(s)} \quad + \quad 3H_{2(g)}$
Magnesium	Mg	A few bubbles of hydrogen gas are produced very slowly. However, when heated strongly in the presence of steam the magnesium reacts very violently. The magnesium glows brightly and hydrogen gas is produced. A white powder—magnesium oxide—is left	magnesium + water $\longrightarrow$ magnesium hydroxide + hydrogen $Mg_{(s)} \quad + 2H_2O_{(l)} \longrightarrow \quad\quad Mg(OH)_{2(aq)} \quad + \quad H_{2(g)}$ magnesium + steam $\longrightarrow$ magnesium oxide + hydrogen $Mg_{(s)} \quad + H_2O_{(g)} \longrightarrow \quad\quad MgO_{(s)} \quad + \quad H_{2(g)}$
Calcium	Ca	Hydrogen gas is produced quite quickly. A cloudy alkaline solution is left behind	calcium + water $\longrightarrow$ calcium hydroxide + hydrogen $Ca_{(s)} \quad + 2H_2O_{(l)} \longrightarrow \quad\quad Ca(OH)_{2(aq)} \quad + \quad H_{2(g)}$
Sodium	Na	Hydrogen gas is produced during a very violent and vigorous reaction. The metal fizzes around the surface reacting very quickly leaving a cloudy alkaline solution	sodium + water $\longrightarrow$ sodium hydroxide + hydrogen $2Na_{(s)} \quad + 2H_2O_{(l)} \longrightarrow \quad\quad 2NaOH_{(aq)} \quad + \quad H_{2(g)}$
Zinc	Zn	No observable reaction* takes place with cold water. When steam is passed over strongly heated zinc powder the zinc glows slightly. Hydrogen gas is produced. Zinc oxide powder is left behind in the boiling tube which is yellow when hot but becomes white when cold	zinc + steam $\longrightarrow$ zinc oxide + hydrogen $Zn_{(s)} + H_2O_{(g)} \longrightarrow \quad ZnO_{(s)} \quad + \quad H_{2(g)}$
Silver	Ag	No reaction	

Table 8.1   *Reacts very slowly with cold water over a very long period of time

Fig. 8.3   Apparatus to investigate the reaction of magnesium with cold water

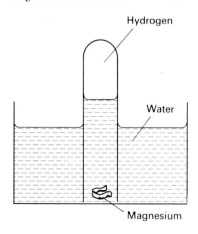

Magnesium

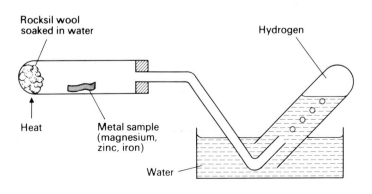

Fig. 8.4   Apparatus to investigate how less reactive metals react with steam

reactivity. The order of reactivity starting with the most reactive metal is:

> sodium
> calcium
> magnesium
> iron }
> zinc }
> lead }
> copper }
> silver }

However, from these observations it is difficult to separate the metals such as zinc and iron or copper, lead and silver. This problem is helped by looking at the way the metals react with oxygen and dilute acid.

Reaction with oxygen

Table 8.2 summarizes the reactions which take place when small samples of metals are heated in air.

Metal	Symbol	Reaction with oxygen	Equation
Copper	Cu	Produces a patchy black coating	copper + oxygen $\longrightarrow$ copper(II) oxide $2Cu_{(s)} + O_{2(g)} \longrightarrow 2CuO_{(s)}$
Lead	Pb	The sample melts: When cooled some yellow patches can be seen on the metal surface	lead + oxygen $\longrightarrow$ lead(II) oxide $2Pb_{(s)} + O_{2(g)} \longrightarrow 2PbO_{(s)}$
Iron	Fe	Produces a dark brown coating	iron + oxygen $\longrightarrow$ iron oxide $3Fe_{(s)} + 2O_{2(g)} \longrightarrow Fe_3O_{4(s)}$
Magnesium	Mg	Burns very brightly producing a white ash	magnesium + oxygen $\longrightarrow$ magnesium oxide $2Mg_{(s)} + O_{2(g)} \longrightarrow 2MgO_{(s)}$
Calcium	Ca	Initially there is no reaction but after some time it suddenly glows and burns with a red flash leaving a white powder	calcium + oxygen $\longrightarrow$ calcium oxide $2Ca_{(s)} + O_{2(g)} \longrightarrow 2CaO_{(s)}$
Sodium	Na	Burns with a yellow flame producing a white powder	sodium + oxygen $\longrightarrow$ sodium oxide $2Na_{(s)} + O_{2(g)} \longrightarrow Na_2O_{2(s)}$
Zinc	Zn	Gives a yellow coating on the surface of the metal which goes white on cooling	zinc + oxygen $\longrightarrow$ zinc oxide $2Zn_{(s)} + O_{2(g)} \longrightarrow 2ZnO_{(s)}$
Silver	Ag	No reaction	—

Table 8.2

Reaction with dilute acid

Table 8.3 summarizes the reactions which take place when small samples of metals are placed in dilute hydrochloric acid. You will notice that the very reactive metals such as sodium and calcium are missing from the table. This is because these metals are so reactive that they are *never* placed in dilute acid.

Element	Symbol	Reaction with dilute hydrochloric acid	Equation
Copper	Cu	No reaction takes place even when the mixture is heated	
Lead	Pb	Over the time of normal practical sessions no reaction takes place*	
Iron	Fe	A very slight reaction takes place at room temperature with the production of a few bubbles of hydrogen. The reaction becomes more vigorous upon heating with more hydrogen being produced	iron + dilute hydrochloric acid $\longrightarrow$ iron(II) chloride + hydrogen $Fe_{(s)} + 2HCl_{(aq)} \longrightarrow FeCl_{2(aq)} + H_{2(g)}$
Magnesium	Mg	A very vigorous reaction. The metal disappears very quickly and hydrogen gas is produced. The reaction mixture becomes quite hot	magnesium + dilute hydrochloric acid $\longrightarrow$ magnesium chloride + hydrogen $Mg_{(s)} + 2HCl_{(aq)} \longrightarrow MgCl_{2(aq)} + H_{2(g)}$
Zinc	Zn	This is a slow reaction. Hydrogen gas is produced. The metal very slowly disappears	zinc + dilute hydrochloric acid $\longrightarrow$ zinc chloride + hydrogen $Zn_{(s)} + 2HCl_{(aq)} \longrightarrow ZnCl_{2(aq)} + H_{2(g)}$
Silver	Ag	No reaction	—

Table 8.3   *A very slow reaction does take place over a long period of time

By combining all the results so far we obtain an overall order of reactivity or **reactivity series** for the metals tested.

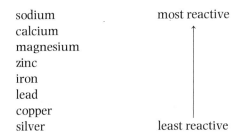

sodium   most reactive
calcium
magnesium
zinc
iron
lead
copper
silver   least reactive

There are many more metals which could be placed in the above reactivity series. Some like gold and platinum are even less reactive than silver and would be placed at the bottom of the series. Others like potassium and caesium are even more reactive than sodium and so would come at the very top of the table. Table 8.4 shows a summary of a more complete reactivity series of metals.

Metal	Symbol	Metal with water	Metal with dilute hydrochloric acid	Metal heated in air
Potassium	K	React with cold water	Violent reaction	Burn to form an oxide but with decreasing vigour
Sodium	Na			
Calcium	Ca			
Magnesium	Mg		React but with decreasing vigour	
Aluminium	Al	Protected by an oxide layer		
Zinc	Zn	React with steam		
Iron	Fe			
Lead	Pb*			React slowly
Copper	Cu	No reaction with either water or steam		
Silver	Ag		No reaction	
Platinum	Pt			Do not react with air
Gold	Au			

Table 8.4   * Lead reacts very slowly with steam

Fig. 8.5(a)   Stainless steel tea set

Fig. 8.5(b)   The roof of Wells Cathedral is covered in lead

Generally, it is the unreactive metals that we find the most uses for. For example, the metals iron and copper can be found in many man-made objects. However, the metal aluminium is an exception to this rule. Aluminium appears in the reactivity series just below magnesium and so it is quite a reactive metal. Fortunately for us, however, aluminium forms quite a thick oxide layer on the surface of the metal which prevents further reaction. This gives us the use of a light and strong metal (see Fig. 8.6).

Fig. 8.6(a)
The trailer of this
lorry is made from
aluminium

Fig. 8.6(b)   Aluminium door handle

There are certain metals you would not expect to find many uses for. For example, you would expect sodium, which is usually stored under oil to prevent it coming into contact with water and air, to be too dangerous to have around. However, because it has a low melting point and is a good conductor of heat, it can be used as a coolant in nuclear reactors.

Uses of the reactivity series

1   Predicting reactions

The reactivity series is useful for predicting how metals will react. It can also be used to predict the reactions of some metal compounds. For example, Tables 8.5, 8.6 and 8.7 summarize how some metal compounds behave when heated. You can see that metal compounds from a similar part of the series behave in a similar manner.

Metal	Symbol	Effect of heat on carbonate	Equation (some examples)
Potassium Sodium	K Na	No reaction	
Calcium Magnesium Aluminium Zinc Iron Lead Copper	Ca Mg Al Zn Fe Pb Cu	Forms the oxide and releases carbon dioxide with increasing ease ↓	calcium carbonate ⟶ calcium oxide + carbon dioxide $CaCO_{3(s)} \longrightarrow CaO_{(s)} + CO_{2(g)}$ zinc carbonate ⟶ zinc oxide + carbon dioxide $ZnCO_{3(s)} \longrightarrow ZnO_{(s)} + CO_{2(g)}$ copper(II) carbonate ⟶ copper(II) oxide + carbon dioxide $CuCO_{3(s)} \longrightarrow CuO_{(s)} + CO_{2(g)}$
Silver Platinum Gold	Ag Pt Au	Too unstable to exist	

Table 8.5

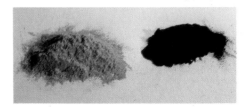

Fig. 8.7   Zinc carbonate, before and after heating

Fig. 8.8   Copper carbonate, before and after heating

Metal	Symbol	Effect of heat on nitrate	Equation (some examples)
Potassium Sodium	K Na	Form the nitrite and oxygen is released	potassium nitrate $\longrightarrow$ potassium nitrite + oxygen $2KNO_{3(s)} \longrightarrow 2KNO_{2(s)} + O_{2(g)}$
Calcium Magnesium Aluminium Zinc Iron Lead Copper	Ca Mg Al Zn Fe Pb Cu	Form the oxide and release oxygen. Brown fumes of nitrogen dioxide (nitrogen(IV) oxide) are also produced	calcium nitrate $\longrightarrow$ calcium oxide + nitrogen(IV) oxide + oxygen $2Ca(NO_3)_{2(s)} \longrightarrow CaO_{(s)} + 4NO_{2(g)} + O_{2(g)}$ zinc nitrate $\longrightarrow$ zinc oxide + nitrogen(IV) oxide + oxygen $2Zn(NO_3)_{2(s)} \longrightarrow 2ZnO_{(s)} + 4NO_{2(g)} + O_{2(g)}$ copper(II) nitrate $\longrightarrow$ copper(II) oxide + nitrogen(IV) oxide + oxygen $2Cu(NO_3)_{2(s)} \longrightarrow 2CuO_{(s)} + 4NO_{2(g)} + O_{2(g)}$
Silver Platinum Gold	Ag Pt Au	Decompose to the metal releasing oxygen and nitrogen(IV) oxide	silver nitrate $\longrightarrow$ silver + nitrogen(IV) oxide + oxygen $2AgNO_{3(s)} \longrightarrow 2Ag_{(s)} + 2NO_{2(g)} + O_{2(g)}$

Table 8.6

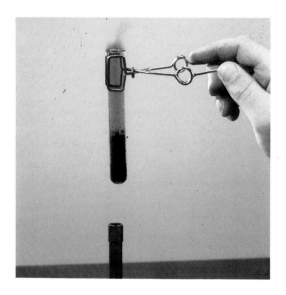

Fig. 8.9   When copper(II) nitrate is heated, brown fumes of nitrogen(IV) oxide are produced

Metal	Symbol	Effect of heat on hydroxide	Equation (some examples)
Potassium Sodium	K Na	No reaction, i.e. no decomposition	
Calcium Magnesium Aluminium Zinc Iron Lead Copper	Ca Mg Al Zn Fe Pb Cu	Decompose to the oxide and release water	calcium hydroxide $\longrightarrow$ calcium oxide + water $Ca(OH)_{2(s)} \longrightarrow CaO_{(s)} + H_2O_{(g)}$ zinc hydroxide $\longrightarrow$ zinc oxide + water $Zn(OH)_{2(s)} \longrightarrow ZnO_{(s)} + H_2O_{(g)}$ copper(II) hydroxide $\longrightarrow$ copper(II) oxide + water $Cu(OH)_{2(s)} \longrightarrow CuO_{(s)} + H_2O_{(g)}$
Silver Platinum Gold	Ag Pt Au	Hydroxides are too unstable to exist	

Table 8.7

2 Solubility

We can also construct a similar table dealing with the solubility of compounds. Table 8.8 shows the solubility in water of the hydroxides and carbonates of the metals in the reactivity series. You will notice from Table 8.8 that the metals in the lower half of the reactivity series form insoluble hydroxides. Pollution problems can be overcome by using this sort of information. Some industrial waste solutions contain quite a high concentration of heavy metals such as zinc and copper. If this waste were released untreated into our rivers it would cause serious pollution problems. However, by adding a relatively cheap alkali such as calcium hydroxide (lime) to the waste solution the copper and zinc hydroxides can be precipitated (see Fig. 8.10) and filtered off. The waste water would then be safe to release into any river.

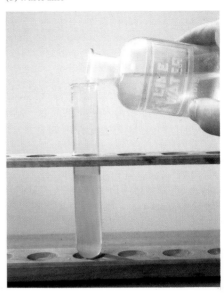

Fig. 8.10   Adding calcium hydroxide to solutions containing (a) waste copper and (b) waste zinc

(a)   Copper hydroxide is precipitated

Metal	Symbol	Metal hydroxide	Metal carbonate
Potassium Sodium	K Na	Very soluble	Very soluble
Calcium Magnesium	Ca Mg	Slightly soluble	
Aluminium Zinc Iron Lead Copper	Al Zn Fe Pb Cu	Insoluble	Insoluble
Silver Platinum Gold	Ag Pt Au	Too unstable to exist	Too unstable to exist

Table 8.8

3 Competition reactions

If a metal is heated with the oxide of a less reactive metal then it will remove the oxygen from it. For example, if iron(III) oxide is mixed and heated with aluminium powder (see Fig. 8.11) then a violent reaction takes place.

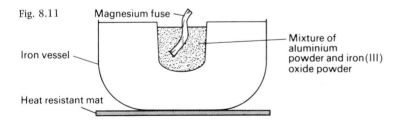

Fig. 8.11

Magnesium fuse

Iron vessel

Mixture of aluminium powder and iron(III) oxide powder

Heat resistant mat

(b)   Zinc hydroxide is precipitated

iron(III) oxide + aluminium ⟶ aluminium oxide + iron

$$Fe_2O_{3(s)} + 2Al_{(s)} \xrightarrow{heat} Al_2O_{3(s)} + 2Fe_{(s)}$$

The aluminium (the more reactive metal) takes the oxygen from iron (the less reactive metal). This is a **redox reaction**. (See Chapter 9, page 128 for further discussion of this type of reaction.)

reduced

$$Fe_2O_{3(s)} + 2Al_{(s)} \longrightarrow Al_2O_{3(s)} + 2Fe$$

oxidized

This particular reaction is known as the **thermit reaction**. It has been

Fig. 8.12   A World War II incendiary bomb

Fig. 8.13 · Welding railway track using the thermit reaction

used extensively for welding railway lines (see Fig. 8.13) as well as for incendiary bombs (see Fig. 8.12). This type of competing reaction, or oxygen-capturing reaction, is also used in the preparation of other metals, such as chromium from its oxide.

Another type of reaction in which metals compete with each other is in **displacement reactions**. In these, as in the previous type of competing reaction, the reactivity series can be used to predict which one will 'win'. In displacement reactions a metal will displace a less reactive metal from solutions of its compounds. For example, zinc metal when placed in a solution of copper(II) nitrate develops a brown coating of copper metal (see Fig. 8.14). In this case the solution loses its blue colour as the zinc continues to displace the copper from the solution of copper(II) nitrate. Eventually the solution becomes colourless zinc nitrate.

$$\text{zinc} + \text{copper(II) nitrate} \longrightarrow \text{zinc nitrate} + \text{copper}$$

$$Zn_{(s)} + Cu(NO_3)_{2(aq)} \longrightarrow Zn(NO_3)_{2(aq)} + Cu_{(s)}$$

4   Extraction of metals

Most metals occur naturally as compounds in the earth's crust called **ores**. These ores are usually oxides, sulphides or carbonates of the metal mixed with impurities. Some of the more common ores are shown in Table 8.9. In most cases the ore must be purified before the metal can be extracted from it . The method then used to extract the metal from its ore depends on the position of the metal in the reactivity series.

Fig. 8.14   Zinc metal after being placed in copper(II) nitrate solution

Fig. 8.15(a)   Bauxite

Fig. 8.15(b)   Cryolite crystals

Fig. 8.15(c)   Haematite

Fig. 8.15(d)   Magnetite

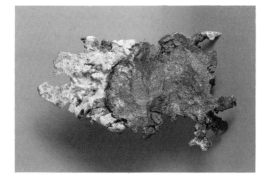

Fig. 8.15(e)   Silver and copper

Fig. 8.15(f)   Gold crystals

Metal	Name of ore	Chemical name	Formula	Usual method of extraction
Sodium	Rock salt	Sodium chloride	NaCl	Electrolysis of molten chloride
Aluminium	Bauxite Cryolite	Aluminium oxide Sodium aluminium fluoride	$Al_2O_3.2H_2O$ Na_3AlF_6	Electrolysis of oxide dissolved in molten cryolite
Zinc	Zinc blende Calamine	Zinc sulphide Zinc carbonate	ZnS $ZnCO_3$	Heating oxide with carbon
Iron	Haematite Magnetite	Iron(III) oxide Mixed iron oxide	Fe_2O_3 Fe_3O_4	Heating oxide with carbon
Copper	Pyrites	Copper iron sulphide	$CuFeS_2$	The sulphide is roasted in air
Silver Gold	Found as the element	—	—	—

Table 8.9

Extraction of reactive metals

If the metal to be extracted is reactive it is usually difficult to extract from its ore. This is because a reactive metal holds onto the element(s) it has combined with. For example, sodium chloride (as rock salt—see Fig. 8.16) is an ionic compound. The Na^+ and Cl^- ions are bonded very strongly to one another and consequently separation of these ions is difficult.

It is not possible to extract a reactive metal by heating the ore with a reducing agent (see Chapter 9, page 128) such as carbon or something similar because no common reducing agent is strong

Fig. 8.16   Mining rock salt

enough to do this. The reactive metals are therefore extracted by electrolysis of their molten compounds. During this process the metal is produced at the cathode whilst a non-metal is produced at the anode. As you might expect, extraction by electrolysis is expensive. For this reason many factories for extracting these metals are situated in regions where there is a good supply of cheap hydro-electric power (see Fig. 8.17).

Sodium

Sodium is extracted from the purified molten ore by electrolysis in a **Down's cell** (see Figs 8.18 and 8.19). During the process the sodium chloride is decomposed into the elements sodium and chlorine:

sodium chloride ⟶ sodium + chlorine

$$2NaCl_{(l)} \xrightarrow{\text{electrolysis}} 2Na_{(l)} + Cl_{2(g)}$$

Sodium chloride is an ionic substance and when it is molten the ions are free to move. The sodium ions (Na^+) are attracted to the iron cathode and deposited as liquid sodium metal, whilst the chloride ions (Cl^-) are attracted to the graphite anode and released as chlorine gas. The liquid sodium collects at the circular cathode and is then passed into a storage tank. The chlorine gas bubbles up under the steel hood above the anode and is collected and stored.

Fig. 8.17 Aluminium smelter at Fort William, Scotland

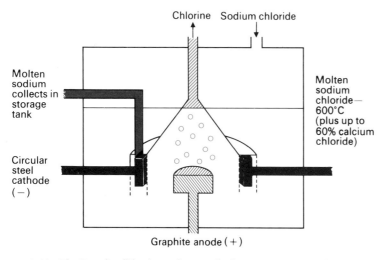
Fig. 8.18 The Down's cell for the production of sodium

Fig. 8.19(a) Down's cells

Fig. 8.19(b) Close-up of a Down's cell

At the *cathode* the sodium ions receive electrons and become sodium atoms:

sodium ion + electron ⟶ sodium atom

$$Na^+ + e^- \longrightarrow Na_{(l)}$$

At the *anode* the chloride ions lose electrons and become chlorine atoms which combine to give chlorine gas molecules:

chloride ion ⟶ chlorine atom + electron

$$Cl^- \longrightarrow Cl + e^-$$

chlorine atoms ⟶ chlorine molecules

$$2Cl \longrightarrow Cl_{2(g)}$$

Sodium metal is used, as already mentioned, as a coolant in nuclear reactors. It is also used in street lamps. Chlorine gas (the by-product) is used in the manufacture of plastics (see Fig. 8.20), in water treatment and in making paper.

Aluminium

Aluminium is found in the earth's crust as the ore bauxite. Bauxite ($Al_2O_3 . 2H_2O$), has to be purified to make pure aluminium oxide. The purified ore is then dissolved in molten cryolite (Na_3AlF_6) and the molten mixture electrolysed in a cell similar to the one shown in Fig. 8.21 (a **Hall cell**). During electrolysis the aluminium oxide is decomposed into its elements aluminium and oxygen:

$$\text{aluminium oxide} \longrightarrow \text{aluminium} + \text{oxygen}$$

$$2Al_2O_{3(s)} \longrightarrow 4Al_{(l)} + 3O_{2(g)}$$

The aluminium ions are attracted to the graphite lining of the tank which acts as the cathode. The molten aluminium then settles to the bottom of the tank and can be syphoned out. The oxide ion (O^{2-}) is attracted to the graphite anodes which have been introduced into the tank from above.

Fig. 8.20   Chlorine is important in the manufacture of plastics

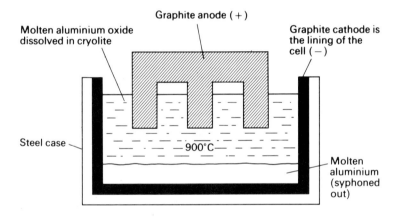

Fig. 8.21   A Hall cell for extracting aluminium by electrolysis

At the *cathode* the aluminium ions collect electrons and aluminium atoms are formed:

$$\text{aluminium ion} + \text{electrons} \longrightarrow \text{aluminium atom}$$

$$Al^{3+} + 3e^- \longrightarrow Al_{(l)}$$

At the *anode* the oxide ions lose electrons to form oxygen atoms which combine to produce oxygen gas molecules:

$$\text{oxide ion} \longrightarrow \text{oxygen atom} + \text{electrons}$$

$$O^{2-} \longrightarrow O + 2e^-$$

$$\text{oxygen atoms} \longrightarrow \text{oxygen molecules}$$

$$2O \longrightarrow O_{2(g)}$$

Aluminium is light, a good conductor of electricity and does not corrode. It is used to make electrical cables and cooking foil as well as alloys such as duralumin (used in the manufacture of aeroplane bodies).

The running costs of both the Down's and Hall cells are quite high because of the large amounts of electrical energy needed to: (a) keep the sodium chloride and cryolite molten (they melt at 801 °C and 1006 °C respectively); and (b) to do the electrolysis. However, in both processes ways have been developed to reduce the costs.

In the Down's cell up to 60% of calcium chloride is added to the sodium chloride electrolyte. The mixture of substances melts at about 600°C. A problem arises, however, in that the mixture contains both sodium and calcium ions. Fortunately the small amount of calcium deposited at the cathode, as well as the sodium, crystallizes out when the mixture cools. A relatively pure sodium metal is left.

In the Hall cell, dissolving the bauxite in molten cryolite allows the working temperature of the cell to be reduced to 900°C. No problems are experienced (as in the Down's cell) with other metals being deposited since cryolite is 'unaffected' by the flow of electricity. Problems do arise, however, with the graphite anodes. At the working temperature of the cell, the oxygen reacts with the graphite (carbon) anodes producing carbon dioxide. Effectively the anodes are burnt away and they have therefore to be replaced frequently.

The extraction of moderately reactive metals

You will notice from Table 8.9 that the metals near the middle of the reactivity series, such as zinc and iron, can be extracted by heating the metal oxide with carbon.

Zinc

The main ore of zinc is zinc blende or zinc sulphide. Firstly, the ore is concentrated. It is then heated very strongly in a current of air. This changes the zinc sulphide to zinc oxide:

zinc sulphide + oxygen $\xrightarrow{\text{heat}}$ zinc oxide + sulphur dioxide

$$2ZnS_{(s)} + 3O_{2(s)} \xrightarrow{\text{heat}} 2ZnO_{(s)} + 2SO_{2(g)}$$

The zinc oxide is then mixed with carbon in a furnace (see Fig. 8.23) and heated strongly. The carbon takes the oxygen from the zinc oxide producing zinc and carbon monoxide. The carbon is acting as a reducing agent (see Chapter 9, page 128):

zinc oxide + carbon $\xrightarrow{\text{heat}}$ zinc + carbon monoxide

$$ZnO_{(s)} + C_{(s)} \xrightarrow{\text{heat}} Zn_{(s)} + CO_{(g)}$$

The temperature inside the furnace is such that the zinc is produced as a gas. It distils off and is condensed.

The carbon monoxide gas produced is burned to generate some of the heat needed for operating the furnace. In this way the running costs are reduced.

Zinc is used to galvanize iron and to make battery cases. It is also used in alloys such as brass.

Fig. 8.22   Opencast zinc mining

Fig. 8.23   Smelting zinc

Fig. 8.24   The product—zinc ingots

Iron

Iron is extracted in very large quantities from its ores haematite (Fe_2O_3) and magnetite (Fe_3O_4), in a blast furnace (see Fig. 8.25 and 8.26). The blast furnace is loaded with limestone (mainly calcium carbonate – $CaCO_3$), coke (nearly pure carbon) and iron ore (usually Fe_2O_3). Hot air is 'blasted' in through holes at the bottom (**tuyères**). This makes the 'charge' in the furnace glow as the carbon burns in the preheated air:

$$carbon + oxygen \longrightarrow carbon\ dioxide$$

$$C_{(s)} + O_{2(g)} \longrightarrow CO_{2(g)}$$

Also, the limestone begins to decompose:

$$calcium\ carbonate \longrightarrow calcium\ oxide + carbon\ dioxide$$

$$CaCO_{3(s)} \longrightarrow CaO_{(s)} + CO_{2(g)}$$

The carbon dioxide gas then reacts with more hot coke forming carbon monoxide:

$$carbon\ dioxide + coke \longrightarrow carbon\ monoxide$$

$$CO_{2(g)} + C_{(s)} \longrightarrow 2CO_{(g)}$$

The carbon monoxide rises up the furnace and reduces (see Chapter 9, page 128) the iron(III) oxide ore, by taking the oxygen from it, at a temperature of approximately 700°C. The molten iron so produced trickles to the bottom of the furnace:

$$iron(III)\ oxide + carbon\ monoxide \longrightarrow iron + carbon\ dioxide$$

$$Fe_2O_{3(s)} + 3CO_{(g)} \longrightarrow 2Fe_{(l)} + 3CO_{2(g)}$$

Fig. 8.25   A blast furnace

Fig. 8.26   Inside a blast furnace

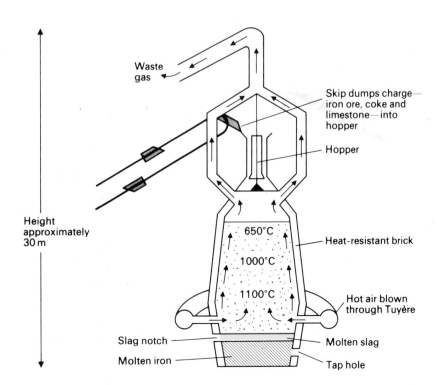

Waste gas

Skip dumps charge— iron ore, coke and limestone—into hopper

Hopper

Height approximately 30 m

650°C

1000°C

1100°C

Heat-resistant brick

Hot air blown through Tuyère

Slag notch

Molten iron

Molten slag

Tap hole

The calcium oxide formed from the limestone reacts with any earthy or sandy materials in the ore to form liquid slag which is mainly calcium silicate. This also trickles down to the bottom of the furnace, but because it is less dense than the molten iron, it floats on top of it.

calcium oxide + silicon dioxide $\longrightarrow$ calcium silicate (slag)

$$CaO_{(s)} \quad + \quad SiO_{2(g)} \quad \longrightarrow \quad CaSiO_{3(l)}$$

Both the molten slag and iron may be run off or **tapped off** at intervals.

Fig. 8.27 Tapping off molten iron

The waste gases, mainly nitrogen and oxides of carbon escape from the top of the furnace and are used to heat incoming air. This helps to reduce the heating costs of the furnace. The other waste product, slag, is used for road building (see Fig. 8.28).

The iron from the blast furnace is known as pig or cast iron and contains about 4% carbon (as well as other impurities). Iron in this form has a limited use since it is brittle and hard. Gas cylinders are sometimes made of cast iron, since they are unlikely to get deformed (bent) during use. Most iron is converted to different iron alloys— steels, such as stainless steel.

Fig. 8.28 Waste slag from the iron and steel industry is used in road foundations

Fig. 8.29 Pig iron is brittle and can snap suddenly!

Extraction of unreactive metals

Unreactive metals such as copper are extracted from their ores by heating the ore in air. When copper pyrites (copper(II) sulphide) is heated in air, initially copper(I) sulphide is produced, but further heating produces copper from the copper(I) sulphide.

$$\text{copper(I) sulphide} + \text{oxygen} \xrightarrow{\text{heat}} \text{copper} + \text{sulphur dioxide}$$

$$Cu_2S_{(s)} \quad + \quad O_{2(g)} \xrightarrow{\text{heat}} 2Cu_{(l)} + \quad SO_{2(g)}$$

Copper is usually purified by electrolysis. The purified copper is easily drawn and is an excellent conductor of electricity. It is used to make water piping, electrical wiring as well as alloys such as brass and bronze (see Fig. 8.30).

Very unreactive metals exist as free metal in the earth's crust. Gold and platinum, because of their resistance to corrosion, are used for jewellery. Gold is also used for tooth fillings (see Fig. 8.31).

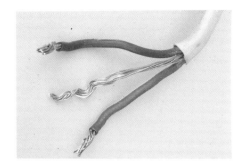

Fig. 8.30(a)   Electrical wiring is made of copper

Fig. 8.30(b)   Copper can be alloyed with zinc to give brass

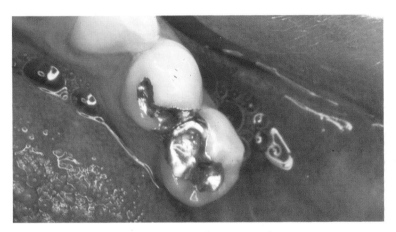

Fig. 8.31   Gold is used in fillings because it does not corrode

Corrosion

After a period of time in the air iron objects become coated with an orange-red powder—**rust**. The rusting, or **corrosion** of iron wastes enormous amounts of money by attacking and gradually eating away nails, nuts, bolts, rivets, screws, car and lorry bodies, and steel plates that are used to make up ships' hulls.

Fig. 8.32   Rust costs money!

Fig. 8.33(a) A copper lightning conductor covered in green patina (see text)

Fig. 8.33(b)   Corrosion of a brass clock face

Corrosion is the name given to the processes which take place when a metal reacts slowly with air, water or any other substance in its environment (surroundings) and so the term is not just restricted to iron. Most of the metals in the reactivity series will corrode to a greater or less extent. Generally, the higher the metal is in the reactivity series the more rapidly it corrodes. For this reason sodium and potassium are kept under oil to protect them from oxygen and moisture in the air. Magnesium and calcium are usually covered with a thin coating of oxide (see Fig. 8.34). Newly formed copper, which is normally pink in colour, becomes brown due to the formation of copper(II) oxide on the surface (see Fig. 8.35). Also, in the open air, copper pipes or roofs soon become covered in a green substance. This is green **patina** which is a mixture of copper(II) sulphate and copper(II) hydroxide (see Fig. 8.33). Gold is unreactive and even after hundreds of years of exposure to the atmosphere it does not corrode.

In cases such as aluminium, corrosion is a useful process and quite advantageous. This is because the oxide layer produced sticks to the surface and protects the metal underneath. For this reason aluminium is used for door and window frames (see Fig. 8.36) as well as in alloys for saucepans, refrigerators and cookers. It is also occasionally used by the construction industry for certain wall sections in buildings.

Fig. 8.34   Magnesium and calcium are covered in a thin coating of oxide

Fig. 8.35   Some of these copper alloy coins have a thin layer of brown copper oxide on the surface

Fig. 8.36(a)   Aluminium-framed greenhouses do not rust!

Fig. 8.36(b)   Aluminium alloy pans are light, strong and corrosion-free

Rusting of iron

Rust is mainly hydrated iron(III) oxide ($Fe_2O_3 . H_2O$). Both oxygen and water are essential for iron to rust. It is found that iron will not rust if one of these two substances is not present (see Fig. 8.37). It is also thought that carbon dioxide is essential for rusting to take place. Another substance which encourages the rusting of iron is salt (sodium chloride).

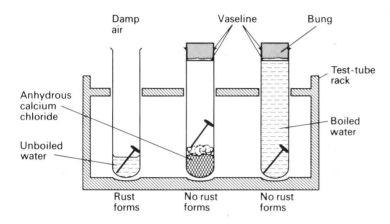

Fig. 8.37   Experiment to show that oxygen and water are needed for iron to rust

Prevention of rusting

When trying to prevent iron from rusting it is important to exclude all contact with oxygen and water. There are several methods which can be employed.

Painting
Bridges, cars, ships and many other large iron and steel structures are painted to prevent rusting (see Fig. 8.38). However, it is essential that the paint is kept in good condition and checked regularly. Damaged paintwork results in rusting (see Fig. 8.39).

Greasing
This is the most common method of protecting moving parts in machinery (see Fig. 8.40). The iron or steel is prevented from coming into contact with air or moisture by coating it with oil.

Fig. 8.38   Spray painting a steel girder

Fig. 8.39   Rusting results when paintwork is not maintained

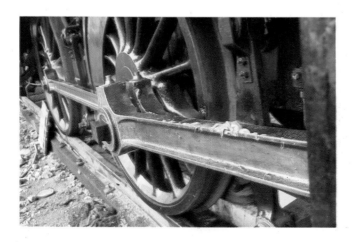

Fig. 8.40   Grease lubricates and protects machinery from rusting

Plating
This involves coating the iron or steel with a layer of another metal. The metal, such as tin, is deposited on the iron or steel by electrolysis, in a process called **electroplating** (see Fig. 8.41). This type of coated steel is used for canning foods—'tin-cans'. Other metals are also used, for example, cycle handle bars are plated with chromium (see Fig. 8.42).

Fig. 8.41   Rolls of electroplated steel about to be made into tin cans

Fig. 8.42   The handle bars of this bike have been chrome-plated

Galvanizing
This involves dipping the object into molten zinc (see Fig. 8.43). When lifted out the object retains a thin surface coat of zinc. Iron coal-bunkers and dustbins are usually coated in this way. If the surface coat of zinc is damaged the iron still does not rust (see Fig. 8.44). This is because zinc is more reactive than iron. The zinc will react in preference to iron to form zinc ions (Zn^{2+}). Since the iron does not react it does not corrode. This is the basis of the next method of protection.

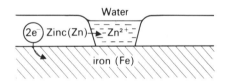

Fig. 8.44   Zinc-coated iron does not rust

Fig. 8.43   Galvanizing a metal object

Sacrificial protection
Gas and water pipes made of iron and steel are connected via a wire to a block of magnesium. Magnesium is more reactive than iron. The magnesium will react in preference to iron to form magnesium ions (Mg^{2+}). The magnesium is sacrificed to protect the iron. Again the iron does not corrode as long as there is magnesium in contact with it (see Fig. 8.45). When the magnesium runs out it can be renewed.

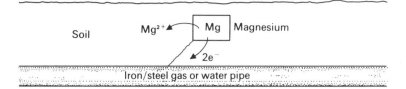

Fig. 8.45   The magnesium is sacrificed to protect the steel pipe

Plastic
Iron or steel can be coated with a thin layer of plastic such as PVC. Dish racks, some forms of wire fencing and garden chairs are often protected in this manner.

Fig. 8.46   Plastic-coated dish rack

Steel and other alloys

It is possible to change the properties of any metal by mixing it with other metals. These mixtures are known as **alloys**. Steel which is a mixture of iron and carbon is also considered to be an alloy.

Steel is perhaps the most important of the alloys we use. There is a range of steels which contain not only iron and some carbon but also other metals such as chromium and nickel (stainless steel). In fact, our lives would be quite different without cars, girders, lorries, trains, ships, kettles, cutlery and the many other items made from steel.

Fig. 8.47   Stainless-steel sink and cutlery

Steel making

There are several methods for making steel but the latest process to be used is that called the **Linz-Danowitz (or L-D) process**. It is also known as the **basic oxygen process**. In this process molten iron from the blast furnace is transferred and poured into the steel making L-D furnace (see Fig. 8.48). Some calcium oxide (lime) is added to remove some impurities as slag. This slag may be skimmed or poured off the surface. A water-cooled steel tube is then introduced into the neck of the furnace and oxygen at a pressure of 5–15 atmospheres is blown onto the surface of the molten metal. The blast of oxygen stirs the metal and oxidizes non-metal impurities such as carbon and phosphorus to gaseous oxides. Samples are continuously taken from the furnace to check the carbon content of the molten metal. When the required amount of carbon has been reached the blast of oxygen is switched off. This furnace can convert 250 tonnes of iron into steel, in less than one hour.

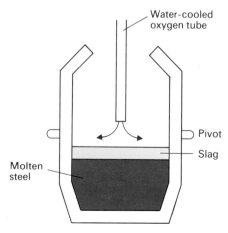

Fig. 8.48   Manufacture of steel by the L-D process

Mild and hard steels are the two most common types of steel. They contain 0.5% and 1.0% carbon respectively. Mild steel is quite easily worked and has lost most of the brittleness. It is used to make car bodies and building structures (see Fig. 8.49). Hard steel is a very hard form of steel which is used for making cutting tools and blades in general (see Fig. 8.50).

If other types of steel are required then up to 30% scrap steel, along with other metal, is added. The carbon is burned off and the resulting material tested until the final composition is that desired. Table 8.10 shows some of the more common types of steel along with their uses.

Fig. 8.49   Steel girders made from mild steel

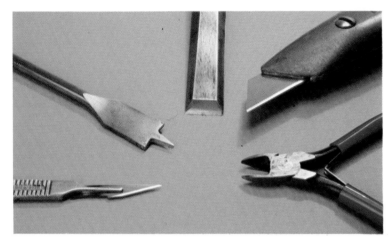

Fig. 8.50   Cutting tools made from hard steel

Fig. 8.51   Drill bits are often made from manganese steel

Steel	Approximate composition	Some uses
Mild steel	99.5% iron, 0.5% carbon	Car bodies, large structures
Hard steel	99% iron, 1% carbon	Cutting tools
Stainless steel	74% iron, 18% chromium, 8% nickel	Cutlery, surgical equipment, kitchen sinks, garden tools
Manganese steel	87% iron, 13% manganese	Drill bits and springs
Tungsten steel	95% iron, 5% tungsten	Edges of cutting tools

Table 8.10

Other alloys

As you saw in the last section it is possible to change the properties of iron by 'alloying'. Generally this is the case with all our useful metals. We can improve the strength, wear and corrosion resistance by this process. Many thousands of alloys are now made. The majority of these alloys have been 'tailor-made' by engineers, technologists and metallurgists to do a particular job. Table 8.11 shows some of the more common alloys in use, together with some of their uses.

Alloy	Approximate composition	Use
Alnico	Aluminium, nickel, cobalt	Permanent magnets
Antimonal lead	99% lead, 1% antimony	Car batteries
Brass	65% copper, 35% zinc	Machine bearings, jewellery, electrical connections
Bronze	90% copper, 10% tin	Machine parts
Constantan	60% copper, 40% nickel	Thermocouple wires
Cupro-nickel	75% copper, 25% nickel 30% copper, 70% nickel	'Silver' coins Turbine blades
Duralumin	95% aluminium, 4% copper (some magnesium, manganese, iron)	Aircraft parts, racing bicycles
Magnalium	70% aluminium, 30% magnesium	Aircraft construction
'Nimonic' alloys	10% nickel, 21% chromium (plus a variety of compositions of aluminium, iron, cobalt, molybdenum, titanium)	Corrosion-resistant parts, electrodes
Pewter	30% lead, 70% tin plus a little antimony	Ornaments, drinking mugs, plates
Solder	70% lead, 30% tin	Welding electrical wires

Table 8.11

Fig. 8.52(a)   Constantan wire

Fig. 8.52(b)   Permanent magnet made from alnico

Fig. 8.52(c)   Pewter mug

─────QUESTIONS─────

1 calcium, magnesium, zinc, iron, copper

From the list of metals given above, choose one which:
a) burns in air, if strongly heated, and forms a yellow solid which turns white on cooling;
b) forms a black coating on its surface when heated strongly in air;
c) reacts vigorously if heated in steam to form a white solid, but has only a slight reaction with cold water;
d) does not react with dilute hydrochloric acid;
e) when mixed with tin forms the alloy pewter;
f) when mixed with aluminium forms the alloy magnalium;
g) is extracted from its ore by heating it in a blast furnace with coke and limestone;
h) is used to galvanize iron objects;
i) is attached to iron pipes to stop them corroding.

2 A is a greenish-blue solid which is insoluble in water. When heated the solid gives off a colourless gas B which turns limewater milky. After heating a black powder C is left.
a) Which metal is probably present in A?
b) What is the name of the gas B?
c) What does this tell you about the chemical name of A?
d) Suggest what the black powder C might be.
e) Write a word equation and a balanced chemical equation for the reaction that takes place when A is heated.

3 A list of metal compounds is given below.

   silver nitrate
   calcium carbonate
   copper nitrate
   potassium hydroxide
   sodium nitrate

Which one of these compounds:
a) is unaffected by heat;
b) produces the metal nitrite and oxygen when heated;
c) is insoluble in water;
d) produces the metal, nitrogen(IV) oxide and oxygen when heated;
e) deposits an orange-brown solid when iron is added to its solution;
f) produces a metal oxide and carbon dioxide when heated strongly?

4 Use the list of metals below to answer questions (a) to (g).

sodium, calcium, magnesium, aluminium, zinc, copper, gold

a) Which of the metals will not react with oxygen to form an oxide?
b) i) Which metal will react violently with cold water?
   ii) Name the two products of the reaction of the metal with water.
c) Which of the metals has a protective coating of oxide on its surface?
d) Which of the metals is usually found in nature as the 'free' element?
e) Which of the metals is found in nature as the ore bauxite?
f) This metal element has a carbonate found in nature as limestone.
g) Write the names of the products which would correctly complete the word equations below. If there is no reaction then state 'no reaction' in your answer.
   i) zinc + copper(II) nitrate solution $\longrightarrow$
   ii) gold + copper(II) oxide $\longrightarrow$
   iii) aluminium + copper(II) oxide $\longrightarrow$
   iv) magnesium + dilute hydrochloric acid $\longrightarrow$

5 Read the following passage carefully.

Many metals are more useful to us when mixed with some other elements. For example, if a metal such as chromium is mixed with iron then an *alloy*—stainless steel—is produced. This alloy is resistant to *corrosion*. Many of the alloys are *tailor-made* by scientists. Some other alloys include solder and brass.

a) Explain the meaning of the terms in italic.
b) i) What metals are found in solder and brass?
   ii) Give one use of each of these alloys.
c) Name three other alloys and give a use for each of them.

6 Three test tubes were set up with iron nails placed in them (see Fig. 1).
a) If you wanted to find out what conditions were necessary for iron to rust, what would you put into each of the test tubes? State the chemicals you would use and anything else you would need to do.

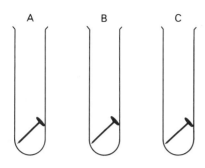

b) The nails were left for a period of two weeks. Describe what each nail would look like at the end of this time.

c) What are the essential conditions for iron to rust?

d) State five methods commonly used to prevent iron rusting.

e) 'Rusting' of iron is a common example of 'corrosion' in metals.
   i) What is the meaning of the term 'corrosion'?
   ii) Name a metal which does not corrode.
   iii) Why is the corrosion of aluminium quite useful to us?
   iv) What is 'patina'?

7 Sodium is extracted in the Down's cell. A diagram of this cell is shown below.

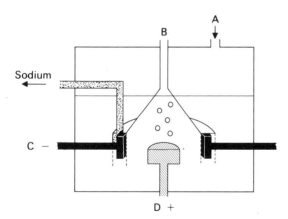

a) Name:
   i) the ore A;
   ii) the substance collected at B;
   iii) the electrode C;
   iv) the electrode D;
b) What materials are the electrodes C and D made from?
c) i) What is the approximate working temperature of the cell?
   ii) Explain why this working temperature is below the normal melting point of ore A.

iii) What substance is added to the ore A to ensure a lower working temperature?

d) Write equations for the formation of sodium metal at electrode C and of substance B at electrode D.

e) Give two uses of sodium and two uses of substance B.

8 a) Study the following passage carefully and then answer the questions related to the metal, aluminium.

For some sixty years, aluminium has been manufactured from bauxite, an ore containing aluminium oxide, found in many parts of the world.
The ore, after extensive purification, is dissolved in molten cryolite and electrolysed in a steel cell lined with carbon, which forms the cathode and uses carbon blocks as the anodes. The process involves a large consumption of electrical power and the frequent replacement of the graphite anodes. Hence, aluminium is an expensive metal. However, its low density and good heat and electrical conducting properties make it a superior metal to steel for many purposes. Coupled with this is its resistance to atmospheric corrosion which is often enhanced by anodizing. This is a process in which the aluminium article is made the anode of an electrolytic cell and oxygen is liberated at the metal surface from an aqueous electrolyte.

   i) Why is aluminium extracted from its oxide by electrolysis rather than by using a chemical reducing agent? (1)
   ii) Explain, with equations, the processes occurring at the anode which make necessary 'the frequent replacement of the graphite anodes' (lines 11–12). (3)
   iii) Give a reason, from information in the passage, for the location of an aluminium extraction plant in the Highlands of Scotland. (1)
   iv) Why is aluminium resistant to atmospheric corrosion? (1)
   v) Suggest how 'anodizing' (line 18) increases the resistance of aluminium to corrosion. (1)
b) Give two different uses of aluminium, one in each case, which depends upon:
   i) its low density and good electrical conduction;
   ii) its low density and resistance to atmospheric corrosion. (2)

(JMB 1981)

111

9 a) The main ores of iron are iron(III) oxide (haematite) and tri-iron tetroxide (magnetite). The ore is mixed with coke and limestone and reduced in a blast furnace. The following is a brief outline of the reactions involved.

$$coke + oxygen \longrightarrow gas\ (A)$$
$$gas\ (A) + coke \longrightarrow gas\ (B)$$
$$iron(III)\ oxide + gas\ (B) \longrightarrow iron + gas\ (A)$$

   i) Name gas (A) and gas (B).   (2)
   ii) Write a symbol equation for the reaction between iron(III) oxide and gas (B).   (2)
   iii) Explain the purpose of adding limestone to the ore in the furnace. Your answer should refer to any chemical reactions involved.   (2)

b) The iron obtained from the blast furnace is called cast iron or pig iron. Most cast iron is turned into steel. This involves removing some impurities completely. The carbon in cast iron is either completely removed and then replaced by a calculated quantity or adjusted to the required proportion. Controlled quantities of other elements are also added to give different varieties of steel.

   i) Name an impurity other than carbon which is present in cast iron and which is removed completely in manufacturing steel.
   Describe and explain a method of steel manufacture which removes this impurity.   (4)
   ii) Name a metallic element which may be added to iron to produce a particular variety of steel.   (1)
   iii) Give two advantages of stainless steel over cast iron.   (2)

c) Electrolysis is used in industry to extract aluminium from its ore. Electrolysis is also used for refining copper to obtain pure copper from impure copper.
   i) Complete Table 1.   (4)

   ii) Write a symbol equation for the change taking place at the anode during the refining of copper.   (1)
   iii) Aluminium can be protected from corrosion by 'anodizing'. Explain what is meant by anodizing and briefly outline how the process is carried out.   (2)
   (JMB/WMEB 1982)

10 a) Zinc is reacted with steam using an apparatus illustrated in the diagram.

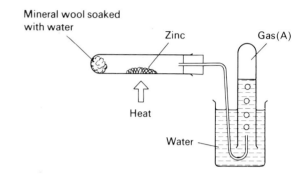

Gas (A), when mixed with air and ignited, gave a small explosion. A solid (B), which is yellow when hot and white when cold, remained in the reaction tube.
   i) Name gas (A).   (1)
   ii) Name the product formed when gas (A) burns in air.   (1)
   iii) Name solid (B).   (1)
   iv) Write a symbol equation for the reaction between zinc and steam.   (2)
   v) Name another metal which could be used safely in place of the zinc, to produce another sample of gas (A).   (1)

Electrolyte	Material used for anode	Material used for cathode	Result at the anode	Result at the cathode
Aluminium oxide in cryolite (molten)		Carbon (graphite)		Aluminium deposited
Copper(II) sulphate solution	Impure copper		Copper from the anode goes into solution	

Table 1

b) Gas (A) is also produced when zinc reacts with dilute hydrochloric acid. Write the name and formula of the other product of this reaction. (2)

c) i) Name one metal which reacts vigorously with cold water to produce gas (A). (1)

ii) Name the other product of this reaction. (1)

(NEA 1984)

11 a) 'For the benefits that society obtains from the intensive use of material, there is often a price to pay in environmental terms.'

Discuss this statement with reference to steel. In your answer consider:

i) the extraction of the necessary raw materials; (8)

ii) the production of steel from them. (3)

b) There has been a world-wide reduction in the demand for steel in recent times. Discuss:

i) the reasons for the reduction in demand; (8)

ii) the sociological effect in the U.K. (4)

(AEB 1984)

12 a) Using your knowledge of the electrochemical series, predict what, if anything, would happen when:

i) zinc is added to lead(II) nitrate solution;

ii) copper is added to dilute hydrochloric acid;

iii) copper is added to silver nitrate solution;

iv) iron is added to magnesium sulphate solution.

Give a reason for each answer and write equations, where appropriate. (10)

b) What do you understand by a redox reaction? Give two examples to illustrate your answer. (5)

(SUJB 1981)

13 Below are pairs of substances. The members of each pair are similar in appearance. However, they can be distinguished by heating each separately in a test tube and then identifying any gas evolved by its colour or by a chemical test. Describe what you would see, the tests you would carry out, and write appropriate word equations and balanced chemical equations for each pair.

a) sodium carbonate and zinc carbonate;

b) lead nitrate and potassium nitrate;

c) silver nitrate and zinc nitrate.

WATER AND HYDROGEN

Fig. 9.1   Water is the commonest compound

Water is the commonest compound on this planet. For instance, about four-fifths of the Earth's surface is covered with sea, and the land is dotted with rivers and lakes. It is vital to our existence and survival because it is one of the main constituents in all living organisms. For example, your bones contain 72% water, your kidneys are about 82% water and your blood is about 90% water (see Fig. 9.2). It is a neutral, colourless liquid which (at 1 atmosphere pressure) boils at 100°C and freezes at 0°C (see Fig. 9.3).

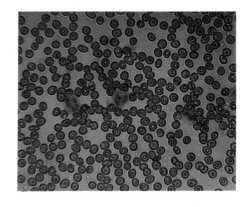

Fig. 9.2   Each blood cell contains some water

Fig. 9.3   Liquid water turns to steam at 100°C and to ice at 0°C

You can test to show that a colourless liquid contains water by adding the unknown liquid to anhydrous copper(II) sulphate. If this changes from white to blue then the liquid contains water. Another test also may be used. Dip blue cobalt chloride paper into the liquid. If the paper goes pink then the liquid contains water (see Fig. 9.5).

You have already learned in Chapter 6 that water (acidified with a little dilute sulphuric acid) may be electrolysed. When this is done the ratio of the volumes of the gas produced at the cathode to that produced at the anode is 2:1. This is what you might expect since its formula is H_2O.

Water pollution and treatment

Water is very good at dissolving substances. It will dissolve solids such as sodium chloride and gases such as oxygen, carbon dioxide and sulphur dioxide. It is therefore unusual to find really pure water on this planet.

As water falls through the atmosphere and down onto, and through, the surface of the Earth it dissolves a great variety of substances. For instance, river water contains dust and grit as well as chemical fertilizers washed off surrounding fields. It may also contain detergents, poisonous metals and solvents from industries near rivers, as well as human waste. Other insoluble impurities include lead 'dust' and oil from exhaust fumes of cars and lorries (see Fig. 9.6). All these natural and man-made impurities must be removed from water.

Fig. 9.4   Anhydrous copper(II) sulphate goes blue when water is added to it

Fig. 9.5   Cobalt chloride paper turns pink when dipped into water

Fig. 9.6   Car exhaust fumes contain carbon monoxide as well as lead dust and oil

Water treatment falls broadly into three categories.

1   Provision of clean water. Every day, on average, we each use 150 litres of water for washing, cooking, drinking, etc. (see Fig. 9.7). Industry uses vast amounts of water, much of it for cooling purposes.

2   Control of impurities added to rivers and the land (see Fig. 9.8).

3   Treatment of sewage.

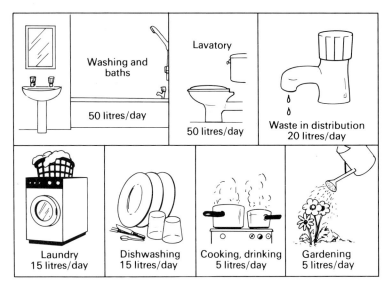

Fig. 9.8   A badly polluted river

Fig. 9.7   Domestic use of water in litres per day

Most of our drinking water is taken from those rivers where pollution is low. Before it is pumped into reservoirs or storage tanks, the river water is first passed through screens that filter out floating debris. To remove various sizes of particles of impurities further filtrations are then carried out through coarse sand (this removes the largest particles), and finer sand (this removes the tiniest particles)— see Fig. 9.9. These sand beds have to be washed clean at the end of every day. Some of the bacteria present in the water are removed by microbes grown especially for that purpose in the sand. Finally, however, to ensure that all the bacteria have been removed and the water is fit to drink or use in industry, small quantities of chlorine gas are dissolved in it. This gas kills the bacteria but is not present in large enough quantities to smell or taste.

Fig. 9.9   Cross-section through a sand filter

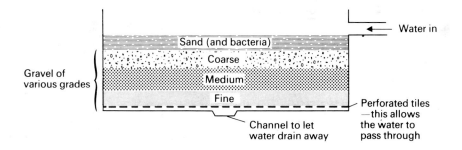

Sewage contains our general waste products. It contains washing water as well as anything else that goes down the toilet, drain or sink. All sewage, therefore, must be treated in a sewage works (see Fig. 9.10) before it can be passed into our rivers or seas. Firstly, the larger pieces of rubbish are removed from the sewage by passing it through large screens. Any sand or grit is then allowed to settle out. The sludge is then allowed to settle into the bottom of the tanks (see Fig. 9.11). Here it is drained away and it is at this stage that it is attacked by tiny living organisms (microbes) which convert the sludge into a low quality fertilizer and release methane gas (a fuel). This refined sludge is sometimes dumped at sea. The water left behind, which is still impure, is allowed to drain through gravel. Microbes have been deposited on the surface of the gravel and these kill off more bacteria. Finally, the relatively pure water is now chlorinated ready for drinking or returning to the river.

Fig. 9.10   Aerial view of a large sewage treatment plant

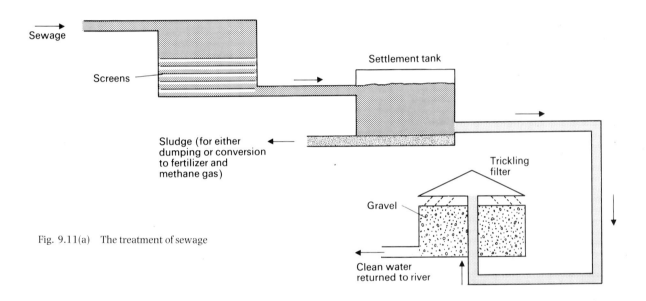

Sewage

Screens

Settlement tank

Sludge (for either dumping or conversion to fertilizer and methane gas)

Trickling filter

Gravel

Clean water returned to river

Fig. 9.11(a)   The treatment of sewage

Fig. 9.11(b)   Settlement tank

Fig. 9.11(c)   Trickling filter in operation

The water cycle

The water cycle is shown in Fig. 9.12. This diagram illustrates how water circulates round the Earth. The driving force for the cycle is the Sun.

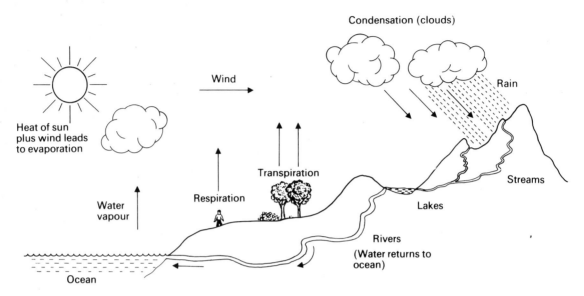

Fig. 9.12   The water cycle

Water vapour in the atmosphere comes from a number of sources: heat from the Sun evaporates water from the sea, causing water vapour to float up into the air; in all living organisms the processes of **respiration** occur during which starchy food material is 'burned' up creating water and carbon dioxide which are expelled into the air; in plants the process of **transpiration** causes water to be drawn from the soil through the roots and allows water to evaporate at the leaves.

As the water vapour in the atmosphere is cooled, it condenses forming millions of tiny water droplets and clouds are formed. If further cooling of the moisture-laden air occurs, rain forms and falls. This rain drains through streams into rivers and then back into the sea. Some water is diverted from the rivers into reservoirs and purified. This water is then used in industry and the home. After use it is dirty and so has to be treated at the sewage works before being returned to a river or the sea. Eventually all water finds its way into the sea. In this way all the water that left the sea eventually returns there and the cycle can continue.

Hardness of water

The water you drink contains some dissolved solids and gases. This dissolved material usually is not harmful and can, in fact, be good for you. Where do these dissolved solids come from? The rain water collects carbon dioxide from the atmosphere as it falls to the ground. When the water combines with the carbon dioxide, a weak acid called **carbonic acid** is produced (see Fig. 9.13).

carbon dioxide + water $\rightleftharpoons$ carbonic acid

$$CO_{2(g)} \quad + H_2O_{(l)} \rightleftharpoons H_2CO_{3(aq)}$$

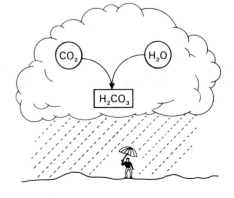

Fig. 9.13   How carbonic acid forms in the atmosphere

The rocks in some parts of the country contain limestone (calcium carbonate) or dolomite (magnesium carbonate). The weak carbonic acid in rain water attacks these rocks and very slowly dissolves them as it passes over and through them. The dissolved substances are called calcium hydrogencarbonate and magnesium hydrogencarbonate respectively.

calcium carbonate + carbonic acid $\rightleftharpoons$ calcium hydrogencarbonate

$$CaCO_{3(s)} + \underbrace{H_2CO_{3(aq)}}_{(H_2O_{(l)} + CO_{2(g)})} \rightleftharpoons Ca(HCO_3)_{2(aq)}$$

Rocks may also contain gypsum (calcium sulphate—$CaSO_4 \cdot 2H_2O$) or anhydrite ($CaSO_4$) which are only sparingly soluble in water.

Temporary hardness is caused by the presence of dissolved calcium (or magnesium) hydrogencarbonate. **Permanent hardness** is caused by the presence of dissolved calcium (or magnesium) sulphate (and sometimes chloride) in water. When water containing these substances is boiled or evaporated a white solid deposit is usually left behind (see Fig. 9.14). This is due to calcium (or magnesium) sulphate and/or calcium carbonate reappearing. The 'furring' in kettles which occurs in hardwater regions is a direct result of these deposits (see Fig. 9.15). Also, blockages in pipes can be caused by such behaviour.

This sort of change in which a solid is deposited can happen quite slowly. For example, the caverns in the Yorkshire Dales contain **stalactites** and **stalagmites** formed from the slow evaporation of water containing calcium hydrogencarbonate (see Fig. 9.16). Calcium carbonate is produced in the following process:

calcium hydrogencarbonate $\longrightarrow$ calcium carbonate + water + carbon dioxide

$$Ca(HCO_3)_{2(aq)} \longrightarrow CaCO_{3(s)} + H_2O_{(g)} + CO_{2(g)}$$

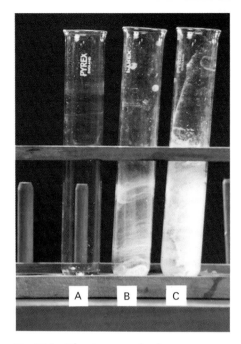

Fig. 9.14 When temporary hard or permanently hard water is evaporated a deposit is left behind (B and C). Evaporating distilled water leaves no deposit (A)

Fig. 9.15 The fur in this kettle was formed from hard water

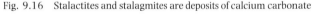
Fig. 9.16 Stalactites and stalagmites are deposits of calcium carbonate

What effect do these dissolved substances have on soap?

An ordinary soap such as sodium stearate, when added to water containing no dissolved solids or gases (soft water) gives a good lather almost immediately (see Fig. 9.17). If the water is either temporarily hard or permanently hard then when soap is added to it no lather is produced initially. In fact, it takes the addition of quite a lot of soap solution to give a good lather (Fig. 9.18). The amount of soap added can be used to estimate the hardness in water (Fig. 9.19). You will notice from Fig. 9.18 that in addition to the lather on the surface of the water, the water itself has become very cloudy. This cloudiness is caused by the presence of solid material (a **precipitate**) produced by the reaction of the dissolved substances with soap. This reaction may be represented by the following equation:

Fig. 9.17 Soft water gives a good lather quickly

$$\text{sodium stearate (soap)} + \text{calcium hydrogen-carbonate (in temporary hard water)} \longrightarrow \text{calcium stearate (scum)} + \text{sodium hydrogen-carbonate}$$

$$2NaSt_{(aq)} + Ca(HCO_3)_{2(aq)} \longrightarrow Ca(St)_{2(s)} + 2NaHCO_{3(aq)}$$

St = stearate
$NaSt = C_{17}H_{35}COONa$

The calcium stearate is the precipitate (more commonly referred to as 'scum').

This reaction may be represented more simply, since it is the calcium ion (or magnesium ion) present in hard water which produces the scum:

$$2NaSt_{(aq)} + Ca^{2+}_{(aq)} \longrightarrow Ca(St)_{2(s)} + 2Na^+_{(aq)}$$

Fig. 9.18 When soap is added to hard water a scum is formed with hardly any lather

Soapless detergents (discussed in more detail in Chapter 11) do not produce scum in hard water. This is an advantage of soapless detergents.

Removal of hardness

Temporary hardness may be removed by boiling. When heated the calcium hydrogencarbonate decomposes producing calcium carbonate which is insoluble.

$$\text{calcium hydrogencarbonate} \xrightarrow{\text{heat}} \text{calcium carbonate} + \text{water} + \text{carbon dioxide}$$

$$Ca(HCO_3)_{2(aq)} \longrightarrow CaCO_{3(s)} + H_2O_{(l)} + CO_{2(g)}$$

Permanently hard water is caused by the presence of calcium (or magnesium) sulphate (and sometimes chlorides). These substances are not decomposed when heated and therefore cannot be removed by boiling. Both types of hardness may be removed by the addition of washing soda (sodium carbonate) crystals.

Permanent hardness

$$\text{calcium sulphate} + \text{sodium carbonate} \longrightarrow \text{calcium carbonate} + \text{sodium sulphate}$$

$$CaSO_{4(aq)} + Na_2CO_{3(aq)} \longrightarrow CaCO_{3(s)} + Na_2SO_{4(aq)}$$

Fig. 9.19 Titrating soap into hard water to determine how hard it is

Temporary hardness

calcium hydrogen-carbonate + sodium carbonate ⟶ calcium carbonate + sodium hydrogen-carbonate

$$Ca(HCO_3)_{2(aq)} + Na_2CO_{3(aq)} \longrightarrow CaCO_{3(s)} + 2NaHCO_{3(aq)}$$

In each case the calcium (or magnesium) ion which causes the hardness is removed as a precipitate and can no longer cause hardness.

$$Ca^{2+}_{(aq)} + CO^{2-}_{3(aq)} \longrightarrow CaCO_{3(s)}$$

Both types of hardness may also be removed by the technique known as **ion-exchange**. The water is passed through a container filled with a suitable resin in the form of small granules (see Fig. 9.20). The calcium (or magnesium ion) causing the hardness is exchanged for a sodium ion which is present on the resin.

Temporary hardness

calcium hydrogen-carbonate + sodium-resin ⟶ calcium-resin + sodium hydrogen-carbonate

$$Ca(HCO_3)_{2(aq)} + Na_2\text{-resin} \longrightarrow Ca\text{-resin} + 2NaHCO_{3(aq)}$$

Permanent hardness

calcium sulphate + sodium-resin ⟶ calcium-resin + sodium sulphate

$$CaSO_{4(aq)} + Na_2\text{-resin} \longrightarrow Ca\text{-resin} + Na_2SO_{4(aq)}$$

When all the sodium ions on the resin have all been exchanged for calcium ions then the resin can be recharged. Both types of hardness may also be removed by distillation of the water, but this is too expensive for large-scale use.

Advantages and disadvantages of hard water

Some of the problems of hard water were highlighted on page 119. Table 9.1 shows some of the advantages as well as disadvantages of hardness in water.

Fig. 9.20(a)   Inside an ion exchanger are small resin granules. These are a compound made of sodium and a resin loosely combined together

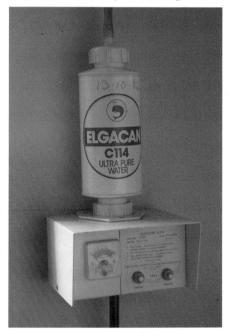

Fig. 9.20(b)   An ion exchange system in operation

Disadvantages of hard water	Advantages of hard water
Causes waste of soap*	Can have a good taste
Can spoil the finish of fabrics	Calcium ions in hard water are required by the body to build strong bones and teeth
Causes kettles to fur	Coats lead pipes with a thin film of insoluble lead sulphate or carbonate and cuts down the possibility of lead poisoning
Can cause pipes to block	Can be good for brewing beer

Table 9.1   *This is not a serious problem

Dissolving

One of the most interesting things about water is that it will dissolve such a variety of substances. For instance, if you stir a spatulafull of salt into a beaker of water it disappears (Fig. 9.21). The salt is still there but it has **dissolved** into the water. Water is a very good **solvent**. A solvent is a substance which dissolves substances (**solutes**) to form **solutions**.

solvent + solute ⟶ solution

In this case the salt is the solute, and when it dissolves we have produced a salt solution. Solutions in which water is the solvent are called **aqueous solutions**.

Even though water is a very good solvent, it cannot go on dissolving more and more of a solute. For example, if a large amount of salt is added to the beaker of water some of the salt may not dissolve. We say that the solution has become **saturated** with the solute (salt). A **saturated solution** is one which contains as much dissolved solute as it can *at a particular temperature*.

Fig. 9.21(a)   Salt being stirred into water

Solubility and temperature

When making a cup of coffee, have you ever noticed that the solids dissolve more easily in hot water than in cold water? It is a well-known fact that the amount of solid that will dissolve in a solution increases with increasing temperature. We say that the **solubility** increases with increasing temperature. Different solutes have different solubilities at a particular temperature. For example, at 50°C, 100 g of water will dissolve 84 g of potassium nitrate but only 33 g of copper(II) sulphate.

The solubility of a solute in water at a given temperature is the number of grams of that solute which can be dissolved in 100 g of water to produce a saturated solution at that temperature.

Fig. 9.21(b)   The salt soon dissolves

Calculating solubilities

Example
81 g of potassium nitrate dissolve in 60 g of water at 70 °C. Calculate the solubility of potassium nitrate in water at that temperature.

Since solubility is related to the amount of substance dissolving in 100 g of water you need to know how much dissolves in that amount. If 60 g of water dissolves 81 g of potassium nitrate then 1 g of water will dissolve 81/60 g of potassium nitrate. Therefore, 100 g of water will dissolve

$$\frac{81}{60} \times 100 = 135 \, \text{g}.$$

The solubility of potassium nitrate in water at 70 °C is 135 g.

Solubility curves

Fig. 9.22 shows how the solubility of potassium nitrate and of copper(II) sulphate varies with temperature. The graphs shown in this figure are known as **solubility curves**. Using curves of this type you can find the solubility of any solute at any temperature over a range of temperatures. For example, the solubility of potassium nitrate at 35 °C is 54 g whilst that of copper(II) sulphate is 26 g.

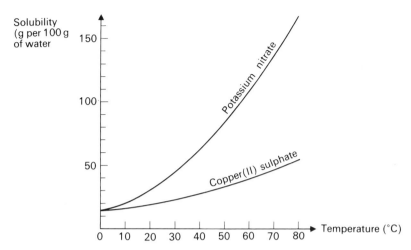

Fig. 9.22   Solubility curves for potassium nitrate and copper(II) sulphate

Hydrogen

Hydrogen is an essential part of water and, therefore, of all living things. It is also found in a vast array of compounds such as methane (natural gas), ethanol (alcohol) and sodium stearate (soap) (see Fig. 9.23). It is the lightest element—it is so light that as the free element it generally escapes from the pull of Earth's gravity. It is the most common element in the universe, for example, the Sun is a huge white hot ball consisting almost entirely of hydrogen (see Fig. 9.24).

Fig. 9.24   The Sun consists almost entirely of hydrogen

(a)   Methane is used for cooking

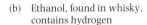

(b)   Ethanol, found in whisky, contains hydrogen

Fig. 9.23   Some compounds in which hydrogen is found

(c)   Soap (sodium stearate) contains hydrogen

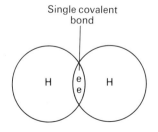

Fig. 9.25   Hydrogen is a diatomic molecule

Each hydrogen atom consists of one proton and one electron (there are no neutrons) and it exists as diatomic molecules by sharing electrons to form a single covalent bond (see Fig. 9.25).

Hydrogen is a very useful gas. Large quantities are required for the manufacture of ammonia gas, most of which is then converted to nitric acid or fertilizers. Also, some metals such as tungsten are extracted from their oxide ores using hydrogen. When hydrogen gas is mixed with other gases including oxygen it produces a very hot flame that may be used for welding (see Fig. 9.26). The gas is used in making organic compounds such as nylon, synthetic petrol and methanol, and it is used to make solid fats that are required to manufacture margarine. Balloons used in cosmic ray research and meteorological balloons can be filled with hydrogen. Lastly, as a liquid, hydrogen is used as a rocket fuel along with liquid oxygen (Fig. 9.27).

Fig. 9.27   As a liquid, hydrogen is used as a rocket fuel

Fig. 9.26   Welding is one of the uses of hydrogen

Making hydrogen in industry

Several methods are used to prepare large quantities of hydrogen for industrial use. Up to 1960 most hydrogen was made by passing steam through white-hot coke (the **Bosch process**). However, production has since switched to the oil industry. When heavier oil fractions (see Chapter 11, page 150) are **cracked** (broken down into smaller more useful molecules) hydrogen is obtained as a byproduct. Most hydrogen, however, is made by passing steam and methane (natural gas) over a hot nickel catalyst. The process is called **steam reforming**. Hydrogen and carbon dioxide are produced:

$$\text{methane} + \text{steam} \xrightarrow[\text{heat}]{\text{catalyst}} \text{carbon dioxide} + \text{hydrogen}$$

$$CH_{4(g)} + 2H_2O_{(g)} \longrightarrow CO_{2(g)} + 4H_{2(g)}$$

Because it is not very soluble the carbon dioxide is removed by dissolving it in water under pressure. Hydrogen is the gas remaining. It is stored in large cylinders like the ones in Fig. 9.28.

Fig. 9.28   Hydrogen is stored in pressurized cylinders

Making hydrogen in the laboratory

You have already seen that hydrogen is released when water is electrolysed (see page 64). It is also released when certain metals react with water or dilute acid (see Chapter 8, page 89). Adding a metal to a dilute acid is the most convenient method for preparing hydrogen in the laboratory.

All acids contain hydrogen and when metals such as zinc are put into them hydrogen gas is produced. When this happens a salt is also formed. Zinc and dilute hydrochloric acid are often used to make the gas in the apparatus shown in Fig. 9.29. Copper(II) sulphate is added to speed up the reaction between the zinc and dilute acid. It acts as a **catalyst**. (Catalysts are discussed in greater detail in Chapter 16.)

zinc + dilute hydrochloric acid $\longrightarrow$ zinc chloride + hydrogen

$$Zn_{(s)} + \quad 2HCl_{(aq)} \quad \longrightarrow \quad ZnCl_{2(aq)} + H_{2(g)}$$

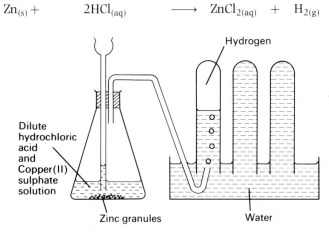

Fig. 9.29   Apparatus for preparing hydrogen

Properties of hydrogen

Hydrogen is a colourless gas with no smell and it is almost insoluble in water. It is also the lightest element (Fig. 9.30) being at least 15 times lighter than other gases in the air. This fact may be illustrated by the experiment shown in Fig. 9.31.

Fig. 9.30   Hydrogen is lighter than air!

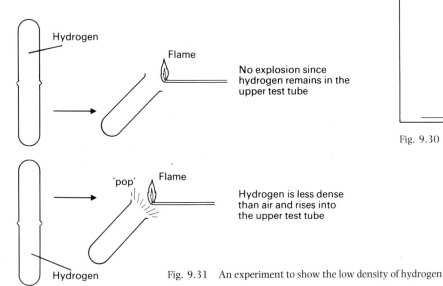

Fig. 9.31   An experiment to show the low density of hydrogen

The extreme lightness of the gas led to its use in the first airships. However, after the Hindenburg disaster in 1937 when the German airship was completely destroyed by fire (see Fig. 9.32) helium gas was used instead of hydrogen. Helium, the second lightest gas, is much safer because of its unreactive nature (Fig. 9.33).

Fig. 9.33   Helium is used today in airships

Fig. 9.32   The Hindenburg airship disaster

The name hydrogen means 'water former'. It combines with oxygen when it burns at a jet and produces water (see Fig. 9.34). This reaction also gives out a lot of energy, which can be used, for example, to propel a space rocket or a car.

$$\text{hydrogen} + \text{oxygen} \longrightarrow \text{water}$$

$$2H_{2(g)} + O_{2(g)} \longrightarrow 2H_2O_{(g)} + \text{energy}$$

This is also the reaction which takes place in the 'pop' test for hydrogen.

Hydrogen will also burn in chlorine gas to form the gas hydrogen chloride (see Fig. 9.35).

$$\text{hydrogen} + \text{chlorine} \longrightarrow \text{hydrogen chloride}$$

$$H_{2(g)} + Cl_{2(g)} \longrightarrow 2HCl_{(g)}$$

This reaction will also occur explosively if the gases are mixed or are left in sunlight.

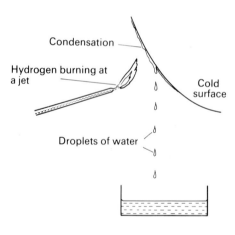

Fig. 9.34   When hydrogen burns water is produced

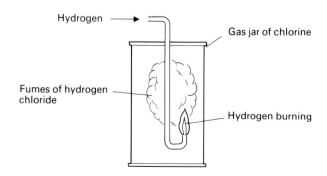

Fig. 9.35   Hydrogen chloride is produced when hydrogen burns in chlorine

Note
It is recommended that the experiments illustrated in Figs 9.34, 9.35 and 9.36 are **not** attempted.

Hydrogen is one of two important non-metallic elements (the other being carbon) which has the ability to remove oxygen from some metal oxides such as copper(II) oxide (see Fig. 9.36).

$$\text{copper(II) oxide} + \text{hydrogen} \xrightarrow{\text{heat}} \text{copper} + \text{steam}$$

$$CuO_{(s)} \quad + \quad H_{2(g)} \quad \longrightarrow \quad Cu_{(s)} + H_2O_{(g)}$$

In this process the hydrogen (or alternatively, carbon) is acting as a **reducing agent** taking the oxygen from the metal oxide.

Lead(II) oxide is another metal oxide which hydrogen will reduce.

$$\text{lead(II) oxide} + \text{hydrogen} \xrightarrow{\text{heat}} \text{lead} + \text{steam}$$

$$PbO_{(s)} \quad + \quad H_{2(g)} \quad \longrightarrow Pb_{(s)} + H_2O_{(g)}$$

In each of the above reactions hydrogen is oxidized to water.

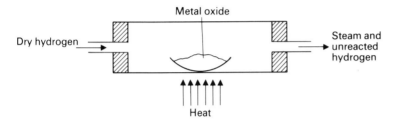

Fig. 9.36   Certain metal oxides are reduced by hydrogen

Oxidation and reduction

'Oxidation' and 'reduction' are chemical processes which take place during some chemical reactions.

As you have already seen in Chapter 2 a substance is oxidized if it gains oxygen:

$$\text{copper} + \text{oxygen} \xrightarrow{\text{heat}} \text{copper oxide}$$

$$2Cu_{(s)} + O_{2(g)} \quad \longrightarrow \quad 2CuO_{(s)}$$

$$\text{magnesium} + \text{oxygen} \xrightarrow{\text{heat}} \text{magnesium oxide}$$

$$2Mg_{(s)} \quad + \quad O_{2(g)} \quad \longrightarrow \quad 2MgO_{(s)}$$

The copper and magnesium have gained oxygen and they have been oxidized to copper(II) oxide and magnesium oxide respectively. The process of **oxidation** has taken place.

Oxidation also takes place if a substance loses hydrogen. For example, hydrogen sulphide gas reacts with chlorine gas (*Note:* both are very poisonous!) producing hydrogen chloride gas and leaving a yellow deposit of sulphur.

$$\text{hydrogen sulphide} + \text{chlorine} \longrightarrow \text{hydrogen chloride} + \text{sulphur}$$

$$H_2S_{(g)} \quad + \quad Cl_{2(g)} \longrightarrow \quad 2HCl_{(g)} \quad + \quad S_{(s)}$$

In this reaction the hydrogen sulphide has lost hydrogen and been oxidized to sulphur. The chlorine gas is doing the oxidizing by removing the hydrogen and is therefore called an **oxidizing agent**. Any substance which brings about oxidation is known as an oxidizing agent.

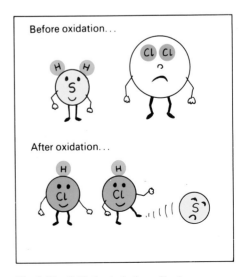

Fig. 9.37   Oxidation is the loss of hydrogen

Reduction is the reverse (or opposite) of oxidation. Therefore, reduction is the removal of oxygen from, or addition of hydrogen to, a substance. For example, in the previous section you learned that when hydrogen gas is burned in air it reacts with oxygen gas forming water.

$$hydrogen + oxygen \longrightarrow water$$

$$2H_{2(g)} + O_{2(g)} \longrightarrow 2H_2O_{(g)}$$

During this reaction the oxygen is gaining hydrogen and so it is reduced to water.

Again, in the previous section you saw that when hydrogen gas is passed over heated copper(II) oxide, copper is produced as well as steam.

$$copper(II)\ oxide + hydrogen \xrightarrow{heat} copper + steam$$

$$CuO_{(s)} + H_{2(g)} \longrightarrow Cu_{(s)} + H_2O_{(g)}$$

During this reaction copper(II) oxide loses its oxygen and is reduced to copper by the hydrogen gas. In this case the hydrogen is responsible for the reduction by removing oxygen and is called a **reducing agent**. Any substance which brings about reduction is known as a reducing agent.

If we examine the last reaction more closely you will notice that whilst the copper(II) oxide is being reduced to copper the hydrogen is being oxidized to water. Any chemical reaction in which oxidation and reduction take place is known as a **redox reaction** or **REDOX process**.

$$
\begin{array}{ccc}
 & R\ E\ D\ O\ X & \\
 \swarrow & & \searrow \\
REDuction & & OXidation
\end{array}
$$

Also, in the reaction of hydrogen with copper(II) oxide, the hydrogen is doing the reducing and so is the reducing agent, whilst the copper(II) oxide is doing the oxidizing and so is the oxidizing agent. The overall process may be summarized:

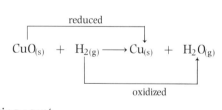

CuO = oxidizing agent
H_2 = reducing agent

Chemists also use another definition of oxidation and reduction which involves electrons. In a chemical reaction if a substance *loses* electrons it is oxidized whilst if it *gains* electrons it has been reduced. For example, when sodium burns in chlorine gas sodium chloride is formed:

$$sodium + chlorine \longrightarrow sodium\ chloride$$

$$2Na_{(s)} + Cl_{2(g)} \longrightarrow 2NaCl_{(s)}$$

An ionic bond is formed between sodium and chlorine in sodium chloride. To do this each sodium atom must lose an electron to each atom of the chlorine. Sodium atoms become sodium ions (Na^+) whilst chlorine atoms become chloride ions (Cl^-). The sodium atoms have been oxidized whilst chlorine atoms have been reduced:

sodium atom $\longrightarrow$ sodium ion + electron

$$Na \longrightarrow Na^+ + e^- \quad (oxidation)$$

chlorine atom + electron $\longrightarrow$ chloride ion

$$Cl + e^- \longrightarrow Cl^- \quad (reduction)$$

The chlorine accepts the electron and is therefore the oxidizing agent. The sodium atom transfers its electron to the chlorine atom and so is the reducing agent.

Oxidation and reduction also take place during electrolysis. For example, in the Down's cell (see Chapter 8, page 98) where molten sodium chloride is electrolysed, sodium ions gain electrons and are deposited at the cathode. The chloride ions lose electrons and are deposited at the anode. Reduction has taken place at the cathode whilst oxidation has taken place at the anode.

At the ANODE—OXIDATION takes place
At the CATHODE—REDUCTION takes place

QUESTIONS

---

1 Water can be formed by burning dry hydrogen at a jet as shown in the diagram below.

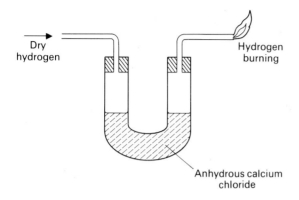

a) Write a word equation and a balanced chemical equation for the reaction which occurs.
b) i) Name chemicals which could be used in the laboratory to prepare hydrogen.
   ii) Write a word equation and a balanced chemical equation for the reaction which occurs in this laboratory preparation.
c) What precautions must be taken before the hydrogen is ignited at the jet?
d) Draw a diagram to show how the water vapour would be condensed and collected.
e) How would the colourless liquid be identified as water?
f) What is the difference between the terms 'dry' and 'anhydrous'?

2 Your friend is helping you to reduce copper(II) oxide using the apparatus below.

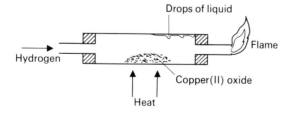

a) Describe the changes you would see in the copper(II) oxide during the experiment.
b) What substance is left in the tube in place of the copper(II) oxide at the end of the experiment?
c) Your friend is rather doubtful about the identity of the substance left in the tube. What simple test could you carry out that might convince him?

d) Name the drops of liquid found at the end of the tube.
e) Give a simple chemical test to prove to your friend that this liquid is indeed what you say it is.
f) Your friend is not convinced this liquid came from the reaction. What simple precautions could be taken at the start of the experiment to show that the liquid could have come only from the reaction and not from other sources?
g) What has been the function of the hydrogen in this experiment?

3 a) Use the data given in Table 1 to plot a solubility curve for ammonium chloride.

Temperature (°C)	Solubility of ammonium chloride (g/100 g)
0	29.2
10	33.0
20	37.1
30	41.8
40	45.8
50	50.8
60	55.2
70	60.2
80	65.6

Table 1

b) Using your solubility curve find the solubility of ammonium chloride at:
   i) 25 °C;
   ii) 45 °C;
   iii) 75 °C.

4 30 g of copper(II) sulphate dissolve in 60 g of water to form a saturated solution at 60 °C. Calculate the solubility in water at that temperature.

5 In the reaction:

$$CuO_{(s)} + Mg_{(s)} \xrightarrow{heat} Cu_{(s)} + MgO_{(s)}$$

a) name and give the formula of the substance which is:
   i) oxidized,
   ii) reduced;
b) name and give the formula of:
   i) the oxidizing agent,
   ii) the reducing agent.
c) The above reaction is an example of a REDOX reaction. What does the term REDOX mean?

6 Table 2 shows the results of testing five different samples of water with soap solution. The soap solution was gradually added to each 50 cm³ sample with shaking until a permanent lather was obtained.

Water sample	Volume of soap solution needed (cm³)	
	Before boiling	After boiling
A	24	2
B	25	11
C	21	21
C after filtering	21	21
C after distilling	2	2

Table 2

Answer parts (a) to (c) which are about the substances present in the water samples and which cause the differences in the volumes of soap solution required for a permanent lather.

a) Of the five water samples:
   i) which two are permanently hard;
   ii) which one is temporarily hard;
   iii) which one has the properties of a mixture of temporarily and permanently hard water? (3)
b) Name a compound which could be present in sample A but not in sample C. (1)
c) Name a compound which could be present in sample C but not in sample A. (1)
d) Explain how the compound you have named in part (c) gets into the water by a naturally occurring process. (1)
e) Why are the results for sample C different after distilling but unchanged after filtering? (2)
(JMB/WMEB 1982)

7 a) Oxidation may be defined as either the addition of oxygen to an element or compound or the removal of hydrogen from an element or compound. Reduction is a reaction which is the opposite of oxidation.
   For the reactions listed below state whether the substance underlined has been oxidized, reduced or undergone neither of these reactions.
   i) carbon monoxide + oxygen
   $\rightarrow$ carbon dioxide
   ii) sulphur + hydrogen → hydrogen sulphide
   iii) copper(II) oxide + magnesium → copper + magnesium oxide (3)

b) Oxidation may also be defined as the removal of electrons. For the reactions listed below state whether the substance underlined has been oxidized, reduced or undergone neither of these reactions.
   i) $2Na_{(s)} + Cl_{2(g)} \rightarrow 2Na^+Cl^-_{(s)}$
   ii) $5Fe^{2+}_{(aq)} + MnO^-_{4(aq)} + 8H^+_{(aq)} \rightarrow 5Fe^{3+}_{(aq)} + Mn^{2+}_{(aq)} + 4H_2O_{(l)}$
   iii) $H^+_{(aq)} + OH^-_{(aq)} \rightarrow H_2O_{(l)}$ (3)
c) When zinc is added to a solution of copper(II) sulphate a redox reaction takes place. A brown precipitate of copper and a colourless solution containing zinc ions are formed. Write the simplest ionic equation for the redox reaction. What is the oxidizing agent in this reaction? (3)
(JMB/WMEB 1982)

8 a) Name a substance which when dissolved in water makes the water:
   i) temporarily hard;
   ii) permanently hard. (2)
b) Name a type of substance which when added to hard water:
   i) produces a lather but does not soften the water;
   ii) produces a lather and forms a white precipitate. (2)
c) State one method which:
   i) can only be used for softening temporarily hard water;
   ii) is used to soften water which is both temporarily and permanently hard. (2)
d) State:
   i) one advantage of hard water;
   ii) one disadvantage of hard water. (2)
(NEA 1984)

9 a) State what is meant by a saturated solution. (1)
b) Table 3 shows the solubility of potassium nitrate in water at various temperatures.

Temperature (°C)	20	30	40	50	60	70
Solubility (g per 100 g water)	32	46	64	86	110	138

Table 3

Plot these results on a grid and draw the solubility curve for potassium nitrate. (3)

c) Use your graph to answer each of the following questions.
   i) What is the solubility of potassium nitrate at 35 °C?
   ii) How much potassium nitrate will saturate 25 g of water at 35 °C?
   iii) How much potassium nitrate would be deposited if a saturated solution, made at 65 °C using 50 g of water, was cooled to 25 °C? (5)

(JMB 1984)

10 a) The usual test for hydrogen is to place a burning splint into a test-tube of the gas open to the air.
   i) What result would you expect if the test-tube did contain hydrogen?
   ii) Write an equation for the reaction occurring. (2)
   b) Use your answers to (a) and your knowledge of the physical properties and industrial sources of hydrogen, to help you to answer the questions which follow.
   Some people have suggested that in the future cars might be powered by hydrogen as a fuel instead of petrol.
   i) Suggest *two advantages* of using hydrogen (instead of petrol) as a fuel to power cars.
   ii) Suggest *one disadvantage* of using hydrogen as a fuel to power cars. (3)

(AEB 1983)

11 a) Some fresh calcium oxide is exposed to the air and weighed at regular intervals. At first there is a fairly rapid increase in mass and this is followed by a much slower increase which eventually ceases. Explain these observations. (8)
   b) Explain why:
   i) calcium carbonate is an essential ingredient of the material which goes into the blast furnace in the extraction of iron; (4)
   ii) calcium carbonate is insoluble in water, yet caves or potholes are common in limestone districts; (4)
   iii) calcium carbonate is insoluble in water, yet some hot-water pipes become blocked up by layers of this carbonate. (4)

(OLE 1983)

12 a) A pupil left the stoppers off three bottles containing liquids on his bench. He returned after the weekend to find the following changes:
   Liquid A had increased in volume;
   Liquid B had decreased in volume;
   Liquid C had remained at more or less the same volume but had turned cloudy.
   If none of the bottles contained water only, use the information above to suggest a possible identity for each of the liquids A, B and C. Explain your reasoning. (4, 4, 4)
   b) i) Explain what is meant by the term *hygroscopic* and give an example of a compound which shows this property. (3)
   ii) A pupil suggests that *writing paper* is hygroscopic. Suggest how this idea could be tested and explain how the test would show a 'positive' result. (5)

(OLE 1984)

13 A town's water supply is obtained by purifying river water.
   a) Write out below the words missing from the following diagram of the water cycle. (2)

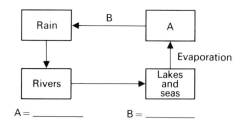

A = _____   B = _____

   b) i) Which process, filtration or distillation, would produce the purest water from river water? Give a reason for your answer. (2)
   ii) Which process, filtration or distillation, is used in this country for producing drinking water from river water.
   In view of your answer to (b)(i) what is the reason for the choice of method? (2)
   c) In recent years pollution of rivers and lakes has become a serious problem. State two main sources of river pollution. (2)
   d) In some areas water is 'recycled'. What does recycling mean and why is it necessary? (2)

(JMB/WMEB 1980)

CARBON

Fig. 10.1 Diamond is a form of carbon

Some elements are an essential part of all living things on this planet. One of these is **carbon**. Small quantities of carbon are found in the Earth's crust as the free element. It is found in two different forms: **diamond** and **graphite** (see Figs 10.1 and 10.2). These forms have different physical properties such as appearance and density but they are the same element and have the same chemical properties. Table 10.1 lists some of the differences between the two forms.

Fig. 10.2 Graphite is another form of carbon

Property	Diamond	Graphite
Appearance	A colourless, transparent crystal which sparkles in light	A dark grey shiny solid
Electrical conductivity	Does not conduct electricity	Conducts electricity
Hardness	A very hard substance	A soft material with a slippery feel
Density	$3.5\,\mathrm{g\,cm^{-3}}$	$2.3\,\mathrm{g\,cm^{-3}}$

Table 10.1

The allotropes of carbon

When an element can exist in more than one physical form in the same state it is said to exhibit **allotropy**. Diamond and graphite are the allotropes of carbon. The structures of these two substances are shown in Figs 10.3 and 10.4. The physical properties of graphite and diamond are different because the carbon atoms are arranged differently in the two forms.

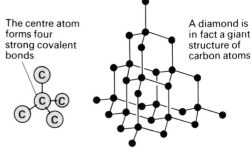

The centre atom forms four strong covalent bonds

A diamond is in fact a giant structure of carbon atoms

Fig. 10.3   The structure of diamond

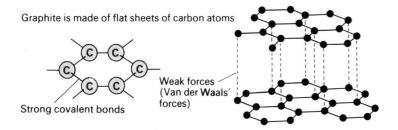

Graphite is made of flat sheets of carbon atoms

Strong covalent bonds

Weak forces (Van der Waals' forces)

Fig. 10.4   The structure of graphite

The graphite structure consists of layers. Within each layer each carbon atom is bonded covalently to three other carbon atoms by three strong covalent bonds. There are, however, only weak forces holding the layers together (van der Waals' forces) and so the layers will easily pass over each other just like a pack of cards (see Fig. 10.5). When you draw with a pencil you leave marks on paper due to the layers of graphite in the pencil lead 'flowing' over one another onto the paper as you draw or write.

With only three covalent bonds formed between carbon atoms within the layers an unbonded electron is present on each carbon atom. These 'spare' electrons form electron clouds between the layers and it is because of these 'spare' (or 'free') electrons that graphite conducts electricity (see Fig. 10.6). A similar process occurs in metals (see Chapter 5, page 61). Also, graphite is less dense than diamond because its structure is less compact.

Fig. 10.5   The layers in graphite can easily slide over one another just like cards

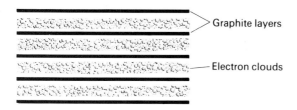

Graphite layers

Electron clouds

Fig. 10.6   A magnified side view of a piece of graphite

In the structure of diamond each carbon atom is bonded to four other carbon atoms by four strong covalent bonds. This bonding scheme gives rise to a very rigid, three-dimensional structure and accounts for the extreme hardness of the substance. Also the electron structure:

$$_6C \quad 2,4$$

is such that each carbon atom is able to share four electrons with the four other carbon atoms it is bonded to. There are no unbonded electrons and so diamond does not conduct electricity.

It is now possible to manufacture both allotropes of carbon. Graphite is made by heating a mixture of coke and sand at a very high temperature in an electric furnace for about 24 hours. Industrial diamonds are made by heating graphite to about $3000°$ C at a very high pressure . Some of the uses of the two allotropes are shown in Table 10.2 and Figs 10.7–10.9.

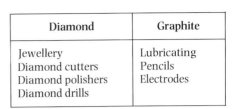

Diamond	Graphite
Jewellery Diamond cutters Diamond polishers Diamond drills	Lubricating Pencils Electrodes

Table 10.2

Fig. 10.7   Diamond-tipped drills are used to drill through very hard substances

Fig. 10.8   Diamonds are perhaps more commonly associated with jewellery

Fig. 10.9   Pencils contain graphite

Some other forms of carbon (not allotropes)

Charcoal and soot are also forms of carbon (see Fig. 10.10) but they do not occur naturally. They are made by heating animal bones, wood or coal in a limited amount of air. Coke is a further form of carbon which is manufactured. It is made by heating coal in the absence of air (see Fig. 10.11). Some of the uses of these forms are shown in Table 10.3.

Fig. 10.10   Soot is not an allotrope of carbon

Fig. 10.11   Coke is produced in large ovens by heating coal in the absence of air

Charcoal	Coke
Used by artists	As an industrial reducing agent
Absorb dangerous gases	As a fuel

Table 10.3

Some properties of carbon

Carbon, in its different forms, will burn in a plentiful supply of oxygen forming carbon dioxide. The temperature at which burning takes place depends upon the form being used.

carbon + oxygen $\longrightarrow$ carbon dioxide

$$C_{(s)} + O_{2(g)} \longrightarrow CO_{2(g)}$$

Carbon will reduce certain metal oxides to the metal. For example, lead(II) oxide will be reduced to lead when heated with carbon.

lead(II) oxide + carbon $\xrightarrow{heat}$ lead + carbon monoxide

$$PbO_{(s)} + C_{(s)} \longrightarrow Pb_{(s)} + CO_{(g)}$$

Other metal oxides can also be reduced by carbon. They include copper and zinc.

Carbon in compounds

Carbon occurs in many naturally-occurring compounds. For example, natural gas (methane) and many of our fuels are compounds of carbon and hydrogen (see Fig. 10.12). Coal is a complex mixture of compounds containing carbon, oxygen and hydrogen. There is a large number of carbonates such as those of calcium, sodium and magnesium (see Fig. 10.13).

(a)

(b)

Fig. 10.12   (a) Petrol and (b) coal both consist of compounds which contain carbon and hydrogen

Fig. 10.13(b)   Chalk is a form of calcium carbonate

Fig. 10.13(a)   Egg shell contains calcium carbonate

Carbon is also present in the food you eat (see Fig. 10.14) as well as in every part of your body. All plant life is made up of compounds containing carbon, hydrogen and oxygen, whilst in the atmosphere there is carbon dioxide.

Fig. 10.14   Do all these foods contain carbon?

The oxides of carbon

There are two oxides of carbon. These are **carbon dioxide** and **carbon monoxide**. Carbon dioxide is the more important of the two and is discussed first.

The air contains a small proportion of carbon dioxide—approximately 0.03% (see Table 12.1). This low value is almost constant and is maintained via the **carbon cycle** (see Fig. 10.15). Some of the carbon dioxide produced by burning and respiration is transferred from the air into plants via the process of **photosynthesis**. This cycle has continued in this manner for millions of years. However, scientists think that problems will arise in the near future through the burning of too much carbon-based fuel. This could upset the balance of the carbon cycle by liberating too much carbon dioxide into the air. If the amount of carbon dioxide builds up in the air then it is thought that the temperature of the Earth will rise. This is called the **greenhouse effect**. Higher temperatures would cause the ice caps to melt and flooding to occur. Weather patterns on our planet would also be affected.

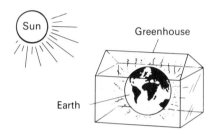

Fig. 10.16   The Earth will get hotter!

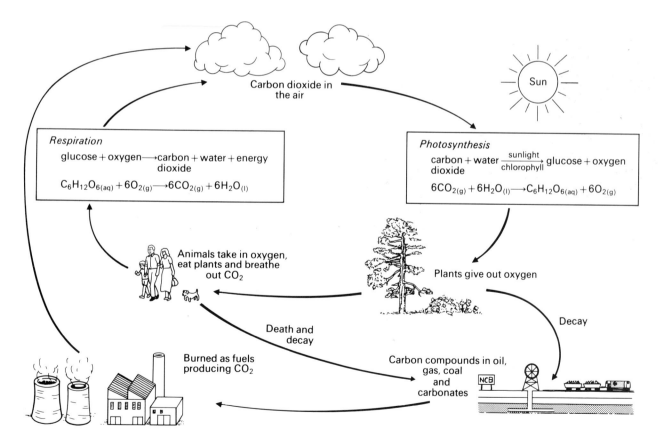

Respiration

glucose + oxygen ⟶ carbon + water + energy
                            dioxide

$C_6H_{12}O_{6(aq)} + 6O_{2(g)} \longrightarrow 6CO_{2(g)} + 6H_2O_{(l)}$

Photosynthesis

carbon + water $\xrightarrow[\text{chlorophyll}]{\text{sunlight}}$ glucose + oxygen
dioxide

$6CO_{2(g)} + 6H_2O_{(l)} \longrightarrow C_6H_{12}O_{6(aq)} + 6O_{2(g)}$

Animals take in oxygen, eat plants and breathe out CO$_2$

Plants give out oxygen

Death and decay

Decay

Burned as fuels producing CO$_2$

Carbon compounds in oil, gas, coal and carbonates

Fig. 10.15   The carbon cycle

Making carbon dioxide

In industry large amounts of carbon dioxide are obtained from the liquefaction of air (see Chapter 12, page 176). Also, when coke is burned in a plentiful supply of air, carbon dioxide is produced.

$$\text{carbon} + \text{oxygen} \xrightarrow{\text{heat}} \text{carbon dioxide}$$

$$C_{(s)} + O_{2(g)} \longrightarrow CO_{2(g)}$$

Large quantities of carbon dioxide are also obtained during the manufacture of hydrogen from natural gas (methane) as well as from fermentation (manufacture of ethanol) (see Chapter 11, page 159).

What is all this carbon dioxide needed for?

Carbon dioxide has a large number of uses (see Fig. 10.17). Large quantities of the gas are used in the making of mineral waters (lemonade, etc.) and beer. It is used in fire extinguishers and, as a solid ('dry ice'), it is used as a refrigerant and for creating the 'smoke' you see at 'pop' concerts. The gas is also used for transferring heat in some nuclear power stations.

Making carbon dioxide in the laboratory

In the laboratory the gas is made by pouring dilute hydrochloric acid onto calcium carbonate in the form of marble chips.

$$\begin{array}{l}\text{calcium} \\ \text{carbonate}\end{array} + \begin{array}{l}\text{dilute} \\ \text{hydrochloric acid}\end{array} \longrightarrow \begin{array}{l}\text{calcium} \\ \text{chloride}\end{array} + \begin{array}{l}\text{carbon} \\ \text{dioxide}\end{array} + \text{water}$$

$$CaCO_{3(s)} + 2HCl_{(aq)} \longrightarrow CaCl_{2(aq)} + CO_{2(g)} + H_2O_{(l)}$$

The apparatus usually used for this preparation is shown in Fig. 10.18.

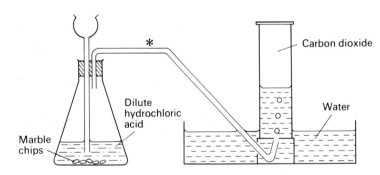

*If dry gas is required, then it is passed through concentrated sulphuric acid (to dry it) and then collected as shown below.

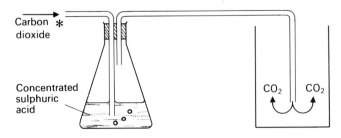

Fig. 10.18   Apparatus for preparing carbon dioxide

Fig. 10.17(a)   Soda water contains dissolved carbon dioxide

Fig. 10.17(b)   Carbon dioxide fire extinguishers are used mainly for electrical fires

Fig. 10.17(c)   Dry ice is solid carbon dioxide

Properties of carbon dioxide

Carbon dioxide is a colourless gas with only the very slightest trace of an odour and a taste as in soda water. It is only sparingly soluble in water. It is denser than air as shown by the fact that the gas falls from an inverted beaker into another beaker (see Fig. 10.19). It does not usually support combustion. When the gas fills the beaker it extinguishes the candle.

When carbon dioxide is bubbled through limewater (calcium hydroxide solution) a white precipitate is formed (see Fig. 10.20). This white solid is calcium carbonate.

carbon dioxide + calcium hydroxide ⟶ calcium carbonate + water

$$CO_{2(g)} + Ca(OH)_{2(aq)} \longrightarrow CaCO_{3(s)} + H_2O_{(l)}$$

This reaction is used as a test for carbon dioxide gas. If enough carbon dioxide is bubbled through the limewater then it will eventually become clear. This is due to the calcium carbonate reacting with the carbon dioxide in the presence of water to produce calcium hydrogencarbonate which is soluble.

calcium carbonate + water + carbon dioxide ⟶ calcium hydrogencarbonate

$$CaCO_{3(s)} + H_2O_{(l)} + CO_{2(g)} \longrightarrow Ca(HCO_3)_{2(aq)}$$

Carbon dioxide does not itself burn. Also, it will not allow a burning wooden spill or candle to continue burning in it. However, a strongly burning reactive metal such as magnesium will decompose the gas to provide oxygen so that it will continue to burn in the gas with much crackling. A white ash of magnesium oxide and black specks of carbon are deposited inside the boiling tube or gas jar (see Fig. 10.21).

magnesium + carbon dioxide ⟶ magnesium oxide + carbon

$$2Mg_{(s)} + CO_{2(g)} \longrightarrow 2MgO_{(s)} + C_{(s)}$$

Carbon dioxide will dissolve slightly in water forming a solution of the weak acid, carbonic acid:

water + carbon dioxide ⇌ carbonic acid

$$H_2O_{(l)} + CO_{2(g)} \rightleftharpoons H_2CO_{3(aq)}$$

When carbon dioxide is bubbled through a solution of sodium hydroxide, sodium carbonate and water are formed.

carbon dioxide + sodium hydroxide ⟶ sodium carbonate + water

$$CO_{2(g)} + 2NaOH_{(aq)} \longrightarrow Na_2CO_{3(aq)} + H_2O_{(l)}$$

Generally carbon dioxide reacts with alkalis to form carbonates. A solution of sodium hydroxide can be used to absorb carbon dioxide from the air. If an excess of carbon dioxide is bubbled through the solution of alkali then a white precipitate may be obtained. This is due to the formation and precipitation of sodium hydrogencarbonate.

sodium carbonate + water + carbon dioxide ⟶ sodium hydrogencarbonate

$$Na_2CO_{3(aq)} + H_2O_{(l)} + CO_{2(g)} \longrightarrow 2NaHCO_{3(s)}$$

Fig. 10.19 When the carbon dioxide is poured into the beaker the candle goes out

Fig. 10.20 A white precipitate of calcium carbonate is produced when carbon dioxide is bubbled through limewater. This precipitate disappears if you bubble more carbon dioxide through

Fig. 10.21 Magnesium oxide and carbon are produced when magnesium burns in carbon dioxide

Carbon monoxide (CO)

This gas is produced when carbon is heated in a limited supply of air:

$$\text{carbon} + \text{oxygen} \xrightarrow{\text{heat}} \text{carbon monoxide}$$

$$2C_{(s)} + O_{2(g)} \longrightarrow 2CO_{(g)}$$

It is also produced by the incomplete combustion of fuels. Petrol engines produce appreciable quantities of carbon monoxide because only a limited amount of air is allowed into the engine.

It is a highly poisonous gas being particularly dangerous because it is colourless and lacks a smell. It is almost insoluble in water and has a density similar to that of air.

Fig. 10.22 Incomplete combustion of petrol in a car engine produces carbon monoxide which is colourless and odourless

Fig. 10.23 Carbon monoxide is a highly poisonous gas!

Carbon monoxide burns in air with a blue flame to produce carbon dioxide.

$$\text{carbon monoxide} + \text{oxygen} \longrightarrow \text{carbon dioxide}$$

$$2CO_{(g)} + O_{2(g)} \longrightarrow 2CO_{2(g)}$$

Carbon monoxide can often be seen burning at the top of fires which use smokeless fuels (see Fig. 10.24).

Carbon monoxide is a good reducing agent. It will reduce many metal oxides to the metal. For example, if passed over heated copper(II) oxide, copper metal is produced.

$$\text{copper(II) oxide} + \text{carbon monoxide} \longrightarrow \text{copper} + \text{carbon dioxide}$$

$$CuO_{(s)} + CO_{(g)} \longrightarrow Cu_{(s)} + CO_{2(g)}$$

This property is made use of in the blast furnace (see Chapter 8, page 101). In this furnace the carbon monoxide formed reduces the iron ore (haematite) to iron.

$$\text{iron(III) oxide} + \text{carbon monoxide} \longrightarrow \text{iron} + \text{carbon dioxide}$$
$$\text{(haematite)}$$

$$Fe_2O_{3(s)} + 3CO_{(g)} \longrightarrow 2Fe_{(l)} + 3CO_{2(g)}$$

In addition to being used as a reducing agent carbon monoxide is used as a fuel. It is also used in the purification of nickel.

Fig. 10.24 Carbon monoxide burns to form carbon dioxide

Carbonates

Another important range of compounds which contain carbon, are the metal carbonates. They are all salts of carbonic acid. Many of these occur naturally in rock formations. For example, calcium carbonate ($CaCO_3$) is found as marble, limestone and chalk whilst magnesium carbonate is found in dolomite (Fig. 10.25). Sodium carbonate (Na_2CO_3) is a common carbonate which is used to soften water (see Chapter 9, page 120).

Properties of carbonates

It is found that most metal carbonates are decomposed upon heating (see Chapter 8, page 93). For example, copper(II) carbonate gives copper(II) oxide and carbon dioxide on heating.

copper(II) carbonate $\xrightarrow{\text{heat}}$ copper(II) oxide + carbon dioxide

$$CuCO_{3(s)} \longrightarrow CuO_{(s)} + CO_{2(g)}$$

Fig. 10.25 These rocks contain dolomite

The carbonates of the more reactive metals are much more difficult to decompose than copper carbonate. You would not expect, therefore, that calcium carbonate would decompose easily. In fact, it requires very strong heating indeed. The carbonates of the most reactive metals such as sodium and potassium do not decompose even at very high temperatures.

Carbonates are generally insoluble in water except for those of ammonium, sodium and potassium carbonates (see Chapter 7, page 80).

Carbonates react with acids to form salts, water and carbon dioxide (see Chapter 7, page 82). For example, copper(II) carbonate reacts with dilute hydrochloric acid to form copper(II) chloride, water and carbon dioxide.

copper(II) carbonate + dilute hydrochloric acid $\longrightarrow$ copper(II) chloride + water + carbon dioxide

$$CuCO_{3(s)} + 2HCl_{(aq)} \longrightarrow CuCl_{2(aq)} + H_2O_{(l)} + CO_{2(g)}$$

Generally, carbonates behave as bases. For this reason calcium carbonate can be used by gardeners to neutralize acids which are present in soil (see Fig. 10.26).

Fig. 10.26 Calcium carbonate will neutralize soil acidity

Test for carbonates

If a small amount of dilute nitric acid is added to some of the suspected carbonate in a test tube, effervescence occurs. If it is a carbonate then carbon dioxide gas is produced which will turn limewater milky.

Calcium carbonate—a useful carbonate

Calcium carbonate exists as limestone, marble and chalk. It is used:
1 to neutralize acids present in soil;
2 to make glass;
3 for extracting iron in a blast furnace;
4 to make cement;
5 to make calcium oxide (quicklime) and calcium hydroxide (slaked lime).

Fig. 10.27 Calcium carbonate is used in glass making

Hydrogencarbonates

Almost all the hydrogencarbonates are known only in solution. They are generally too unstable to exist as solids. The metal hydrogen-carbonate is formed when the metal carbonate reacts with carbon dioxide dissolved in water. For example, calcium carbonate forms calcium hydrogencarbonate under these circumstances. Calcium hydrogencarbonate is responsible for temporary hardness in water (see Chapter 9, page 119). Another example is that of sodium carbonate which reacts with carbon dioxide dissolved in water to form sodium hydrogencarbonate.

$$\text{sodium carbonate} + \text{carbon dioxide} + \text{water} \longrightarrow \text{sodium hydrogencarbonate}$$

$$Na_2CO_{3(aq)} + CO_{2(g)} + H_2O_{(l)} \longrightarrow 2NaHCO_{3(aq)}$$

Hydrogencarbonates decompose more readily than the original carbonate. For example, sodium carbonate does not decompose on heating. However, sodium hydrogencarbonate decomposes very readily releasing carbon dioxide and water vapour.

$$\text{sodium hydrogencarbonate} \xrightarrow{\text{heat}} \text{sodium carbonate} + \text{carbon dioxide} + \text{water}$$

$$2NaHCO_{3(s)} \longrightarrow Na_2CO_{3(s)} + CO_{2(g)} + H_2O_{(g)}$$

Sodium hydrogencarbonate is often called 'bicarb' (bicarbonate of soda). It is used in baking powder which is used as a raising agent in baking bread and cakes (see Fig. 10.28). The heat of the oven causes it to decompose. In doing so the release of carbon dioxide gas makes the bread or cakes 'rise'.

Hydrogencarbonates will also act as bases and neutralize acids. For example sodium hydrogencarbonate will react with dilute hydro-chloric acid liberating carbon dioxide and forming water and sodium chloride.

Fig. 10.28 One raising agent used to make bread is sodium hydrogencarbonate

$$\text{sodium hydrogen-carbonate} + \text{dilute hydrochloric acid} \longrightarrow \text{carbon dioxide} + \text{sodium chloride} + \text{water}$$

$$NaHCO_{3(s)} + HCl_{(aq)} \longrightarrow CO_{2(g)} + NaCl_{(aq)} + H_2O_{(l)}$$

For this reason these compounds are added to tablets sold under the heading of 'indigestion remedies'. The hydrogencarbonate is added to reduce the amount of hydrochloric acid found normally in your stomach.

Fig. 10.29(a) This will neutralize the acid!

Fig. 10.29(b) This indigestion remedy contains some types of hydrogencarbonate

---
QUESTIONS
---

1 a) Carbon occurs as two allotropes. One is very hard and is called _____. Because of its hardness it is used for _____. The other is soft and is called _____. Because of its slippery nature it is used for _____.
   i) Complete the above paragraph by filling in the spaces.
   ii) Which allotrope conducts electricity?
   iii) Give one other use for each of the allotropes.
   b) Draw diagrams to show the bonding and structure in the two allotropes of carbon.

2 Complete the following paragraph about carbon monoxide.
   When any fossil fuel burns in a limited supply of air a poisonous gas called carbon monoxide (formula: _____) is formed. The gas burns in air with a _____ coloured flame to form _____ (formula: _____). Carbon monoxide can often be seen burning on top of fires burning _____. Carbon monoxide is a good _____ agent. It will _____ many metallic oxides to the _____. For example, if passed over heated copper(II) oxide, _____ is produced.

3

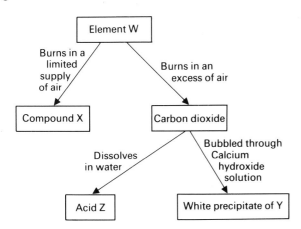

a) Name and give the symbol or formula of:
   i) element W;
   ii) compound X;
   iii) white precipitate Y;
   iv) acid Z.
b) Write a word equation and a balanced chemical equation for the reaction in which:
   i) compound X was formed;
   ii) acid Z was formed.
c) Describe what would happen if carbon dioxide were bubbled continuously through calcium hydroxide solution.

d) Name one place where acid Z is found.
e) Give two large-scale uses of carbon dioxide.

4 D is a yellow powder which when heated strongly with charcoal produces small beads of a shiny metal. The beads leave a grey mark when rubbed on paper.
a) What is the metal in the beads?
b) During the heating of D with charcoal a gas B is given off. Write down the names of the elements which are present in D.
c) What is the chemical name and formula of D?
d) What is the name given to the process in which a metal is obtained from one of its compounds by heating with charcoal?
e) Write a word equation and a balanced chemical equation for the reaction which has taken place.

5 The diagram below shows a simplified version of the carbon cycle.

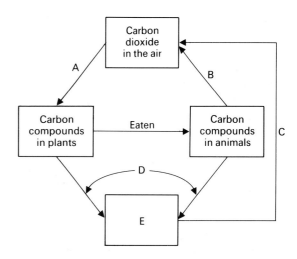

a) Name the processes labelled A, B, C and D.
b) Process A can be written:

   carbon dioxide + substance F → glucose + substance G

   i) Identify substances F and G.
   ii) For process A to take place certain conditions are essential. What are these conditions?
c) There are a number of substances which could be placed in the box labelled E. They are all used as sources of energy. Name two such substances.
d) Scientists talk these days of the 'greenhouse effect'. What is the 'greenhouse effect' and what are its possible consequences?

143

6 a) Carbon dioxide is prepared by reacting dilute hydrochloric acid with calcium carbonate.
   i) Name *two* other products formed during the reaction. (2)
   ii) Explain why carbon dioxide is *not* usually prepared by mixing dilute sulphuric acid and calcium carbonate. (2)

 b) When a gas jar containing carbon dioxide is held over a burning wooden splint and the cover removed, the flame goes out.

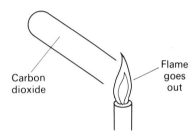

Carbon dioxide — Flame goes out

   State *two* properties of carbon dioxide which are illustrated by this observation. (2)

 c) When a piece of burning magnesium is lowered into a gas jar containing carbon dioxide, the magnesium continues to burn. A white powder and particles of a black solid are formed.
   i) Name the white powder. (1)
   ii) Name the black solid. (1)
   iii) Explain why magnesium continues to burn in carbon dioxide but the wooden splint goes out. (2)

(JMB/WMEB 1981)

7 a) i) Name the gaseous ingredient of 'fizzy' drinks such as lemonade. (1)
   ii) This gas dissolves in water to give an acidic solution. Name the acid present. (1)
 b) Why do these drinks only fizz after the bottle (or can) is opened? (3)

(AEB 1984)

8 a) i) Write an equation for the overall chemical reaction taking place in respiration. (2)
   ii) State, with a reason, whether you consider the above chemical reaction to be endo-ergic (endothermic) or exoergic (exothermic). (3)
 b) Proper maintenance of appliances in which gas is burned is essential, otherwise carbon monoxide may be formed.
   i) Write a balanced equation showing natural gas (methane) burning in air to produce carbon monoxide and water. (2)
   ii) Describe the physiological effects of carbon monoxide. (3)

(AEB 1982)

9 a) Explain briefly what is meant by the term *allotropy*. (2)
 b) The diagrams below represent the crystal structures of two giant molecular solids A and B.

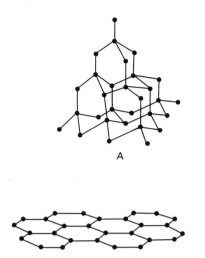

A

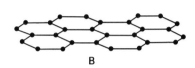

B

   i) Identify A and B. (2)
   ii) Select one physical property and briefly explain how it is different for A and B. (6)

(AEB 1982)

10 a) How would you prepare and collect a sample of carbon dioxide? Write an appropriate equation. (4)
 b) Name the products and write equations for the reactions which take place when carbon dioxide is:
   i) bubbled into sodium hydroxide solution (caustic soda);
   ii) passed over strongly-heated carbon. (4)
 c) How many moles of carbon dioxide are evolved when 10 g of calcium carbonate are heated until there is no further change in mass? (3)
 d) What is temporarily hard water and how is it formed? (4)

(SUJB 1984)

11 Limestone is a naturally-occurring form of calcium carbonate. It is an important raw material used in many different industries.
 a) Explain why the quarrying of limestone can cause environmental problems. (1)
 b) One of the properties of limestone is its reaction with acids.

i) How can buildings made of limestone be damaged by atmospheric pollution? (1)

ii) Why do some farmers put powdered limestone on their fields? (1)

iii) Write a word equation for the reaction of calcium carbonate with nitric acid. (1)

c) Name a building material which is made by heating a mixture of limestone and clay. (1)

d) Name one other industrial process in which limestone is used. (1)

e) When limestone is heated strongly, carbon dioxide is given off and a white solid (A) is formed. When a few drops of water are added to solid (A), it swells and crumbles to a white powder (B). On adding more water, stirring and filtering, a colourless solution (C) is formed.

i) Give the name or formula of: solid (A); powder (B). (2)

ii) Describe one other observation you would make when drops of water are added to solid (A). (1)

iii) State one laboratory use for solution (C). (1)

(NEA 1985)

ORGANIC CHEMISTRY

Fig. 11.1   All living things contain carbon

All organisms are composed of compounds which contain carbon. In this chapter we are going to study some of these compounds in more detail. This branch of chemistry is called **organic chemistry**.

Crude oil—an important source of organic chemicals

Some of the simplest organic compounds are found in crude oil. These compounds are made up of molecules containing carbon and hydrogen only and because of this are known as **hydrocarbons**. The atoms within these molecules are held together by single covalent bonds. Crude oil is a very complex mixture of these hydrocarbons. The molecules vary in size from those which contain one or two carbon atoms to those which contain about a hundred carbon atoms. Each of the compounds in this mixture has a different boiling point. To separate the different parts of this mixture chemists use a technique called **fractional distillation**. This process is usually carried out at an oil refinery (see Fig. 11.3) as a continuous process and takes place in a tall **fractionating tower** like the one in Fig. 11.4. A diagram of a cross-section of a fractionating tower is shown in Fig. 11.5.

Fig. 11.2   Crude oil is a thick, smelly, black liquid

Fig. 11.3   Night view of BP's Vohburg refinery, Bavaria, Germany

Fig. 11.4   Fractional distillation of crude oil at BP's Europort refinery, Holland

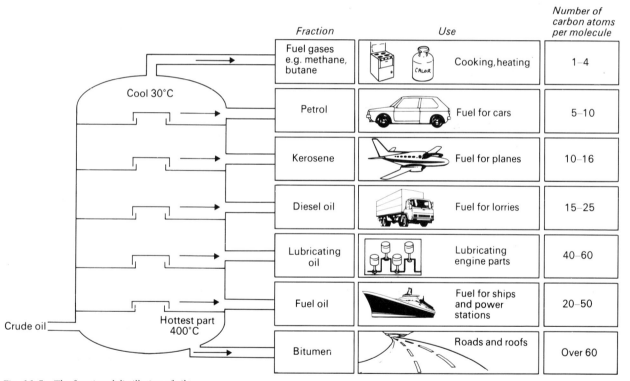

Fig. 11.5   The fractional distillation of oil

In an oil refinery, crude oil is heated to about 400°C to vaporize (turn into gas) all the different parts in the mixture. This mixture of vapours passes into the fractionating tower near the bottom. The tower is hotter at the bottom than at the top. The bigger hydrocarbon molecules which have higher boiling points condense in the lower half of the tower. The smaller molecules with lower boiling points condense in the upper half of the tower. The liquids are collected on different **trays**. In this way the crude oil is separated into different **fractions**. These fractions are then further refined by further distillations to produce purer single organic chemicals.

Alkanes

Alkanes are a family of compounds obtained by the fractional distillation of crude oil. The hydrocarbon molecules within the alkane family are said to be **saturated** since each molecule contains carbon atoms bonded to four other atoms by single covalent bonds. Table 11.1 shows the first six members of the alkane family.

Alkane	Formula	Structural formula	Boiling point (°C)	Physical state at room temperature	Molecular model
Methane	CH_4	H–C–H (with H above and below)	−164	Gas	
Ethane	C_2H_6	H–C–C–H	−87	Gas	
Propane	C_3H_8	H–C–C–C–H	−42	Gas	
Butane	C_4H_{10}	H–C–C–C–C–H	0	Gas	
Pentane	C_5H_{12}	H–C–C–C–C–C–H	36	Liquid	
Hexane	C_6H_{14}	H–C–C–C–C–C–C–H	69	Liquid	

Table 11.1   The first six alkanes

You will notice from the table that each successive member of the family has one more carbon atom and two more hydrogen atoms in its molecule (i.e. an increase of one —CH_2— unit). Also, the members of the alkane family have similar structural formulae and similar names—they all end in *-ane*. A family of compounds with the above factors in common is called a **homologous series**.

If a family of compounds is a homologous series then it can be represented by a general formula. For example, in the case of the alkanes:

$$C_nH_{2n+2}$$

When $n = 1$ the formula is:

$$C_1H_{(2 \times 1 + 2)} = CH_4$$

When $n = 4$ the formula is:

$$C_4H_{(2 \times 4 + 2)} = C_4H_{10}$$

and so on.

In the fractionating tower boiling points increase as molecular size increase. Physical state also depends on the size of the molecule. Under normal conditions, the compounds with very small molecules are gases, those with between 5 and 16 carbon atoms in a molecule are liquids, whilst those with more than 16 carbon atoms per molecule are solids.

Isomerism

Certain alkanes have the same formula but different arrangements of atoms. For example, there are two different compounds with the formula C_4H_{10}. The structural formulae of these substances along with their names are shown in Fig. 11.7.

Compounds like those in Fig. 11.7 are known as **isomers**. Isomers are substances having the same molecular formula but different structural formula. All the hydrocarbons with four or more carbon atoms per molecule possess isomers.

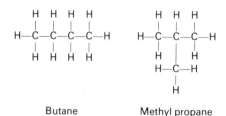

Butane   Methyl propane

Fig. 11.7   Two substances with the formula C_4H_{10}

Some properties of alkanes

The alkanes do not react with a wide range of chemicals. For example, they are generally not affected by acids or alkalis. In fact, they do not react with many other substances.

Alkanes such as methane will burn well in a good supply of air forming carbon dioxide and water. Plenty of heat energy is produced and so alkanes are generally used as fuels.

$$\text{methane} + \text{oxygen} \longrightarrow \text{carbon dioxide} + \text{water} + \text{heat}$$

$$CH_{4(g)} + 2O_{2(g)} \longrightarrow CO_{2(g)} + 2H_2O_{(g)}$$

Methane as natural (or North Sea) gas is used for cooking (see Fig. 11.8). It is also used for heating our homes and schools.

Butane and propane burn with a hot flame. They are easily liquefied and sold as Calor gas (or Camping gaz) and Propagas respectively. In areas where there is no supply of natural gas central heating systems can be run using propane gas (see Fig. 11.9).

Alkanes will react with chlorine or bromine in the presence of sunlight (or ultraviolet light). For example, methane reacts with chlorine forming chloromethane and hydrogen chloride gas.

$$\text{methane} + \text{chlorine} \xrightarrow{\text{sunlight}} \text{chloromethane} + \text{hydrogen chloride}$$

$$CH_{4(g)} + Cl_{2(g)} \longrightarrow CH_3Cl_{(g)} + HCl_{(g)}$$

This reaction is known as a **substitution reaction**. In this type of reaction one hydrogen atom of a methane molecule is substituted by a chlorine atom.

Uses of alkanes

Alkanes are used mainly as fuels (see Chapter 17, page 227). Some of the heavier alkanes are used as waxes, lubricating oils, and also in the manufacture of alkenes.

Fig. 11.8   This gas cooker is burning methane

Fig. 11.9   Propane gas can be used as a fuel for central heating

Alkenes

This is another hydrocarbon family. The **alkenes** are more reactive than the alkanes. This is because each of the alkene molecules contains a double covalent bond between two carbon atoms. Molecules which have a double bond of this kind are said to be **unsaturated**. Table 11.2 shows the first three members of the alkene family.

Alkene	Formula	Number of carbon atoms per molecule	Structural formula	Boiling point (°C)	Physical state at room temperature	Molecular model
Ethene	C_2H_4	2	H C=C H / H H	-104	Gas	
Propene	C_3H_6	3	H H H / H—C—C=C / H H	-47	Gas	
Butene	C_4H_8	4	H H H H / H—C—C—C=C / H H H	-6	Gas	

Table 11.2   The first three alkenes

You will notice from Table 11.2 that again each successive member increases its carbon and hydrogen content by a $—CH_2—$ unit. The compounds also all contain one $C=C$ double bond per molecule. They all have similar names, they all end in *-ene*. They form a homologous series with general formula C_nH_{2n}.

Where do alkenes come from?

Alkenes are not found to any great extent in nature. The ones we require can usually be obtained from a fraction of oil. To obtain alkenes, chemists use a process called **catalytic cracking**. In this process the alkane molecules to be 'cracked' (split up) are passed over a mixture of chromium and aluminium oxides heated to about 500°C.

hexadecane $\longrightarrow$ heptane + propene + ethene

$C_{16}H_{34(g)} \longrightarrow C_7H_{16(g)} + C_3H_{6(g)} + C_2H_{4(g)}$ + others

long carbon chain alkane   shorter carbon chain alkane

This sort of process can be illustrated in the laboratory. If rocksil wool is soaked in liquid paraffin (alkanes were formerly known as paraffins) and the hot paraffin vapour passed over a heated porous pot, then the large paraffin molecules are split up into smaller ones (see Fig. 11.11). During the cracking process some alkenes are produced.

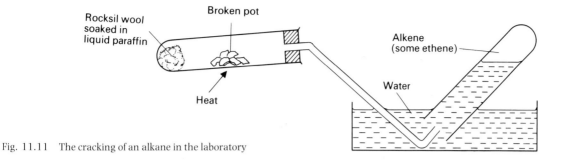

Fig. 11.11   The cracking of an alkane in the laboratory

Some properties of alkenes

As a family of compounds, alkenes have similar chemical properties. For example, they all burn in a plentiful supply of air forming carbon dioxide and water. During this reaction heat energy is also produced.

ethene + oxygen $\longrightarrow$ carbon dioxide + water + heat

$$C_2H_{4(g)} + 3O_{2(g)} \longrightarrow 2CO_{2(g)} + 2H_2O_{(g)}$$

However, these substances are not used as fuels since they do not burn as well as alkanes, they are too expensive to produce and they have other properties which make them far too useful to burn.

A major difference between the alkanes and the alkenes is that whilst the alkanes will undergo substitution reactions, alkenes will undergo **addition reactions**. This difference provides a means of distinguishing alkenes from alkanes. If an alkene such as ethene is shaken in a test tube containing bromine water a reaction takes place. During this reaction the orange colour of the bromine water disappears (see Fig. 11.12). A colourless substance has been formed by the reaction of the bromine with ethene. The bromine has 'added' across the double bond to form dibromoethane.

Fig. 11.12   An alkene decolourizes bromine water whilst an alkane does not

ethene + bromine $\longrightarrow$ dibromoethane

$$C_2H_{4(g)} + Br_{2(aq)} \longrightarrow C_2H_4Br_{2(l)}$$

This is better shown by the structural formula involved:

$$\begin{array}{c} H \quad\quad H \\ \diagdown \quad\diagup \\ C{=}C \\ \diagup \quad\diagdown \\ H \quad\quad H \end{array} + Br{-}Br \longrightarrow \begin{array}{c} H \quad H \\ | \quad | \\ H{-}C{-}C{-}H \\ | \quad | \\ Br \quad Br \end{array}$$

If an alkane such as ethane or hexane is shaken with bromine in solution then no colour change takes place. This is because there are no double bonds present between the carbon atoms in alkanes, so that the addition reaction is not possible. The bromine water therefore stays orange in colour.

Hydrogen will also 'add' across the double bond, forming ethane.

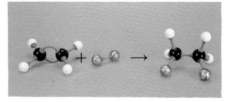

Fig. 11.13   The addition of bromine to ethene using molecular models

ethene + hydrogen $\longrightarrow$ ethane

$$C_2H_{4(g)} + H_{2(g)} \longrightarrow C_2H_{6(g)}$$

or

$$\begin{array}{c} H \quad\quad H \\ \diagdown \quad\diagup \\ C{=}C \\ \diagup \quad\diagdown \\ H \quad\quad H \end{array} + H{-}H \longrightarrow \begin{array}{c} H \quad H \\ | \quad | \\ H{-}C{-}C{-}H \\ | \quad | \\ H \quad H \end{array}$$

For this reaction to take place high temperature, pressure and a nickel or platinum catalyst are needed.

Many other substances will also 'add' across the alkene double bond. For example, ethanol is formed when water (as steam) is added across the double bond of ethene. For this reaction to take place the reactants have to be passed at 60 atmospheres pressure over a phosphoric acid catalyst at 300°C.

$$\text{ethene} + \text{water} \longrightarrow \text{ethanol}$$

$$C_2H_{4(g)} + H_2O_{(g)} \longrightarrow C_2H_5OH_{(g)}$$

or

$$
\begin{array}{c}
\underset{H}{\overset{H}{C}}=\underset{H}{\overset{H}{C}} + H{-}OH \longrightarrow H{-}\underset{H}{\overset{H}{C}}{-}\underset{H}{\overset{H}{C}}{-}O{-}H
\end{array}
$$

An important addition reaction of ethene

Ethene is used as a starting material for making the plastic **polythene**. When ethene is heated to a high temperature of 200°C under a very high pressure of 2000 atmospheres a white waxy solid is formed. This is the plastic polyethene—usually known as polythene.

In polyethene the ethene molecules have joined together to form very long hydrocarbon chains. They have joined together very much like poppet beads or paper clips as shown in Fig. 11.14.

Fig. 11.14 Ethene molecules join together very much like these poppet beads or paper clips

$$\text{ethene} + \text{ethene} + \text{ethene} \longrightarrow \text{part of a polyethene chain}$$

Even larger numbers of units can be written generally:

Where n is a very large number.

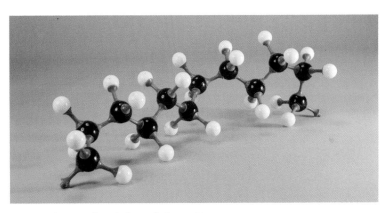
Fig. 11.15 Part of a polythene chain

When many small molecules like ethene join together to form long chains of atoms, the process is called **polymerization**. The small molecules, like ethene, which join together in this way are known as **monomers**. The final product is known as a **polymer**. A polymer chain may contain thousands of monomer units joined together. In any piece of plastic there will be many millions of polymer chains. Since the monomer units add together to form the polymer the process is called **addition polymerization**.

Other addition polymers

Other plastics are produced by addition polymerization in a similar way to that used for making polyethene. For example, PTFE (poly-tetrafluoroethene) and PVC (polyvinyl chloride or polychloroethene) are made from monomer units which are similar to ethene.

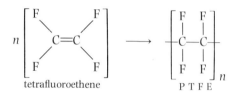

PTFE
monomer
(tetrafluoroethene)

PVC
monomer
(vinyl chloride or chloroethene)

During polymerization:

$$n \begin{bmatrix} \underset{F}{\overset{F}{\diagdown}} C = C \underset{F}{\overset{F}{\diagup}} \end{bmatrix} \longrightarrow \begin{bmatrix} \overset{F}{\underset{F}{\overset{|}{C}}} - \overset{F}{\underset{F}{\overset{|}{C}}} \end{bmatrix}_n$$

tetrafluoroethene   P T F E

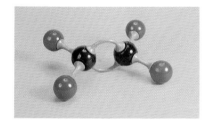

Fig. 11.16(a)   The PTFE monomer

Fig. 11.16(b)   Part of a PTFE chain

and

$$n \begin{bmatrix} \underset{H}{\overset{H}{\diagdown}} C = C \underset{Cl}{\overset{H}{\diagup}} \end{bmatrix} \longrightarrow \begin{bmatrix} \overset{H}{\underset{H}{\overset{|}{C}}} - \overset{H}{\underset{Cl}{\overset{|}{C}}} \end{bmatrix}_n$$

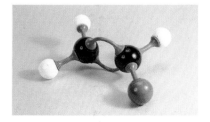

Fig. 11.17(a)   The PVC monomer

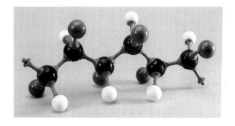

Fig. 11.17(b)   Part of a PVC chain

The uses of these plastics are summarized in Table 11.3 and Fig. 11.18.

Plastic	Uses	Thermosoftening or thermosetting
Polythene	Plastic bowls, plastic bags, dustbins, binliners	Thermosoftening
PTFE	Linings of non-stick pans, soles of irons, floors of ovens	Thermosoftening
PVC	Records, clothing, guttering	Thermosoftening
Polystyrene	Polystyrene tiles, packaging, plastic cups	Thermosoftening
Perspex	Rulers, car windscreens, clear plastic in advertising signs	Thermosoftening
Nylon	Clothing, rope, bristles for different types of brushes	Thermosoftening
Terylene	Clothing	Thermosoftening
Phenolic	Plugs, electrical fittings	Thermosetting
Melamine	Ashtrays, 'unbreakable' mugs and plates	Thermosetting

Table 11.3

(a) PTFE lining of pans

(b) A polypropene crate

(c) Polythene binliner

(d) Polythene sandwich

Fig. 11.18 Some uses of plastics

154

Condensation polymers

Another type of plastic

When polyethene is made from ethene, all the monomer molecules are identical. Some polymers can be made by reacting different 'starting' molecules together. For example, nylon can be made by reacting two different chemicals together. The two chemicals used consist of molecules which are more complex than ethene. They are called diaminohexane and hexanedioic acid. In nylon the polymer chain is built up of the two molecules arranged alternately. It is as if you had two different-coloured poppet beads and they are joined together as shown in Fig. 11.19. In this sort of polymerization, chemicals such as water are also formed. Because of this, it is called **condensation polymerization**. Another condensation polymer is Terylene. Some of the uses of these polymers are shown in Table 11.3 and Fig. 11.18.

Fig. 11.19 A condensation polymer chain looks like this

Thermosoftening and thermosetting plastics

Plastics can be put into one of two groups. **Thermosoftening plastics** (or **thermoplastics**) are those which soften on heating. **Thermosetting plastics** are those which do not soften on heating and only char on continued heating.

You will notice from Table 11.3 that the first seven plastics shown are thermosoftening, whilst the last two are thermosetting. Thermosetting plastics have polymer chains which are linked (bonded) to each other. This is called **cross linking** (see Fig. 11.20). Thermosoftening plastics do not have their polymer chains joined in this way. When thermosoftening plastics are heated their polymer chains flow over one another and the plastic softens. However, in the case of thermosetting plastics the bonds between the polymer chains hold the chains firmly in place and no softening of the plastic takes place.

(a)   (b)

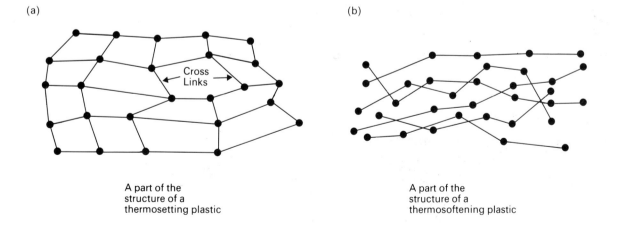

A part of the
structure of a
thermosetting plastic

A part of the
structure of a
thermosoftening plastic

Fig. 11.20 Polymer chains in thermosetting and thermosoftening plastics

Forming plastics

Raw plastics are made into usable objects by the process known as **forming**. The method of forming used depends on the type of plastic being handled. With thermosoftening plastics the methods normally used are as follows.

1 Vacuum forming. A thermosoftening plastic sheet is placed over a mould, the sheet is then softened by heating and sucked over the cold mould. The coolness of the mould hardens the plastic into the required shape. Examples of objects made by this process are toys, baths and refrigerator liners.

2 Blow moulding. For hollow objects the forming method often used is blow moulding. A thin tube of softened thermosoftening plastic is blown into a cold mould. The mould is in two halves if the shape is complicated. Examples of objects made by this process are plastic bottles and dolls.

3 Injection moulding. Softened plastic is forced into a cold mould, and the plastic hardens to the required shape. Examples of objects made by this process are washing up bowls, buckets and dustbins.

If objects are to be made with thermosetting plastics then the method used is usually compression moulding.

Fig. 11.21   Compression moulding

Fig. 11.22   These trays have been produced by injection moulding

Problems with plastics

Plastics are now used as replacement materials for wood, glass, metals and paper as well as for many natural fibres such as cotton and wool. They have 'taken over' in the last twenty years because they are quite cheap, light and can be easily moulded into any shape as well as being relatively unreactive and colourful. However, plastics can also be a problem. Normally the plastic waste produced at factories manufacturing plastics causes no problem since it can be **recycled** (re-used). However, we produce a tremendous amount of unsightly plastic litter which does not rot away. Also this plastic waste can be dangerous—when dumped in the countryside it can cause the death of farm or other animals (see Fig. 11.23).

Further pollution problems also arise when plastics are burned because they often produce poisonous fumes (see Fig. 11.24).

What possible solutions to this problem of plastic waste do we have? In recent years the disposal of plastic litter has become an increasing problem (see Fig. 11.25). Several schemes have been used to overcome this problem. These include plastic waste being used: to fill disused quarries—landscaping; to make black polythene bags and sheets—recycling; to make building materials such as floor fillings.

Fig. 11.23   How could this plastic bottle be a danger to the cow?

Fig. 11.25   Burying plastic litter

Fig. 11.24   Clouds of poisonous black smoke are produced when plastics burn

Biodegradable plastics

Recently, scientists have developed chemical additives, which when mixed with raw plastics, help them decompose more quickly. Plastics which have these additives are called **biodegradable** plastics. 'Bio' refers to living things and 'degradable' means 'able to rot away'. When plastics of this type are thrown away, they will be 'attacked' by bacteria and weather and will eventually rot away.

Fig. 11.26   Plastic packaging from a weekly shop!

Starch—a natural polymer

Starch occurs in potatoes, rice, wheat and all green plants. It belongs to the family of compounds called **carbohydrates**. These compounds contain carbon, hydrogen and oxygen (the hydrogen and oxygen atoms are in the same ratio as in water, i.e. $2:1$). Some of the simplest carbohydrates are known as **monosaccharides**. Examples of this type of carbohydrate are glucose and fructose. Both these substances have the same formula, $C_6H_{12}O_6$; they are therefore isomers. They both dissolve in water and have a sweet taste.

A more complicated type of carbohydrate are those known as **disaccharides**. Sucrose (ordinary sugar—see Fig. 11.28) and maltose are examples of this type of compound. Like monosaccharides these substances dissolve in water and are also sweet to taste. However, the disaccharides contain two monosaccharide units. The formula for sucrose is $C_{12}H_{22}O_{11}$.

Starch belongs to the more complicated group known as **polysaccharides**. These are natural condensation polymers made up of many thousands of $C_6H_{10}O_5$ units. Starch does not form a true solution and it does not have a sweet taste. The general formula for starch is $(C_6H_{10}O_5)_n$, where 'n' is a large number—usually bigger than 200.

Fig. 11.27   Starch is found in all these foodstuffs

Fig. 11.28   All these contain sugar (sucrose)

Hydrolysis of starch

Starch can be broken down in two ways. Both of these reactions take place in the presence of water. The reactions are known as **hydrolysis** reactions.

If starch solution is boiled with dilute hydrochloric acid for about one hour then the natural polymer is broken down into its monomer, glucose—a monosaccharide.

$$\text{starch} \quad + \text{water (with dilute acid)} \xrightarrow{\text{heat}} \text{glucose}$$

$$(C_6H_{10}O_5)_n + \qquad nH_2O \qquad \longrightarrow nC_6H_{12}O_6$$

In this case the hydrochloric acid is acting as a catalyst.

The second method involves mixing the starch solution with some saliva. If this mixture is left to stand for a few minutes then the enzyme present in saliva, amylase, will break-up the natural polymer to produce the disaccharide, maltose ($C_{12}H_{22}O_{11}$).

$$\text{starch} \quad + \text{water (in saliva)} \longrightarrow \quad \text{maltose}$$

$$(C_6H_{10}O_5)_n + \qquad nH_2O \qquad \longrightarrow nC_{12}H_{22}O_{11}$$

Enzymes are natural catalysts present in animals and plants. You will notice that enzymes do not require a high temperature to break down the starch. Enzymes are very efficient at this process. In our bodies the salivary amylase has the job of breaking down the starch in our food.

The above hydrolysis reactions are summarized in Fig. 11.30.

In both of these hydrolysis reactions you can see whether all the starch has been hydrolysed so that none is left in the solution. This is done by taking a few drops of the solution and adding some iodine to it. In the presence of starch the iodine solution will go a deep blue (see Fig. 11.31). If there is no deep blue colour when the iodine solution is added all the starch has been broken down.

Fig. 11.29   The enzyme amylase will break up starch!

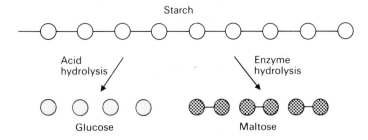

Fig. 11.30   Summary of starch hydrolysis

The products of the two hydrolysis reactions may be identified using a technique which you will have used earlier in your chemistry course—**chromatography**. The chromatography paper is 'spotted' with the samples from the two reactions as well as pure glucose and maltose. When this is developed, after some hours in a solvent, the spots may be identified (see Fig. 11.32).

Fig. 11.31   The iodine solution on the left turns dark blue in the presence of starch

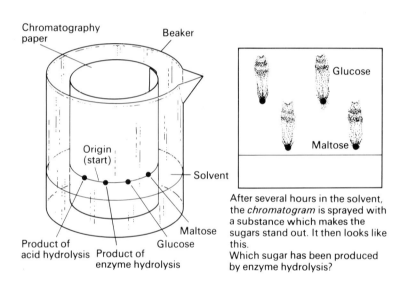

After several hours in the solvent, the *chromatogram* is sprayed with a substance which makes the sugars stand out. It then looks like this.
Which sugar has been produced by enzyme hydrolysis?

Fig. 11.32   The products of hydrolysis may be identified by chromatography

Fig. 11.33(a)   Fermentation just beginning

Fermentation

It is possible to break up the glucose produced by acid hydrolysis into even smaller molecules. This is done in the process of **fermentation**. In fermentation, a glucose solution is mixed with yeast and the temperature maintained between 18 °C and 20 °C (see Fig. 11.33). The enzymes in the yeast break down the glucose forming ethanol and carbon dioxide

$$\text{glucose} \xrightarrow{\text{yeast}} \text{ethanol} + \text{carbon dioxide}$$

$$C_6H_{12}O_{6(aq)} \longrightarrow 2C_2H_5OH_{(l)} + 2CO_{2(g)}$$

Fig. 11.33(b)   The carbon dioxide produced during fermentation fills the plastic bag

Fig. 11.34   All the wine and beer on these shelves has been made by fermentation

Fig. 11.35   Grape picking in the south of France

Fermentation is used to make 'alcoholic' drinks like wine and beer. Wine is made by fermenting grape juice which contains glucose (see Fig. 11.35). Beer is made from barley (with hops added for flavour (see Fig. 11.36). Wine normally contains about 10% ethanol, whilst beer contains only about 4% ethanol. More concentrated forms of 'alcoholic' drinks, such as whisky and brandy, come under the heading of spirits. These higher concentrations of ethanol are produced by distillation after fermentation (see Fig. 11.37).

As you will know, it is the ethanol content in these drinks which can make people drunk. It is also the ethanol in these drinks which causes the headaches, dizziness and vomiting that is associated with being drunk. Ethanol can cause damage to vital organs in your body. Excessive ethanol intake over a period of time can cause irreparable damage to the liver. Cirrhosis of the liver can result in death. Ethanol is also addictive. Ethanol abuse is a very serious social problem in our society.

Fig. 11.36   The froth produced during beer fermentation

Ethanol

Ethanol is a colourless, neutral, liquid which does not conduct electricity. It has a boiling point of $78\,^{\circ}C$. It is the commonest member of the family of compounds known as **alcohols**. In fact, it is itself commonly referred to as 'alcohol'.

ethanol $+$ oxygen $\longrightarrow$ carbon dioxide $+$ water $+$ energy

$$C_2H_5OH_{(l)} + 3O_{2(g)} \longrightarrow 2CO_{2(g)} + 3H_2O_{(g)}$$

It is already used as a fuel as methylated spirit (see Fig. 11.38). Some countries have already experimented with ethanol as a fuel for cars. Up to 20% of ethanol can be added to petrol used in car engines without the need to make adjustment to the carburettor (see Fig. 11.39). Many other useful materials such as flavourings and synthetic rubber, are also made from ethanol.

The vast majority of the world's supply of ethanol is produced by fermentation although a small amount is produced by the hydration of ethene. It is a very good solvent and evaporates easily (very volatile). It is therefore used extensively as a solvent in aftershave, paints, glues and many other everyday products (see Fig. 11.40).

Fig. 11.37   Pot stills in a whisky distillery

Fig. 11.38   This camping stove uses methylated spirit as a fuel

Fig. 11.39   This Brazilian car runs on 'Alcool'—a petrol–ethanol mixture

Ethanol can be oxidized to ethanoic acid (an organic acid) by powerful oxidizing agents such as potassium dichromate(VI). During the reaction, the orange colour of the solution of potassium dichromate(VI) changes to a dark green (see Fig. 11.41).

$$\text{ethanol} + \text{oxygen} \xrightarrow{\text{heat}} \text{ethanoic acid} + \text{water}$$
$$\begin{bmatrix}\text{from} \\ \text{potassium} \\ \text{dichromate(VI)}\end{bmatrix}$$

$$C_2H_5OH_{(l)} + 2[O] \longrightarrow CH_3COOH_{(aq)} + H_2O_{(l)}$$

or

Fig. 11.40   The common solvent is ethanol

Name	Formula	Number of carbon atoms per molecule	Structural formula	Physical state at room temperature
Methanol	CH$_3$OH	1		Liquid
Ethanol	C$_2$H$_5$OH	2		Liquid
Propanol	C$_3$H$_7$OH	3		Liquid

Table 11.4   Some alcohols

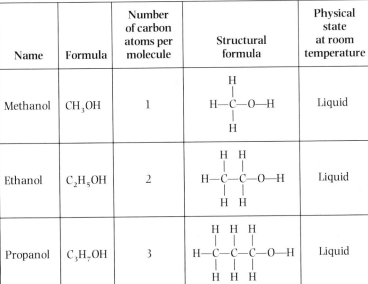

Fig. 11.41   Potassium dichromate(VI) (on the left) slowly turns green (on the right) as the ethanol is oxidized

Organic acids

This family of organic compounds contains one well-known substance—ethanoic acid. It is better known as the main constituent in vinegar. Another organic acid which is present in stinging nettles and in ant stings is methanoic acid. Table 11.5 shows the relevant data about these two acids.

This family of organic compounds has similar names ending in -*oic*. They contain the functional group —COOH. They form a homologous series with a general formula $C_nH_{2n+1}COOH$.

Fig. 11.42(a) Vinegar contains ethanoic acid

Name	Formula	Number of carbon atoms per molecule	Structural formula	Physical state at room temperature
Methanoic acid	HCOOH	1	H—C with =O and O—H	Liquid
Ethanoic acid	CH_3COOH	2	H—C(H)(H)—C with =O and O—H	Liquid

Table 11.5

Fig. 11.42(b) Methanoic acid is present in nettles

Some properties of organic acids

Like all acids they affect indicators. Some will react with metals such as magnesium. Whereas the mineral acids such as sulphuric acid and hydrochloric acid are called strong acids (Chapter 7, page 77), methanoic acid, ethanoic acid and the other organic acids are weak acids. A solution of ethanoic acid has a pH of about 3.

As acids they will react with bases to form salts. For example, ethanoic acid will react with sodium hydroxide forming the salt, sodium ethanoate and water.

ethanoic acid + sodium hydroxide $\longrightarrow$ sodium ethanoate + water

$$CH_3COOH_{(aq)} + NaOH_{(aq)} \longrightarrow CH_3COONa_{(aq)} + H_2O_{(l)}$$

Organic acids will also react with alcohols to form sweet-smelling substances called **esters**. For example, ethanoic acid will react with ethanol to produce the ester ethyl ethanoate and water. This reaction needs a few drops of concentrated sulphuric acid added as a catalyst.

ethanoic acid + ethanol $\underset{\text{acid}}{\overset{\text{concentrated sulphuric}}{\rightleftharpoons}}$ ethyl ethanoate + water

$$CH_3COOH_{(l)} + C_2H_5OH_{(l)} \rightleftharpoons CH_3COOC_2H_{5(l)} + H_2O_{(l)}$$

or

$$
\begin{array}{ccccccccc}
& H & O & & H & H & & H & O & & H & H \\
& | & \| & & | & | & & | & \| & & | & | \\
H-C-C & + & \boxed{H}-O-C-C-H & \rightleftharpoons & H-C-C & & H & H & + & H_2O \\
& | & \boxed{O-H} & & | & | & & | & O-C-C-H & & \\
& H & & & H & H & & H & | & | & \\
& & & & & & & & H & H &
\end{array}
$$

The ⇌ sign means that the reaction is reversible. In these processes not all the ethanoic acid and ethanol have changed into products. This reaction is called an **esterification reaction**.

Members of the 'ester' family have strong and pleasant smells. Many of them occur naturally and are responsible for the smell and flavour in fruits and flowers. They are used therefore in some food flavourings. Esters are also used in perfumes, solvents, and in the production of some antibiotics (see Fig. 11.43).

Fig. 11.43   Some uses of esters

(a) Perfumes

(b) Food flavourings

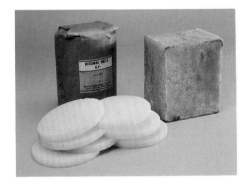

(c) Beeswax

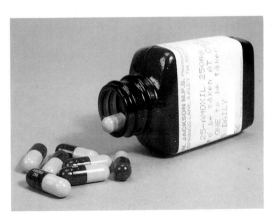

(d) Antibiotics

Soaps and soapless detergents.

Fig. 11.44   Are any of these 'soaps'?

Fig. 11.45   These contain fats

Soaps are made from **fats** which are complicated ester molecules. Fats can either be plant fats like olive oil or animal fats such as lard (see Fig. 11.45). To form the soap the fat is boiled with an alkali such as sodium hydroxide. This type of reaction is called **saponification** and is really the reverse of esterification.

$$\text{fat} + \text{sodium hydroxide} \xrightarrow{\text{boil}} \text{soap} + \text{another complicated molecule}$$

A simple soap is sodium stearate:

$$C_{17}H_{35}COO^-Na^+$$

This substance consists of a long hydrocarbon chain (see Fig. 11.46). The hydrocarbon chain is 'hydrophobic'—water hating—whilst the ionic head of the soap molecule is 'hydrophilic'—water loving.

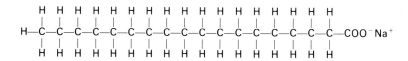

Simplified diagram of a soap molecule

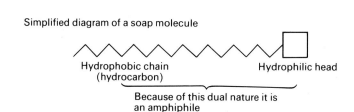

Fig. 11.46   A soap molecule

How a soap works

When soap is put into water which has some greasy cloth (or dish) in it, the hydrocarbon end (hydrophobic part) of each soap molecule becomes attracted to the grease and becomes embedded in it (see Fig. 11.47). The ionic head group (hydrophilic part) remains in the water. When the water is stirred, the grease is slowly released and completely surrounded by the soap molecules. The grease is thus removed from the cloth or dish.

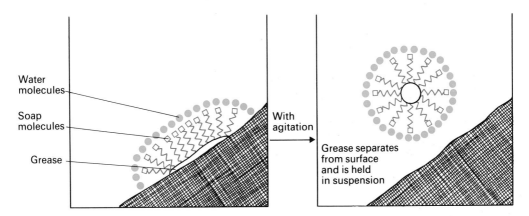

Fig. 11.47   How a soap works

In Chapter 9, page 120 we discussed the way in which soap reacts with dissolved substances to form a scum. This problem was overcome when **soapless detergents** were manufactured. These new substances do not form a scum with hard water.

Soapless detergents

Soapless detergents are not made from vegetable or animal fats. Instead they are made from alkanes obtained from crude oil. The alkanes used have hydrocarbon chains of between 12 and 20 carbon atoms joined together. Soapless detergents are made by firstly reacting the hydrocarbon with concentrated sulphuric acid and then with sodium hydroxide. This results in a molecule of the type shown below.

$$\underset{\displaystyle \quad}{H-\overset{\displaystyle H}{\underset{\displaystyle H}{C}}-\overset{\displaystyle H}{\underset{\displaystyle H}{C}}-\overset{\displaystyle H}{\underset{\displaystyle H}{C}}-\overset{\displaystyle H}{\underset{\displaystyle H}{C}}-\overset{\displaystyle H}{\underset{\displaystyle H}{C}}-\overset{\displaystyle H}{\underset{\displaystyle H}{C}}-\overset{\displaystyle H}{\underset{\displaystyle H}{C}}-\overset{\displaystyle H}{\underset{\displaystyle H}{C}}-\overset{\displaystyle H}{\underset{\displaystyle H}{C}}-\overset{\displaystyle H}{\underset{\displaystyle H}{C}}-\overset{\displaystyle H}{\underset{\displaystyle H}{C}}-\overset{\displaystyle H}{\underset{\displaystyle H}{C}}-\overset{\displaystyle H}{\underset{\displaystyle H}{C}}-\overset{\displaystyle H}{\underset{\displaystyle H}{C}}-\overset{\displaystyle H}{\underset{\displaystyle H}{C}}-\overset{\displaystyle H}{\underset{\displaystyle H}{C}}-CSO_3^- Na^+}$$

$$C_{17}H_{35}SO_3^- Na^+$$

Like soap molecules these also have a hydrophobic and a hydrophilic part. They remove grease in a similar way.

Since soapless detergents were first made and used in the 1950s there have been problems with them. Millions of tonnes of detergent were pumped into rivers because the bacteria present in sewage works purification processes could not break down these organic molecules. This resulted in plants and animals in some of these rivers being almost totally killed off. Also, foam was produced in large quantities which, when the rivers passed through towns and cities, was blown onto the streets. This problem has largely been overcome today since detergents have been developed which are biodegradable. This means that they can be broken down by bacteria in the water and air into harmless chemicals.

Organic chemistry and medicines

We live in a society which demands effective treatment for its diseases. The treatment of illness today usually involves chemicals called **drugs**. The use of chemical substances to kill germs and bacteria which invade your body is called **chemotherapy**. The first person to develop this idea was Paul Ehrlich, a German scientist who, in 1910, discovered that a drug called Salvarsan could be used as a treatment for the disease syphilis. Since those early days many such drugs have been developed. For example, sulphonamide drugs such as sulphapyridine have had a great success in treating pneumonia. The structure of the sulphapyridine molecule is very complicated and is shown in Fig. 11.49.

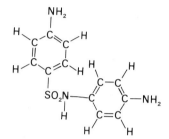

Fig. 11.49 The structure of sulphapyridine

Fig. 11.48 Dispensing drugs in hospital

Antibiotics are a group of substances produced by microorganisms which behave in ways which make them useful in chemotherapy. The first antibiotic—penicillin—was discovered by Sir Alexander Fleming in 1928, although it was not used as a medicine until much later. Penicillin is a very popular antibiotic and has certainly proved its worth in the fight against bacteria such as pneumococci, which cause pneumonia, and meningococci which cause meningitis. Many tonnes of this antibiotic are produced annually in the U.K. Since the discovery of penicillin, many other antibiotics have been discovered or made. They include chloramphenicol and streptomycin.

Many other drugs have also been developed to deal with complaints ranging from sleeplessness to high blood pressure. High blood pressure (hypertension) is treated by a drug called methyldopa—its structure is shown in Fig. 11.50.

It should be noted that all drugs are 'alien substances', foreign to the body. Dosage is important as some often have side-effects.

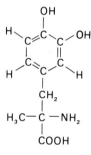

Fig. 11.50 The structure of methyldopa

Drug abuse

One of the serious problems our society has to try to solve is that of drug abuse. Some of the useful drugs developed by chemists can be habit forming. These *addictive* drugs include barbiturates (in sleeping tablets), morphine (a pain killer) and amphetamine (a stimulant). The drugs produce psychological problems in the addicts to such an extent that they lose interest in themselves and their families. They often lose their jobs as a consequence of the addiction. Also their health usually suffers to such an extent that premature death occurs.

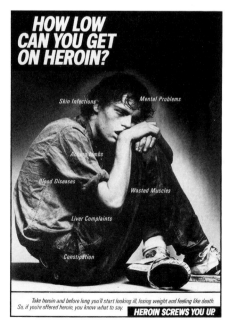

Fig. 11.51 Drug addiction can kill

———————————————————————— QUESTIONS ————————————————————————

1 a) Name the process by which a large molecule, such as starch, is broken down using an enzyme or a dilute acid.

b) Complete the following chart which represents the breaking down of starch:

$$starch \xrightarrow[\text{enzyme}]{\text{dilute acid}} \underline{\quad A \quad} + \underline{\quad B \quad}$$

$$\xrightarrow[\text{yeast}]{} \underline{\quad C \quad} + \begin{array}{l}\text{carbon}\\\text{dioxide}\end{array}$$

$$\underline{\quad C \quad} \xrightarrow[\text{catalyst}]{\text{heat and}} \underline{\quad D \quad}$$

c) What effect will D have on bromine water?

d) What does this tell you about D?

e) A polymer is made up of small molecules called _____.

f) i) Which plastic would you use D to make?
   ii) Give two uses of this plastic.

2 Below are two lists. One is of plastics and the other of uses to which these plastics are put.

a) The pairing is wrong. Make a list of the plastics with their correct uses.

Plastic	Uses
polytetrafluoroethene (PTFE)	ropes
nylon	glass substitute
polyvinyl chloride (PVC)	lining for non-stick pans
expanded polystyrene	plugs
melamine	records
perspex	ashtrays
phenolic plastic	packaging

b) Which of the above plastics are:
   i) thermosoftening;
   ii) thermosetting?

3 Write brief notes on the following, using as many sources of information as you can find.
a) The problems of plastics.
b) Alcohol abuse.
c) Carbohydrates.
d) Biodegradable plastics.
e) Life without plastics.

4 Read the following paragraph and then answer the questions below.

Chemotherapy is now a very important method of fighting illness and disease. Many *drugs* have been developed since Salvarsan was produced by Paul Ehrlich in 1910. One such group of drugs are the sulphonamide drugs. Other types of drug have also been developed—the *antibiotics*. These have proved especially useful in the fight against pneumonia and meningitis.

a) What are the meanings of the terms in italic?
b) Name the disease that the drug Salvarsan was used to treat.
c) Name one sulphonamide drug and state which illness it has been used to treat.
d) i) Which antibiotic has been successful in the treatment of pneumonia and meningitis?
   ii) Who discovered this antibiotic?

5 Drug abuse is a rapidly growing problem in our society. Using information from newspapers and magazines, as well as any other source, make a list of addictive drugs and discuss the problems drug abuse can cause. Can you propose any solutions to the drug abuse problem?

6 Ethyl ethanoate can be prepared by the following reaction:

$$C_2H_5OH + CH_3CO_2H \rightleftharpoons CH_3CO_2C_2H_5 + H_2O$$

a) What is meant by the symbol $\rightleftharpoons$?
b) State the essential experimental conditions required to make ethyl ethanoate by this reaction.
c) Name the homologous series of which ethyl ethanoate is a member.   (4)
(Cambridge 1984)

7 Name the homologous series represented by each of the following general formulae:
a) C_nH_{2n+2};
b) $C_nH_{2n+1}OH$.
State *two* general characteristics of an homologous series, other than the existence of a general formula.   (4)
(Cambridge 1984)

8 Many chemicals are made from crude oil. Four such groups of chemicals are polymers, fertilizers, weedkillers and soapless detergents.

a) The diagram shows the primary fractional distillation of crude oil.

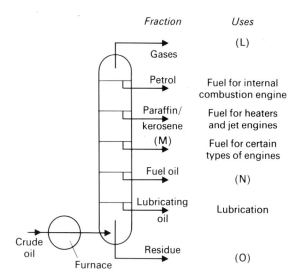

i) Give the use (L). (1)
ii) Name the fraction (M). (1)
iii) Give the use (N). (1)
iv) Name product (O). (1)

b) Crude oil is a mixture of alkanes. Alkanes can be gases or low boiling point liquids and are non-conductors of electricity.
Name the type of chemical bonding present in alkanes.
By showing all the outer energy level electrons draw a diagram to illustrate the chemical bonding in a molecule of ethane, C_2H_6. (3)

c) Alkenes are some of the most important starting materials in the petrochemical industry. Ethene, C_2H_4, is an example of an alkene and it is a starting point for making many organic chemicals, e.g. poly(ethene), PVC and ethanol.
i) Draw structural formulae to show how the monomer unit chloroethene, C_2H_3Cl, produces the polymer poly(chloroethene) which is also known as polyvinyl chloride (PVC). (3)
ii) Some polymers are said to be thermoplastic and others thermosetting. Explain the difference between the two types of polymers. (2)
iii) The conversion of ethene to ethanol is an example of an addition reaction. Describe the conditions used for this industrial reaction. (3)
Write an equation for the reaction. (3)
Explain what is meant by an addition reaction. (2)

(JMB/WMEB 1982)

9 a) The first two members of the alkane series are methane (CH_4) and ethane (C_2H_6). The first two members of the alkene series are ethene (C_2H_4) and propene (C_3H_6).
i) Write the name and formula for the third member of the alkanes. (1)
ii) Write the general formula for the alkane series. (1)
iii) Write the name and formula for the third member of the alkenes. (1)
iv) Write the general formula for the alkene series. (1)

b) Write the structural formula for ethane and ethene. Methane is given as an example (see Table 1). (2)

Methane	Ethane	Ethene
H | H—C—H | H		

Table 1

c) Describe one test which could be used to distinguish between samples of ethane and ethene. State the result of the test with each compound. (2)

d) i) Name the reagent which is used to convert ethene to ethane. (1)
ii) State the conditions needed for the reaction. (1)

(NEA 1984)

10 Below is a simple representation of a detergent molecule.

a) Using representations like the one above, fill in the diagram below to show how you would expect detergent molecules to interact with grease and water. (2)

b) Describe one similarity in structure between the above detergent molecule and a soap molecule. (1)

c) Most detergents produced today are biodegradable.
   i) Explain what this term means. (1)
   ii) Why is it necessary that detergents should be biodegradable? (2)
d) i) What happens when soap is dissolved in water containing calcium ions in solution? (2)
   ii) Give the name of *one* calcium compound commonly found in solution in natural waters.
(AEB 1982)

11 a) In bread making, yeast is added to the mix and then the dough is left to stand for a period of time whilst it rises (increases in volume) before baking.
   i) What gas is responsible for causing the dough to increase in volume? (1)
   ii) How is this gas formed? (3)
   iii) What happens to the yeast on baking? (1)
   b) i) Name *one* other raising agent used in baking which produces the same gas. (1)
   ii) Under what condition(s) is the gas liberated by this agent? Give the equation. (3)
(AEB 1982)

12 The *principal components* of petrol are hydrocarbons of the *alkane* series together with *additives*. The combustion of the petrol in the cylinder of the engine depends upon mixing petrol vapour with air. A mixture with a high proportion of petrol vapour is called a rich mixture and a mixture with a high proportion of air is called a weak mixture.
When the engine is running on a rich mixture the inside of the tail pipe of the exhaust will often develop a black deposit. When the engine is running on a weak mixture the inside of the tail pipe will often develop a light deposit containing some lead compounds.
a) i) Give the general formula for the *alkane* series. (1)
   ii) Give the name and formula of *one* of the principal components of petrol. (2)
b) i) Name *one* common *additive* in petrol. (1)
   ii) What is the function of the additive you have named? (2)
c) i) How can you account for the formation of the black deposit when the engine is running with a rich mixture? (3)
   ii) How can you account for the light deposit formed when the engine is running with a weak mixture? (3)
d) Describe *one* pollution problem that can arise from the use of *additives* in petrol. (2)
(AEB 1982)

13 Organic chemicals may be classified under general names such as alkanes, alkenes, alcohols, carboxylic acids, esters, polyesters, addition polymers. For each of the compounds represented by the following structural formulae, choose from the above list the class to which it belongs.

a) $CH_3CH_2C{\overset{O}{\underset{OH}{\lessgtr}}}$ (1)

b) $\underset{H_3C}{\overset{H_3C}{>}}C=C\underset{H}{\overset{CH_3}{<}}$ (1)

c) $\underset{H_3C}{\overset{H_3C}{>}}C\underset{CH_3}{\overset{CH_3}{<}}$ (1)

d) $\underset{H_3C}{\overset{H_3C}{>}}C\underset{CH_2OH}{\overset{CH_3}{<}}$ (1)

e) $\left[-C_6H_4-\overset{O}{\overset{||}{C}}-O-CH_2CH_2-O-\overset{O}{\overset{||}{C}}-\right]_n$ (1)

(AEB 1983)

14 Give the name *or* the structural formula of the main organic product formed when each of the following procedures is carried out:
a) A mixture of methane and chlorine is exposed to ultraviolet light. (1)
b) A mixture of ethene and steam is passed over an acid catalyst at high temperature and pressure. (1)
c) A mixture of propene and hydrogen is passed over a hot metal catalyst. (1)
d) Ethene is subjected to a high pressure in the presence of a small amount of oxygen. (1)
e) **Ethene is bubbled into bromine water at room temperature.** (1)
(AEB 1982)

15 a) Polymers are important materials in the service of man. For each of the uses given suggest a suitable polymer and give the characteristic property that makes it suitable.
   i) Manufacture of items of clothing with a 'permanent' crease.
   ii) The manufacture of self-lubricating bearings, for example, the lining of an artificial hip joint. (6)
b) Explain the basis for the classification of some polymers as condensation polymers. (2)
(AEB 1983)

16 a) Crude oil is a valuable source of fuels and of organic chemicals. It is refined by fractional distillation. Use the data in Table 2 to answer the questions which follow.

Fraction	Boiling point in °C
A	40
B	80
C	200
D	350
E	above 350

Table 2

Give the letter which is most appropriate as an answer to each of the following questions and explain, where possible, the reasons for your choice. Each letter may be used once, more than once, or not at all.
  i) Which fraction would contain the most volatile compounds?
  ii) Which fraction would be collected at the bottom of the fractionating column?
  iii) Which fraction would be used as a fuel for cars?
  iv) Which fraction would contain the smallest molecules?
  v) Which *two* fractions would be most likely to be used as fuels for vehicles other than cars? (5)
b) i) Explain what you understand by the term *catalytic cracking*.
  ii) Write an equation to show how octane can be produced by catalytic cracking of *either* $C_{15}H_{32}$ or $C_{17}H_{36}$. (4)
c) Alkenes are used as source materials for industrial organic chemicals. Choose two different alkenes and, *in each case*, give:
  i) the name and structural formula of the alkene;
  ii) the name of an addition polymer which can be manufactured from this alkene;
  iii) the structure of *one repeating unit* of the polymer;
  iv) an important use of the polymer. (8)
(AEB 1983)

17 a) i) Name the essential material which must be added to an aqueous solution of sucrose in order to prepare an aqueous solution of ethanol. State the name given to this type of process.

  ii) Give a diagram of the apparatus you would use to obtain a more concentrated solution of ethanol from the solution produced in (i). (6)
b) Ethanol can be manufactured from ethene. For this reaction give the essential reaction conditions and write the equation. (2)
c) Ethyl ethanoate ($CH_3CO_2C_2H_5$) can be prepared from ethanol and ethanoic acid.
  i) Write the equation for the reaction.
  ii) Calculate the theoretical yield of ethyl ethanoate which can be obtained from 23 g of ethanol.
  iii) Experimentally it was found that 33 g of ethyl ethanoate were obtained from 23 g of ethanol. Calculate the percentage yield. (3)
d) Ethanol is the second member of the homologous series of alcohols.
  i) Give the name and full structural formula of the first member of this series.
  ii) Give three general properties of an homologous series. (4)
(Cambridge 1982)

18 The apparatus below has been recommended for the distillation of liquid mixtures.

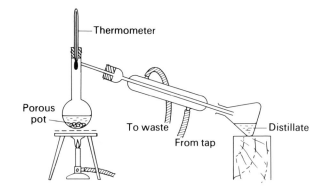

a)

Liquid	Boiling point (°C)
methanol	65
ethanol	78
butanol	118
hexanol	157

From the table of alcohols above, state which pair of liquids
  i) could be separated *most* effectively using this apparatus. (2)
  ii) could be separated *least* effectively using this apparatus. (2)
b) Suggest *one way* in which an apparatus for more effective fractional distillation would differ from that shown above. (2)
(OLE 1984)

12

THE AIR

Fig. 12.1   The Earth is surrounded by a layer of gases we call 'the air'

The air (or atmosphere) is a mixture of gases. It is mainly nitrogen and oxygen with small amounts of some others. Without this gaseous envelope around the Earth we would not survive. In Chapter 10 you learned how you rely on using oxygen to stay alive:

oxygen + glucose $\longrightarrow$ carbon dioxide + water + energy

$$6O_{2(g)} + C_6H_{12}O_{6(aq)} \longrightarrow 6CO_{2(g)} + 6H_2O_{(l)}$$

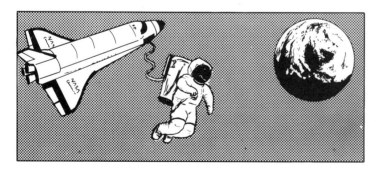

Fig. 12.2   An astronaut needs a personal 'air' supply

Fig. 12.3   Without air would this fire burn?

Scientists have also shown that the air is important for a whole range of familiar chemical processes. For example, without the oxygen in the air your family car would not go very far and your coal or gas fire could not burn (see Fig. 12.3).

The reactive part of the air

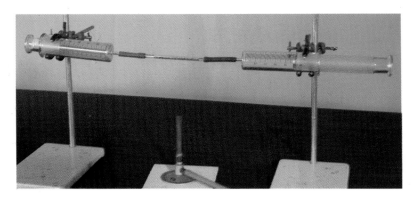

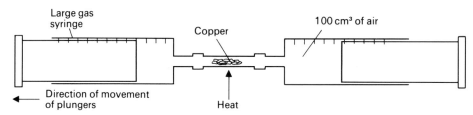

Fig. 12.4   The apparatus used to find out the volume of oxygen in the air

When copper is heated in air, the metal turns black. To produce the black coating the copper must have combined with something out of the air. The gas which has combined with the copper is known as the reactive part of the air. Fig. 12.4 shows the apparatus which can be used in the laboratory to find out how much of this reactive gas there is in the air. When the 100 cm³ of air is passed backwards and forwards over the heated copper turnings the amount of gas in the syringe is reduced. The copper also goes black. Some data obtained from an experiment like the one above are given below.

Fig. 12.5   Copper turnings before and after heating

Volume of air at the start of the experiment = 100 cm³
Volume of air at the end of the experiment =   79 cm³
Volume of the reactive gas used up =   21 cm³

The percentage of the reactive gas in the air is

$$\frac{21}{100} \times 100 = 21\%$$

This reactive gas is oxygen. It takes up approximately one-fifth of the air by volume. It is known as the 'reactive part of the air' reacting with metals such as copper to produce metal oxides.

copper + oxygen ⟶ copper(II) oxide

$$2Cu_{(s)} + O_{2(g)} \longrightarrow 2CuO_{(s)}$$

The remaining, less reactive, part of the air is a mixture of gases, the major component being nitrogen. This gas makes up approximately four-fifths of the air by volume. It makes up almost 78 cm³ of the remaining 79 cm³. Nitrogen is a very unreactive gas.

Other gases which scientists have found in the air are carbon dioxide and water vapour as well as argon, neon, krypton, xenon and helium (the noble or inert gases). Table 12.1 shows a typical composition analysis of pure *dry* air ('clean' air). Before air is dried it normally contains up to 1% water vapour although this will vary according to whether or not it is a damp or dry day.

Component	Approximate percentage (%) composition by volume
Oxygen	21
Nitrogen	78
Argon	0.9
Carbon dioxide	0.03
Neon	0.002
Helium, krypton, xenon	0.00055

Table 12.1   The composition of pure dry air

Air pollution

There are several impurities found in the air besides water vapour. These other substances are known as **pollutants** and they cause **air pollution**. Some of them are detailed below.

1 **Sulphur dioxide** is formed when fuels such as coal and oil are burned at home and in power stations. Also petrol contains small amounts of sulphur. This is converted into sulphur dioxide in the petrol engine. This gas gives rise in part to **acid rain** which not only damages buildings, but also plants and trees (see Fig. 12.6). Sulphur dioxide attacks the lungs and makes us more vulnerable to diseases like bronchitis.

2 **Carbon monoxide** is produced in quite large quantities by petrol and diesel engines. It is formed when fuels do not have enough air to burn completely. The gas is very poisonous. It reacts with blood stopping it carrying oxygen around the body. In Japan, traffic police have to wear gas masks to protect them from this type of pollution.

3 **Nitrogen(IV) oxide** is also found in car exhaust fumes. It is formed in the hotter parts of the engine. It is part of acid rain and will also affect our lungs in a similar manner to sulphur dioxide (see Figs 12.7 and 12.8).

4 **Smoke** often contains, amongst other materials, tiny particles of carbon. The smoke makes buildings dirty and unsightly and contributes to lung disease. Before the Clean Air Act of 1956 sights such as that shown in Fig. 12.9 were not uncommon. However, since then matters have improved.

5 **Lead** comes from lead tetraethyl a substance which is added to petrol as an 'antiknock' agent. The lead is present in exhaust fumes. It can cause brain damage, especially in young children.

Fig. 12.6   Acid rain has caused the damage to these trees

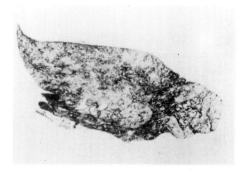

Fig. 12.7   Lung section of a middle-aged town-dweller

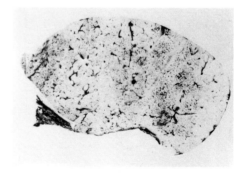

Fig. 12.8   Lung section of a countryman of the same age

Fig. 12.9   London before the Clean Air Act

Fig. 12.10   London after the Clean Air Act

Air pollution is very costly. Upwards of £6000 million are spent on the problem of air pollution every year. It has been generally recognized that air pollution must be reduced. For this reason many cities have **smokeless zones**. In these areas only smokeless fuel is burned in homes and factories. Unfortunately, the burning of smokeless fuels does not reduce the emission of sulphur dioxide. Cars can be fitted with specially-designed exhaust systems which contain substances (catalysts) which will decompose the dangerous nitrogen dioxide gas into nitrogen and oxygen which are 'safe'. Lead does not have to be added to petrol. Petrol engines can be modified to use lead-free petrol. Factories and power stations have increased the height of their chimneys. These taller chimneys spread out the smoke they produce over a larger area which makes the problem less localised. Fine dust particles and some of the noxious gases can be removed from industrial smoke. One method of doing this involves 'washing' the smoke with water before it is released to the atmosphere.

More about oxygen

Joseph Priestley (in Britain) and Carl Wilhelm Scheele (in Sweden) identified oxygen independently in 1773–4. However, the gas was named by the French scientist Antoine Lavoisier.

Oxygen is a colourless, odourless gas which is slightly soluble in water. Fish and all forms of aquatic life rely on this property (see Fig. 12.11). It is the most abundant element in the Earth's crust (see Fig. 2.5) but it is not easily obtained from the rocks. It can be prepared quite easily in the laboratory using the apparatus shown in Fig. 12.12. In this preparation hydrogen peroxide solution is poured onto manganese(IV) oxide which acts as a catalyst. Hydrogen peroxide decomposes very slowly. However, when manganese(IV) oxide is added the chemical breakdown proceeds much more quickly.

Fig. 12.11   Fish can 'breathe' the oxygen dissolved in water

$$\text{hydrogen peroxide} \xrightarrow{\frac{\text{manganese(IV)}}{\text{oxide}}} \text{water} + \text{oxygen}$$

$$2H_2O_{2(aq)} \longrightarrow 2H_2O_{(l)} + O_{2(g)}$$

We can show the gas produced in this reaction is oxygen by the fact that it relights a glowing splint.

Fig. 12.12   The apparatus used to prepare oxygen

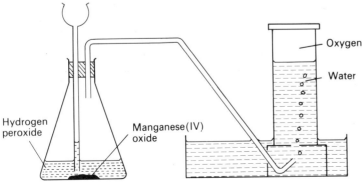

Some properties of oxygen

Oxygen is a reactive gas. When it reacts with metal and non-metal elements, compounds called **oxides** are produced. We have already examined in Chapter 8 the reactions of metals with oxygen from the air. Many of these metals will react more vigorously when ignited in air and then plunged into a gas jar of oxygen (see Fig. 12.13). For example, magnesium burns brightly in air producing a white ash of magnesium oxide. When burning magnesium is plunged into a gas jar of oxygen it burns violently with a blinding white light.

$$\text{magnesium} + \text{oxygen} \longrightarrow \text{magnesium oxide}$$

$$2Mg_{(s)} + O_{2(g)} \longrightarrow 2MgO_{(s)}$$

Metals like sodium and calcium also react more vigorously producing the corresponding oxide.

Non-metals behave in a similar way. They burn more brightly in oxygen producing the corresponding oxides. Sulphur produces sulphur dioxide.

$$\text{sulphur} + \text{oxygen} \longrightarrow \text{sulphur dioxide}$$

$$S_{(s)} + O_{2(g)} \longrightarrow SO_{2(g)}$$

Phosphorus produces phosphorus(V) oxide

$$\text{phosphorus} + \text{oxygen} \longrightarrow \text{phosphorus(V) oxide}$$

$$4P_{(s)} + 5O_{2(g)} \longrightarrow P_4O_{10(s)}$$

When solutions of the metal and non-metal oxides are tested with universal indicator paper it is found that, in general, metal oxides produce alkaline (basic) solutions whilst non-metal oxides produce acidic solutions. For example:

$$\text{calcium oxide} + \text{water} \longrightarrow \text{calcium hydroxide}$$

$$CaO_{(s)} + H_2O_{(l)} \longrightarrow Ca(OH)_{2(aq)}$$

$$\text{sulphur dioxide} + \text{water} \longrightarrow \text{sulphurous acid}$$

$$SO_{2(g)} + H_2O_{(l)} \longrightarrow H_2SO_{3(aq)}$$

A summary of the above reactions is shown in Table 12.2.

Fig. 12.13 Magnesium burns very brightly and strongly in oxygen. Magnesium oxide is produced

Element	How does it burn in air?	How does it burn in oxygen?	Appearance of residue	Colour of universal indicator in solution of oxide	Is the product acid or alkaline?
Magnesium	Bright flame	Brilliant white flame	White ash	Blue	Alkaline
Sodium	Pale yellow flame	Bright light yellow flame	Pale yellow powder	Blue	Alkaline
Calcium	Red flame	Bright red flame	White powder	Blue	Alkaline
Phosphorus	Pale yellow flame	Vigorously with a bright yellow flame	White powder	Red	Acid
Sulphur	Pale blue flame	Brilliant blue flame	Colourless gas	Red	Acid

Table 12.2

Some oxides are neither acidic or basic, they are neutral oxides. Examples of neutral oxides are carbon monoxide (CO), water (H_2O) and dinitrogen oxide (N_2O). (Dinitrogen oxide is also referred to as nitrous oxide—laughing gas.) The oxides of some metals react with both acids and alkalis. They are called **amphoteric oxides**. Examples of this type of oxide include zinc oxide and aluminium oxide.

In Chapter 11 you saw that alkanes such as methane (natural gas) burn in a good supply of oxygen forming carbon dioxide and water and releasing energy.

$$\text{methane} + \text{oxygen} \longrightarrow \text{carbon dioxide} + \text{water} + \text{energy}$$

$$CH_{4(g)} + 2O_{2(g)} \longrightarrow CO_{2(g)} + 2H_2O_{(g)}$$

If there is a limited supply of oxygen then carbon monoxide is produced.

Extracting gases from the air

Air is a very useful resource. We have developed many uses for the gases which make up this mixture. The gases are extracted by fractional distillation of liquid air. The stages in this process are:

1 Initially the air is filtered to remove any dust.
2 It is then pumped through sodium hydroxide solution to remove any carbon dioxide.

$$\text{sodium hydroxide} + \text{carbon dioxide} \longrightarrow \text{sodium carbonate} + \text{water}$$

$$2NaOH_{(aq)} + CO_{2(g)} \longrightarrow Na_2CO_{3(aq)} + H_2O_{(l)}$$

Any water vapour is then removed by passing the air into a drying tower containing a drying agent such as silica gel.
Note It is important to remove every trace of carbon dioxide and water vapour since in the next stages these would freeze and block the pipes.
3 The remaining gases in the air—nitrogen, oxygen and noble gases—are now compressed to about 200 atmospheres and cooled. The cooling is done by the gas mixture being recirculated from the next stage.
4 The cold compressed air is now allowed to expand through a small hole. This process causes further cooling. It is similar to gas escaping from a bicycle tyre. It feels cool.
5 The now cold gas mixture is returned to the compressor. On the way it cools the gas mixture coming in. This process is repeated several times and eventually liquid air is formed.
6 The liquid air is finally passed into a fractionating column. In here it is fractionally distilled.

Table 12.3 shows the temperatures at which the various gases 'boil off'. A plant for carrying out this process is shown in Fig. 12.15. The gases so produced are then stored under pressure in very strong cylinders (see Fig. 12.16).

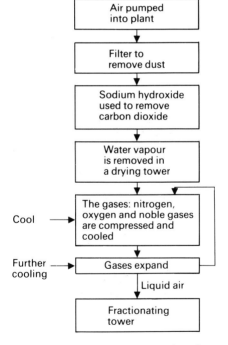

Fig. 12.14   A flow diagram showing how the different gases present in the air are extracted

Fig. 12.15   Gases are extracted from the air in this plant

Gas	Boiling point (°C)
Helium	−269
Neon	−246
Nitrogen	−196
Argon	−186
Oxygen	−183
Krypton	−157
Xenon	−108

Table 12.3

Some uses of oxygen

Large quantities of oxygen are used in industry in converting pig iron into steel (see Chapter 8, page 107), and when mixed with gases like ethyne (acetylene) it is used to produce a very hot flame for welding (see Fig. 12.17). Oxygen is used in hospitals to help those with breathing difficulties (see Fig. 12.18), and to revive patients after operations. Sportsmen such as divers and mountaineers use it (see Fig. 12.19). Oxygen is carried in space rockets so that the kerosene and hydrogen fuels can burn. For example, the Saturn V Apollo moon missions used 1450 tonnes (1.25 million litres) of liquid oxygen in stage 1 to burn 550 tonnes of kerosene in 2.5 minutes.

Fig. 12.16   Pressurized cylinders are used to store the gases shown in Table 12.3

Fig. 12.17   Oxygen is used to produce a very hot flame for welding

Fig. 12.19   Why do mountaineers sometimes carry their own supply of oxygen?

Fig. 12.18   Patients with breathing difficulties are given oxygen in hospital

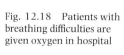

Some uses of nitrogen

Many chemical reactions require a non-reactive atmosphere and the inert nature of nitrogen makes it highly suited for this purpose. Nitrogen's non-reactive nature makes it also very useful for filling empty oil tankers to reduce the possibility of fire or explosion (see Fig. 12.20). In liquid form it is used as a refrigerant. Nitrogen is also used in the production of ammonia, nitric acid, explosives, dyes and fertilizers (see Fig. 12.21).

Fig. 12.21   Dyes contain nitrogen in their molecular structure

Fig. 12.20   Empty oil tankers are filled with nitrogen to prevent fire and explosions

Some uses of noble gases

Argon, the most plentiful of the noble gases in the air, is used to fill light bulbs (see Fig. 12.22). Neon glows red when electricity is passed through it and so it finds a use in advertising signs (see Fig. 12.23). Helium, a very light gas, is used almost entirely as an alternative to hydrogen in weather balloons. Also, helium is used, when mixed with oxygen, by divers (see Fig. 12.24). Since the noble gases are extremely unreactive, they provide a useful inert atmosphere for some chemical reactions as well as being used in electric arc welding to prevent oxidation of the metals being welded at high temperatures.

Fig. 12.22   This bulb is full of argon

Fig. 12.24   Deep-sea divers breathe a helium–oxygen mixture

Fig. 12.23   The 'castle' sign contains neon

—————————————————————————— QUESTIONS ——————————————————————————

1 a) Oxygen has an atomic number of 8.
   What is the electronic structure of the oxygen atom?

   b) Oxygen molecules are *diatomic*. Explain the meaning of the term in italic.

   c) Draw a diagram (outermost electron shells only) to show the electron structure of a molecule of oxygen. What type of bonding does the molecule contain?

2 a) The apparatus shown below can be used to prepare oxygen.

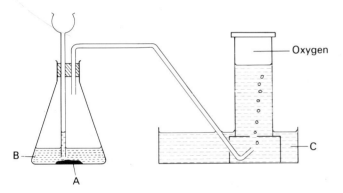

   i) Name and give the formulae of the substances labelled A, B, and C.

   ii) What is the function of the solid A?

   iii) Write a word equation and a balanced chemical equation for the reaction in which oxygen is produced.

   b) When oxygen reacts with metallic and non-metallic elements, oxides are produced.

   i) How could you distinguish between a metal oxide and a non-metal oxide?

   ii) Name a neutral oxide.

   iii) Some oxides are said to be *amphoteric*. Explain the meaning of the term in italic.

   iv) Name two amphoteric oxides.

   c) Give two large-scale uses of oxygen.

3 a) Explain what is meant by the term 'air pollution'.

   b) Name two air pollutants produced by the combustion of petrol in an internal combustion engine.

   c) Name a different air pollutant produced by the burning of coal.

   d) Give three ways in which attempts have (or are) being made to cut down the amount of air pollution.

   e) Explain what is meant by a 'smokeless zone'.

4 Give an account of one example of air pollution. Indicate clearly the nature of the pollutant, its effects and how it can be monitored.

5 Read the following description of an industrial process.
   Air is dried and then carbon dioxide is removed. The remaining gases are liquefied and then separated by fractional distillation. These gases are listed below with their boiling points:

Argon	$-186\,^{\circ}C$
Helium	$-269\,^{\circ}C$
Krypton	$-157\,^{\circ}C$
Neon	$-246\,^{\circ}C$
Nitrogen	$-196\,^{\circ}C$
Oxygen	$-183\,^{\circ}C$
Xenon	$-108\,^{\circ}C$

   a) How can the air be freed from solid matter before the carbon dioxide and moisture are removed? (1)

   b) Before distilling the air it is cooled to about $-200\,^{\circ}C$.

   i) Why is it necessary to remove carbon dioxide and water vapour before cooling and distilling? (1)

   ii) Which of the gases will *not* become liquid at $-200\,^{\circ}C$? (2)

   iii) The substances which have liquefied at $-200\,^{\circ}C$ are separated by fractional distillation of the liquid mixture. Which substance is the first to change from a liquid to a gas as the temperature is slowly increased? (1)

   c) Choose any *two* gases from the list and give one important use for each gas. (2)

   d) Carbon dioxide can exist in three states of solid, liquid or gas.

   i) In which state will the carbon dioxide particles be closest together and in a regular pattern? (1)

   ii) In which state will there be most space between the carbon dioxide particles? (1)

   (JMB/WMEB 1979)

6 Two gas syringes are connected as shown in the diagram below and the copper is heated strongly. By moving the syringes in and out, the air is passed over the hot copper until no further change in volume takes place. The apparatus is then allowed to cool to the original temperature before a final reading of the gas volume is taken.

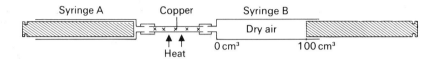

a) Why is the apparatus allowed to cool before the final volume is read? (1)

b) What would be the expected final volume of gas in the syringe? (1)

c) i) Explain briefly why there is a change in volume and write an equation for any reaction which occurs. (3)
    ii) What would be the final appearance of the surface of the copper? (1)

d) Name:
    i) the main residual gas in the syringe; (1)
    ii) one other gas present in the syringe. (1)

(AEB 1984)

7 In order to determine the proportion of one of the major components of air, the air was passed in turn through sodium hydroxide solution, through concentrated sulphuric acid and into a glass syringe. The volume of remaining gas was measured and the gas was passed repeatedly over red hot copper until no further contraction in volume occurred. The gas was then allowed to cool and its volume was measured.

> Volume of gas before passing over hot copper $= 90.0 \, cm^3$.
>
> Volume of gas after passing over hot copper $= 70.2 \, cm^3$.

a) Why was the air passed through sodium hydroxide solution? (1)

b) Why was it passed through concentrated sulphuric acid? (1)

c) How would the appearance of the copper before heating and after cooling differ? (1)

d) Which gas was removed by the copper? (1)

e) Name the main gas remaining in the syringe at the end of the experiment and calculate the approximate percentage of this gas in the air from the data provided. (3)

f) Give the name of another element which would still be present in the residual gas. (1)

(JMB 1977)

8 a) Describe briefly how oxygen is obtained for large-scale use from the air. (4)

b) Explain the involvement of atmospheric oxygen in the carbon cycle by describing
    i) one process by which oxygen is removed from the air, and
    ii) the replacement of oxygen into the air. (6)

c) What changes, if any, would be seen if the following were placed in separate jars or tubes of oxygen? Write equations for any reactions which occur.
    i) Burning sulphur.
    ii) pH indicator.
    iii) Burning magnesium ribbon. (5)

(JMB 1982)

9 a) State whether the elements:
    i) magnesium;
    ii) sulphur;
    iii) argon;
    react with oxygen. Describe the reactions, and give the names of any products obtained. (4)

b) Describe briefly how you would carry out the reactions in the laboratory with
    i) magnesium,
    ii) sulphur, in order to collect a sample of each product. (4)

c) The products obtained in (b) each dissolve in water with a reaction.
    i) State the name of each solution produced.
    ii) Give one way in which these solutions show chemically contrasting properties. (3)

d) Suggest one possible way in which your answer to (c) could be used to distinguish between metals and non-metals. (1)

(AEB 1981)

13

NITROGEN AND ITS COMPOUNDS

(a) Nitrogen-containing fabric dyes

(b) The plastic used to make the toothbrushes contains nitrogen

(c) Fertilizers contain nitrogen

Fig. 13.1   Nitrogen atoms are found in many compounds

Nitrogen is a colourless gas with no smell and very little solubility in water. It makes up about four-fifths of the atmosphere (78%). It is an unreactive diatomic gas (N_2) and special conditions are often required to make it react with other elements. Nitrogen can be made to combine with oxygen, hydrogen and some reactive metals such as magnesium, but only with some difficulty.

At very high temperatures nitrogen reacts with oxygen to produce oxides of nitrogen such as nitrogen(II) oxide (NO) and nitrogen(IV) oxide (NO_2).

$$\text{nitrogen} + \text{oxygen} \rightleftharpoons \text{nitrogen(II) oxide}$$

$$N_{2(g)} + O_{2(g)} \rightleftharpoons 2NO_{(g)}$$

In the presence of a catalyst nitrogen combines with hydrogen to produce ammonia, a very useful substance. A high temperature and pressure are also required for this reaction. (It is discussed in detail on page 187.)

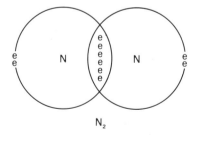

$$N \equiv N$$

Very strong triple covalent bond
It is difficult to break, hence
it is an unreactive gas

Fig. 13.2   The nitrogen molecule

The reactive metal magnesium when burning strongly in air will form a small amount of magnesium nitride in addition to a large amount of magnesium oxide.

$$\text{magnesium} + \text{nitrogen} \longrightarrow \text{magnesium nitride}$$

$$3Mg_{(s)} + N_{2(g)} \longrightarrow Mg_3N_{2(s)}$$

Nitrogen cycle

In spite of its unreactive nature, nitrogen is a very important element. Nitrogen-containing compounds called **proteins** are found in all plants and animals. Proteins are essential for healthy growth. Leguminous plants like beans and clover have root nodules (see Fig. 13.3) which contain a type of bacteria that can absorb free nitrogen from the atmosphere and change it into a form used to make proteins. This is called **fixing nitrogen**. Most plants cannot absorb nitrogen directly from the air but still need a supply of nitrogen to make proteins. They can obtain the nitrogen they need from the soil. As dead plants and animals decay, some soluble nitrogen-containing compounds, usually nitrates, are produced and can be absorbed by these plants. Some of these nitrates are converted into nitrogen by bacteria in the soil. This is then released back into the atmosphere.

Unlike the dead and decaying plants which put nitrogen-containing compounds back into the soil, food crops which are harvested are unable to do this. Thus land which is used for growing food crops can become infertile. For the soil to remain fertile, the nitrates need to be replaced. This is done in a number of natural ways. Lightning produced in thunderstorms causes nitrogen and oxygen to combine giving oxides of nitrogen. These dissolve in water producing nitric acid which reacts with substances in the soil forming nitrates.

Fig. 13.3(a)   Runner beans

Fig. 13.3(b)   The bacteria in these runner bean root nodules change nitrogen into nitrates

Fig. 13.3(c)   Clover

Fig. 13.4   Food crops when harvested cannot put nitrogen-containing compounds into the soil

Plants and animals are eaten. Waste products are created. Natural manures (or fertilizers), such as farmyard manure, are very rich in nitrogen-containing compounds. They are spread directly onto the soil. Bacteria feed on this material and convert it into nitrates.

Fig. 13.3(d)   Clover root nodules also contain bacteria which are capable of fixing nitrogen

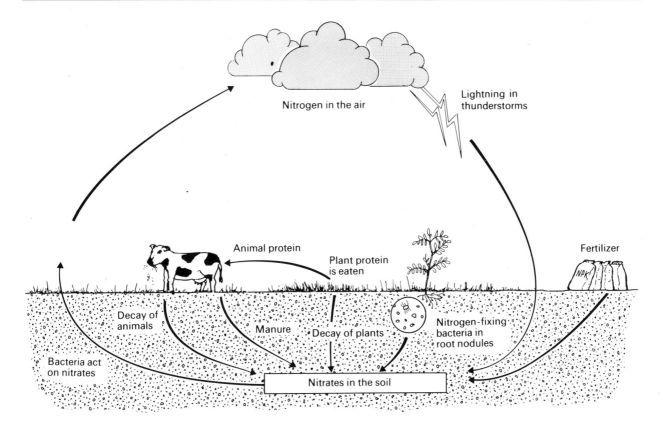

Fig. 13.5   The nitrogen cycle

As you can see, nitrogen is being removed and returned to the soil. This is a natural process known as the **nitrogen cycle** (see Fig. 13.5). However, this natural process cannot supply the amounts of nitrogen required to produce the food output we require today. To overcome this problem scientists have developed new nitrogen-containing compounds to use as fertilizers. These **artificial fertilizers** (see Fig. 13.6) are being used on an increasingly large scale by farmers to maintain an ever-increasing production of crops. One of the most commonly used fertilizers is ammonium nitrate. To make this substance ammonia gas and nitric acid are required. We shall see how ammonium nitrate is made in the next section.

Fig. 13.6   A compound fertilizer containing ammonium nitrate is loaded into a fertilizer spreader which then automatically dispenses fertilizer as the tractor moves along

Ammonia (NH₃)

Ammonia is a colourless gas with a very choking smell. It is less dense than air. It is usually made in the laboratory by heating an ammonium compound with an alkali. The usual substances used are ammonium chloride and calcium hydroxide. The apparatus used for this preparation is shown in Fig. 13.9.

$$\text{ammonium chloride} + \text{calcium hydroxide} \longrightarrow \text{calcium chloride} + \text{water} + \text{ammonia}$$

$$2NH_4Cl_{(s)} + Ca(OH)_{2(s)} \longrightarrow CaCl_{2(s)} + 2H_2O_{(g)} + 2NH_{3(g)}$$

Fig. 13.7 Many household cleaners contain 'ammonia'

The ammonia gas is dried by passing it through a drying tower containing calcium oxide. The dry ammonia rises up into the flask.

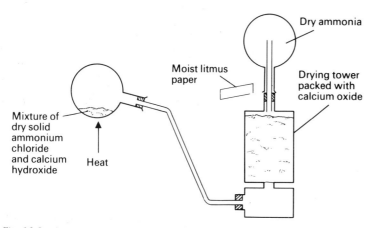

Fig. 13.9   Apparatus used for preparing ammonia

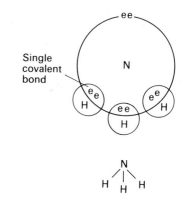

Fig. 13.8   The ammonia molecule

Some properties of ammonia

Ammonia is very soluble in water. It is so soluble that one volume of water will dissolve over 700 times its own volume of ammonia. The 'fountain' experiment shows just how soluble it is (see Fig. 13.11). As the ammonia dissolves in water inside the glass tube, water rushes up to replace the dissolved gas. This creates the 'fountain' effect you see inside the flask. If universal indicator solution has been put into the water in the trough it goes blue when it comes in contact with the dissolved ammonia. This is because ammonia solution is a weak alkali. A little of the ammonia has reacted with the water producing ammonium hydroxide.

$$\text{ammonia} + \text{water} \rightleftharpoons \text{ammonium hydroxide}$$

$$NH_{3(g)} + H_2O_{(l)} \rightleftharpoons NH_4OH_{(aq)}$$

then

$$\text{ammonium hydroxide} \rightleftharpoons \text{ammonium ions} + \text{hydroxide ions}$$

$$NH_4OH_{(aq)} \rightleftharpoons NH^+_{4(aq)} + OH^-_{(aq)}$$

Ammonia when dissolved in water is better known as 'aqueous ammonia' (or ammonia solution). This is because most aqueous ammonia is a solution and not a hydroxide. Ammonia gas will also turn damp pH paper blue. This colour change can be used as a test for the gas.

Fig. 13.10   It's dangerous to leave the stopper off the ammonia bottle

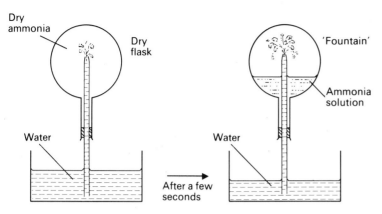

Fig. 13.11   The fountain experiment

When open bottles of concentrated ammonia and concentrated hydrochloric acid are placed side by side, white fumes are seen above the open necks of the bottles (see Fig. 13.12). The white solid in these fumes is ammonium chloride. It is formed by the ammonia gas (from the ammonia bottle) reacting with hydrogen chloride gas escaping from the concentrated hydrochloric acid bottle.

ammonia + hydrogen chloride $\longrightarrow$ ammonium chloride

$$NH_{3(g)} \quad + \quad HCl_{(g)} \quad \longrightarrow \quad NH_4Cl_{(s)}$$

If solid ammonium chloride is heated quite strongly in a test tube it decomposes reversing the above reaction (see Fig. 13.13).

ammonium chloride $\xrightarrow{heat}$ ammonia + hydrogen chloride

$$NH_4Cl_{(s)} \quad \longrightarrow \quad NH_{3(g)} \quad + \quad HCl_{(g)}$$

This is called **thermal dissociation**. However, when the ammonia gas and hydrogen chloride so produced reach the cooler parts of the test tube they react together to form ammonium chloride again.

Ammonia will react as a reducing agent. If passed over heated copper(II) oxide (see Fig. 13.14) ammonia will reduce it to copper. Ammonia itself is oxidized to water and nitrogen.

ammonia + copper(II) oxide $\xrightarrow{heat}$ copper + water + nitrogen

$$2NH_{3(g)} \quad + \quad 3CuO_{(s)} \quad \longrightarrow 3Cu_{(s)} + 3H_2O_{(g)} + \quad N_{2(g)}$$

Fig. 13.12   When ammonia and hydrogen chloride mix, white clouds of ammonium chloride are produced

Fig. 13.14   Ammonia will reduce black copper(II) oxide to pink/brown copper

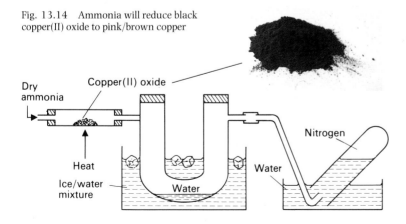

Fig. 13.13   Ammonium chloride thermally dissociates when heated. The ammonia and hydrogen chloride so produced recombine higher up the test tube

Ammonia will not allow substances to burn in it. It will also not burn in air. It will, however, burn in pure oxygen, with a pale or yellowish green flame.

$$\text{ammonia} + \text{oxygen} \longrightarrow \text{nitrogen} + \text{water}$$

$$4NH_{3(g)} + 3O_{2(g)} \longrightarrow 2N_{2(g)} + 6H_2O_{(g)}$$

If ammonia is heated with oxygen in the presence of a platinum catalyst a very different reaction occurs. This time nitrogen monoxide and water are formed.

$$\text{ammonia} + \text{oxygen} \xrightarrow[\text{heat}]{\text{platinum}} \text{nitrogen monoxide} + \text{water}$$

$$4NH_{3(g)} + 5O_{2(g)} \longrightarrow 4NO_{(g)} + 6H_2O_{(g)}$$

This oxidation process is the initial stage in the production of nitric acid (see page 189).

More about ammonia solution

Ammonia solution will react with acids to form salts (see Chapter 7). In these reactions ammonia is acting as a base. For example, if dilute nitric acid is added to a solution containing ammonia, ammonium nitrate is produced (an ammonium salt).

$$\text{ammonia solution} + \text{dilute nitric acid} \longrightarrow \text{ammonium nitrate}$$

$$NH_{3(aq)} + HNO_{3(aq)} \longrightarrow NH_4NO_{3(aq)}$$

Similar reactions occur between ammonia and sulphuric and hydrochloric acids.

$$\text{ammonia solution} + \text{dilute sulphuric acid} \longrightarrow \text{ammonium sulphate}$$

$$2NH_{3(aq)} + H_2SO_{4(aq)} \longrightarrow (NH_4)_2SO_{4(aq)}$$

$$\text{ammonia solution} + \text{dilute hydrochloric acid} \longrightarrow \text{ammonium chloride}$$

$$NH_{3(aq)} + HCl_{(aq)} \longrightarrow NH_4Cl_{(aq)}$$

Fig. 13.15(a)   The brown precipitate is iron(III) hydroxide

As solids, both ammonium nitrate and ammonium sulphate are commonly used as fertilizers. Manufacture of ammonium nitrate on a large scale is by 'blowing' ammonia gas through concentrated nitric acid.

Ammonia solution will also form precipitates with solutions of certain metal salts. For example, iron(III) chloride will react with ammonia solution forming ammonium chloride and a brown precipitate of iron(III) hydroxide (see Fig. 13.15(a)).

$$\text{iron(III) chloride} + \text{ammonia solution} \longrightarrow \text{iron(III) hydroxide} + \text{ammonium chloride}$$

$$FeCl_{3(aq)} + 3NH_4OH_{(aq)} \longrightarrow Fe(OH)_{3(s)} + 3NH_4Cl_{(aq)}$$

Ammonia solution reacts with copper(II) sulphate solution forming initially a pale blue precipitate of copper(II) hydroxide (Fig. 13.15(b)).

$$\text{copper(II) sulphate} + \text{ammonia solution} \longrightarrow \text{copper(II) hydroxide} + \text{ammonium sulphate}$$

$$CuSO_{4(aq)} + 2NH_4OH_{(aq)} \longrightarrow Cu(OH)_{2(s)} + (NH_4)_2SO_{4(aq)}$$

If more ammonia solution is now added until it is in excess the pale blue precipitate dissolves leaving a very deep blue solution called tetra-ammine copper(II) sulphate (see Fig. 13.15(c)).

Fig. 13.15(b)   The pale blue precipitate is copper(II) hydroxide

Chemical test for the ammonium ion (NH₄⁺)
Ammonium compounds contain the ammonium ion. The suspected ammonium salt is heated in a test tube with a small amount of a strong alkali such as sodium hydroxide. If ammonia gas is produced then the substance does contain the ammonium ion.

Manufacture of ammonia by the Haber process

This process was developed by a German scientist called Fritz Haber in 1913. His process was developed to make ammonia in large quantities to satisfy (1) the need for Germany to produce large quantities of explosives in the build-up to World War I, and (2) the very much increased demand for artificial fertilizers. The Haber process makes use of the reversible reaction:

$$\text{nitrogen} + \text{hydrogen} \rightleftharpoons \text{ammonia}$$

$$N_{2(g)} + 3H_{2(g)} \rightleftharpoons 2NH_{3(g)}$$

This type of reaction is known as a **synthesis reaction**, since a compound is formed directly from the elements from which it is made. The nitrogen for this process has always been obtained from the air after purification (see Chapter 12, page 176). The majority of the hydrogen used is obtained from methane (natural gas) or naphtha (a petrol-like fraction of oil) by a process called **steam reforming**. Purified methane or naphtha at a pressure of 30 atmospheres is passed over a nickel catalyst at a temperature of 750°C.

$$\text{methane} + \text{steam} \xrightarrow[\substack{\text{30 atmospheres} \\ 750°C}]{\text{Ni catalyst}} \text{carbon monoxide} + \text{hydrogen}$$

$$CH_{4(g)} + H_2O_{(g)} \rightleftharpoons CO_{(g)} + 3H_{2(g)}$$

The carbon monoxide reduces the steam to hydrogen and is itself oxidized to carbon dioxide which can be absorbed in hot potassium carbonate solution.

$$\text{steam} + \text{carbon monoxide} \rightleftharpoons \text{hydrogen} + \text{carbon dioxide}$$

$$H_2O_{(g)} + CO_{(g)} \rightleftharpoons H_{2(g)} + CO_{2(g)}$$

Fig. 13.15(c)   The dark blue solution is called tetra-ammine copper(II) sulphate

Fig. 13.16   ICI's Billingham complex—fertilizer and ammonia plant

The nitrogen and hydrogen are then mixed in the ratio of 1 volume to 3 volumes respectively and passed into a compressor. The pressure is increased to 200 atmospheres. The gas mixture is then passed over a finely divided catalyst of iron mixed with potassium hydroxide (see Fig. 13.17) in the reaction vessel. The working temperature is in the range 380–450°C. The catalyst works most efficiently in this temperature range. The gas mixture leaving the reaction vessel contains only about 15% of ammonia. This ammonia is removed by cooling and condensing it as a liquid. The remaining gases are then recirculated into the reaction vessel to react together again to produce more ammonia.

The ammonia plants once started up are run for 365 days a year. They are highly automated and can be largely operated from a central control room (see Fig. 13.18).

Running a plant of this size and complexity requires very large amounts of energy. The economical use of available energy is very important and can save many thousands of pounds. For example, the production of ammonia is exothermic and the heat produced can be used elsewhere in the process to warm the incoming gases.

In environmental terms, the present-day Haber process is what we might term a 'clean' process. The only waste materials are the spent catalysts and large quantities of warm water (used for cooling purposes). Ammonia is synthesized at ICI's large and complex Billingham site (see Fig. 13.16). On this site four ammonia plants have been developed in addition to plants for manufacturing fertilizers. This site was originally chosen for ammonia production because of close proximity to the Durham coalfields and hence excess electricity supply. Today it is conveniently positioned for access to North Sea gas—a source of hydrogen (see Fig. 13.19).

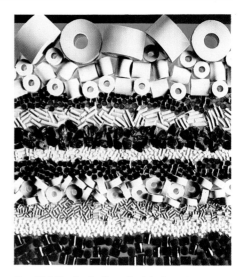

Fig. 13.17   A selection of catalysts

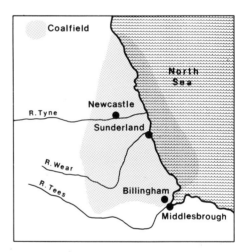

Fig. 13.19   The Billingham site is close to the Durham coalfields and North Sea gas fields

Fig. 13.18   The control room of the 'cracker' plant at ICI Wilton, Middlesbrough

Uses of ammonia

Ammonia is used extensively to make nitrogen-containing fertilizers such as ammonium nitrate, ammonium sulphate, urea and ammonium phosphate (see page 191). It is also used for making nitric acid (essential for the manufacture of fertilizers and a wide range of other substances), nylon and rayon (see page 155).

Fig. 13.20   A lot of ammonia is converted into fertilizers

Nitric acid (HNO$_3$)

In the previous section we noted that ammonia is produced at the very large ICI plant at Billingham. It is central to the operation of the whole complex leading directly to the manufacture of a second nitrogen-containing product—nitric acid.

Manufacture of nitric acid

The essential details of the process for producing nitric acid are given below. The whole process is shown in diagrammatic form in Fig.13.22.

Air and ammonia are pre-heated to about 300 °C and passed into a reaction vessel containing a platinum/rhodium catalyst (90% platinum). The reaction is highly exothermic and more air than is required for the reaction is used to keep the temperature in the vessel within the range 800–900 °C. In the reaction vessel nitrogen monoxide and water are produced.

Fig. 13.21   Nitric acid is a very useful but dangerous substance

$$\text{ammonia} + \text{oxygen} \longrightarrow \text{nitrogen monoxide} + \text{water}$$

$$4NH_{3(g)} + 5O_{2(g)} \longrightarrow 4NO_{(g)} + 6H_2O_{(g)}$$

The gases emerging are then cooled and mixed with air in the oxidizer and further oxidation to nitrogen(IV) oxide results.

$$\text{nitrogen monoxide} + \text{oxygen} \longrightarrow \text{nitrogen(IV) oxide}$$

$$2NO_{(g)} + O_{2(g)} \longrightarrow 2NO_{2(g)}$$

Absorption of the nitrogen(IV) oxide in water in the presence of air produces nitric acid.

$$\text{nitrogen(IV) oxide} + \text{oxygen} + \text{water} \longrightarrow \text{nitric acid}$$

$$4NO_{2(g)} + O_{2(g)} + 2H_2O_{(l)} \longrightarrow 4HNO_{3(aq)}$$

All the above reactions are exothermic.

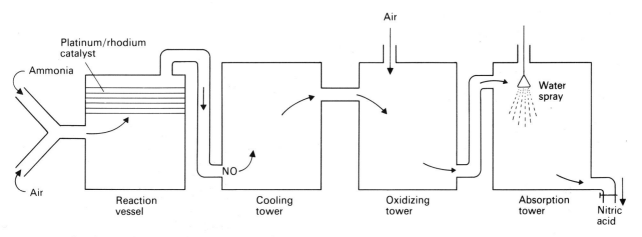

Fig. 13.22   Flow diagram for the manufacture of nitric acid

Waste oxides of nitrogen present a potential pollution problem. They are normally discharged into the atmosphere and older nitric acid plants could be recognized by the brown fumes emerging from tall chimneys. Improvements in plant design have reduced such discharges to very low concentrations.

Some properties of nitric acid

Dilute nitric acid

In this form it will carry out the usual reactions of an acid. It will affect indicators. For example, it will turn pH paper or blue litmus, red. Dilute nitric acid will also react with bases such as sodium hydroxide or copper(II) oxide and form a salt and water.

sodium hydroxide + dilute nitric acid ⟶ sodium nitrate + water

$$NaOH_{(aq)} + HNO_{3(aq)} \longrightarrow NaNO_{3(aq)} + H_2O_{(l)}$$

copper(II) oxide + dilute nitric acid ⟶ copper(II) nitrate + water

$$CuO_{(s)} + 2HNO_{3(aq)} \longrightarrow Cu(NO_3)_{2(aq)} + H_2O_{(l)}$$

It will also react with carbonates such as potassium carbonate producing a salt, carbon dioxide and water.

potassium carbonate + dilute nitric acid ⟶ potassium nitrate + carbon dioxide + water

$$K_2CO_{3(s)} + 2HNO_{3(aq)} \longrightarrow 2KNO_{3(aq)} + CO_{2(g)} + H_2O_{(l)}$$

However, dilute nitric acid behaves differently to acids like sulphuric and hydrochloric acid in that it does not usually produce hydrogen gas when it reacts with metals (except magnesium). For example, copper reacts with dilute nitric acid forming copper(II) nitrate (a salt), nitrogen monoxide and water.

copper + dilute nitric acid ⟶ copper(II) nitrate + nitrogen monoxide + water

$$3Cu_{(s)} + 8HNO_{3(aq)} \longrightarrow 3Cu(NO_3)_{2(aq)} + 2NO_{(g)} + 4H_2O_{(l)}$$

You will notice that dilute nitric acid reacts with quite unreactive metals.

Concentrated nitric acid

In this form nitric acid is a very powerful oxidizing agent which will oxidize both metals and non-metals. For example, it will oxidize carbon to carbon dioxide.

carbon + concentrated nitric acid ⟶ carbon dioxide + nitrogen(IV) oxide + water

$$C_{(s)} + 4HNO_{3(l)} \longrightarrow CO_{2(g)} + 4NO_{2(g)} + 2H_2O_{(l)}$$

It will oxidize metals such as copper to copper ions in copper(II) nitrate (see Fig. 13.23).

copper + concentrated nitric acid ⟶ copper(II) nitrate + nitrogen(IV) oxide + water

$$Cu_{(s)} + 4HNO_{3(l)} \longrightarrow Cu(NO_3)_{2(aq)} + 2NO_{2(g)} + 2H_2O_{(l)}$$

Concentrated nitric acid is such a powerful oxidizing agent that it will oxidize flesh and wood as well as rubber. It is therefore a dangerous acid.

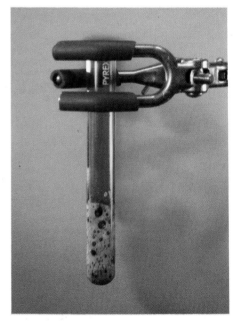

Fig. 13.23 Concentrated nitric acid reacts vigorously with copper. Poisonous fumes of nitrogen(IV) oxide are given off

Uses of nitric acid

Large amounts of nitric acid are used in the making of fertilizers such as ammonium nitrate. Also, it is used as a nitrating agent in the production of explosives such as T.N.T. (tri-nitrotoluene). Dyes as well as man-made fibres are also other products obtained using nitric acid (see Fig. 3.24).

Nitrates

These are the salts of nitric acid. They all dissolve in water. You have already seen in Chapter 8 (page 94) that nitrates decompose on heating (thermal decomposition). The amount of decomposition depends on the reactivity of the metal present. For example, when sodium nitrate is heated, sodium nitrite and oxygen are produced.

$$\text{sodium nitrate} \xrightarrow{\text{heat}} \text{sodium nitrite} + \text{oxygen}$$

$$2NaNO_{3(s)} \longrightarrow 2NaNO_{2(s)} + O_{2(g)}$$

However, when silver nitrate is heated it decomposes to the metal.

$$\text{silver nitrate} \longrightarrow \text{silver} + \text{oxygen} + \text{nitrogen(IV) oxide}$$

$$2AgNO_{3(s)} \longrightarrow 2Ag_{(s)} + O_{2(g)} + 2NO_{2(g)}$$

Chemical test for nitrates
A few drops of sodium hydroxide solution is added to a dilute solution of the suspected nitrate. Devarda's alloy (an alloy of aluminium, copper and zinc) is then added and the mixture boiled. If ammonia gas is given off then the compound was a nitrate.

Uses of nitrates
Potassium nitrate is used in gun powder and fireworks, whilst silver nitrate is used as a chemical test for chlorides (see Chapter 15, page 213). Sodium, potassium and ammonium nitrates are used as fertilizers.

Fig. 13.24 Some man-made fibres and dyes are made using nitric acid

Fertilizers

It will be clear that the two industrial processes so far described in this chapter are part of an overall scheme, the end product of which is a range of nitrogen-containing fertilizers (see Table 13.1).

Why do we need artificial fertilizers?

The existence of the Billingham plant (Fig. 13.16) and of others like it, suggests a very substantial market for their nitrogen-containing fertilizers. Why is this so? We have known for many years that healthy plant growth depends upon the existence in the soil of essential nutrients. These nutrients include nitrogen, phosphorus and potassium, which are particularly important in promoting the growth of agricultural crops, as well as a number of other elements, some of which are required only in very small quantities, e.g. calcium, magnesium, sodium, sulphur, copper, iron, zinc, manganese and boron. Adding manure and compost to the soil is one important way of returning to the soil some of the nutrients used by plants as they grow. However, the intensive cultivation of crops developed to feed a rapidly-growing world population often removes nutrients from the soil more quickly than they can be replaced by natural means. Artificial fertilizers are therefore added to the soil to make sure that it can continue to support the growth of crops. Artificial

Fertilizer	Formula
Ammonium nitrate	NH_4NO_3
Urea	$CO(NH_2)_2$
Ammonia solution	$NH_{3(aq)}$
Ammonium sulphate	$(NH_4)_2SO_4$
Ammonium phosphate	$(NH_4)_3PO_4$

Table 13.1 Some fertilizers which contain nitrogen

fertilizers may also, of course, enable plants to be grown on land previously unable to support the growth of crops because it lacked some, or all, of the essential nutrients.

If artificial fertilizers are not used properly, problems can arise. For example, an excess of nitrates in the soil can be washed, by rainfall, into rivers, streams or lakes, thus disturbing the natural balance of plant and animal life in these waters or heavily contaminating a source used as part of a domestic water supply.

Commercial fertilizers

Commercial compound fertilizers must by law indicate the proportion by percentage of the elements they contain, usually nitrogen (N), phosphorus (P) and potassium (K). Such percentages are known as the NPK values of fertilizers.

N—nitrogen fertilizers are those shown in Table 13.1
P—phosphorus-containing substances include calcium superphosphate, $Ca(H_2PO_4)_2$
K—the potassium-containing substance is potassium chloride

Fig. 13.25 shows a series of commercially available fertilizers.

Fig. 13.25 Which fertilizer contains most nitrogen?

Problems with fertilizers

The ever-growing use of fertilizers is not without its problems. For example, finite natural resources such as natural gas are being used up in the manufacture of fertilizers. Additionally, it has been estimated that some 15 large plants for ammonia synthesis will need to be built annually to keep pace with demand. We are also becoming increasingly aware of possible side effects of the high rates of fertilizer application to the land. This can particularly affect lakes and rivers (see Fig. 13.26). The 'wash off' of fertilizers particularly nitrates and phosphates into rivers, streams and lakes can encourage the very rapid growth of algae or other plants. The rapid growth of algae is often referred to as 'a bloom'. Such 'blooms' can severely upset the natural balance of the lakes and streams. As the algae die and decay, oxygen is removed from the water and this adversely affects other organisms. In extreme cases no normal aquatic life can survive. There are also worries about the effect of agricultural fertilizers, especially nitrates, on the quality of public water supplies.

Fig. 13.26 An algae-covered stream

1 The diagram below shows a simplified version of the nitrogen cycle.

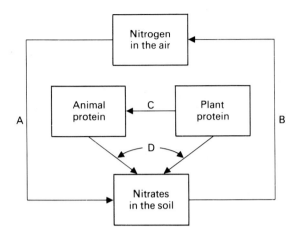

a) Name the processes labelled A, B, C, and D.
b) Name one family of plants which can absorb nitrogen directly from the air and give two examples of this type of plant.
c) What does the term 'fixing nitrogen' mean?
d) Name two man-made substances in which nitrogen has been fixed.

2 a) Give the names of two reagents you would normally use to prepare ammonia gas in the laboratory.
b) Explain how you would dry the ammonia before collection.
c) Explain why it is possible to collect ammonia as shown below.

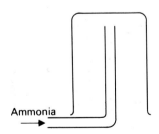

Ammonia

d) i) Name and give the formula of the substance formed when excess ammonia reacts with dilute sulphuric acid.
ii) Give one large-scale use for the product formed in this reaction.
e) Describe what you would see when an excess of ammonia solution is added 'dropwise' to a solution of copper(II) sulphate.

3 The process for manufacturing nitric acid is shown in diagram form below.

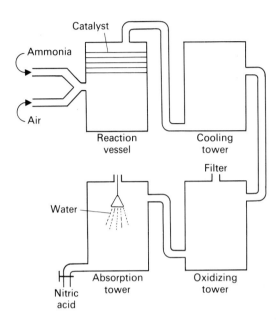

a) What is the catalyst used in the reaction vessel?
b) In the reaction vessel, ammonia is oxidized to nitrogen monoxide(NO) and water. Write a balanced chemical equation for this reaction.
c) The gaseous mixture from the reaction vessel is then cooled and passed into the oxidizing tower. Write a word equation and a balanced chemical equation for the oxidation.
d) The absorption of nitrogen(IV) oxide in water then produces nitric acid. Name one pollution problem associated with this absorption.
e) Give two large-scale uses of nitric acid.
f) i) Give two examples of how dilute nitric acid will behave as an acid.
ii) Give two examples (one with a non-metal and one with a metal) of the oxidizing action of concentrated nitric acid.
g) How does dilute nitric acid react with copper metal?

4 a) i) Name a metallic nitrate which upon heating gives oxygen as the only gaseous product.
ii) Write a word equation and balanced chemical equation for the reaction.
b) i) Name a metal nitrate which upon heating produces two gaseous products.
ii) Write a word equation and a balanced chemical equation for the decomposition.

c) You are given a sample of a substance which is thought to be a nitrate. How could you test this substance to show that it is a nitrate?

d) Give one use of each of the following nitrates: ammonium nitrate, potassium nitrate, silver nitrate.

5 a) Why have commercial fertilizers become necessary in present methods of food production?

b) Discuss some of the problems associated with the use of these commercial fertilizers.

6 a) A market gardener purchases two different fertilizers. One is labelled 17.17.17 and the other 22.11.11.
   i) What comment can you make about the second fertilizer? (1)
   ii) For what specific benefit to his crops do you think the gardener intends to use this second fertilizer? (1)

b) A common nitrogenous fertilizer can be manufactured by the process outlined below. Name the substances A to E. (5)

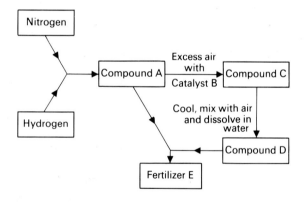

c) Name *one* compound, other than E, used as a nitrogenous fertilizer. (1)

d) In many fertilizers, the 'combined nitrogen' is present in a positive ion. How would you test the fertilizer for the presence of this positive ion? (2)

(JMB 1982)

7 a) Give an account of the industrial production of ammonia from nitrogen and hydrogen by the Haber process. Include in your answer a brief statement of how the starting materials are obtained. (11)

b) State and explain one important industrial use of ammonia. (3)

c) When dry ammonia is passed over heated copper(II) oxide a colourless liquid, a red-brown powder and a colourless gas are obtained.
   i) Name the products.
   ii) Write an equation for the reaction, stating the type of reaction.
   iii) Explain how the products formed show that ammonia contains nitrogen and hydrogen. (6)

(WJEC 1982)

8 Table 1 shows the amounts of three essential elements applied as man-made fertilizers in Britain from 1874 to 1975. Study it carefully and then answer the questions below.

Name of element / Year	Mass of elements applied in man-made fertilizers/thousands of tonnes		
	Nitrogen	Phosphorus	Potassium
1874	35	30	3
1939	61	76	63
1952	184	123	145
1965	574	212	358
1975	984	172	330

Table 1

a) Which nutrient element has shown the greatest percentage increase in application as fertilizer in the last century? Explain your answer. (2)

b) Explain *two* possible reasons for the general increase in the rate of application of fertilizers. (4)

c) In what form do plants take up the chemicals applied to the soil as fertilizers? (2)

d) Two typical nitrogen-containing fertilizers are ammonium nitrate, NH_4NO_3, and ammonium phosphate, $(NH_4)_3PO_4$. Which of these fertilizers contains the greater proportion of nitrogen? (Show your working.) (4)
(Relative atomic masses: $A_r(N) = 14$; $A_r(H) = 1$; $A_r(O) = 16$; $A_r(P) = 31$.)

e) Suggest *three* other factors which ought to be taken into account when comparing the usefulness of two fertilizers. (3)

f) State *one* alternative to the use of man-made fertilizers. Omitting considerations of cost, state *one* advantage and *one* disadvantage of the alternative you have chosen. (3)

(AEB 1983)

9 Ammonia is a key substance in the manufacture of fertilizers such as ammonium sulphate.
   a) Name the sources of
      i) the hydrogen and
      ii) the nitrogen used in the large-scale manufacture of ammonia. (2)
   b) Write balanced equations for:
      i) the formation of ammonia from hydrogen and nitrogen;
      ii) the formation of ammonium sulphate from ammonia and sulphuric acid. (4)
   c) What mass of nitrogen, to the nearest tonne, is contained in 100 tonnes of ammonia? (4)
   d) The first stage in the large-scale conversion of ammonia to nitric acid is represented by the equation:

$$4NH_{3(g)} + 5O_{2(g)} \rightarrow 6H_2O_{(g)} + 4NO_{(g)}$$

   Calculate the volume of oxygen required to react with 1 dm³ of ammonia at the same temperature and pressure. (2)
   e) State one commercial use for nitric acid other than fertilizer manufacture. (1)
   (AEB 1983)

10 a) Nitrogen is an element essential for the development of plants and animals. The percentage of nitrogen in the atmosphere remains constant by the operation of the nitrogen cycle in nature.
      i) Name the type of compound containing nitrogen which is present in all plants and animals. (1)
      ii) Most plants take in nitrogen in a combined form. State the atmospheric conditions necessary for nitrogen from the air to be converted directly to nitrogen compounds. (1)
      iii) Some plants are able to use nitrogen directly from the atmosphere. Give one example of such a plant. (1)
      iv) Describe two natural processes by which nitrogen in plants is eventually returned to the soil. (2)
   b) Ammonia is prepared in the laboratory by the action of heat on a mixture of an ammonium compound and an alkali. The dry gas is collected by upward delivery.
      i) Name a suitable ammonium compound. (1)
      ii) Name a suitable alkali. (1)
      iii) Name two other products of the reaction. (2)
      iv) Write a symbol equation for the reaction. (2)
      v) Which one of the following is used to dry ammonia? (1)
         A calcium carbonate
         B anhydrous calcium chloride
         C calcium oxide
         D anhydrous copper(II) sulphate
         E concentrated sulphuric acid
      vi) State two properties of ammonia which determine the method of collection. (2)
      vii) Explain why dry ammonia has no effect on dry indicator paper but a solution of ammonia has a pH value greater than 7. (2)
   c) When concentrated nitric acid is added to a solution containing iron(II) ions, Fe^{2+}, a brown gas (X) is given off and a solution containing iron(III) ions, Fe^{3+}, is formed.
      i) State, giving a reason for your answer, the type of reaction taking place when iron(II) ions are converted to iron(III) ions. (3)
      ii) Write an ion-electron equation for the conversion of iron(II) ions to iron(III) ions. (1)
      iii) Give the name or formula of gas (X). (1)
   (NEA 1985)

SULPHUR

Fig. 14.1   Fireworks contain sulphur

Sulphur is a yellow, brittle, non-conducting solid (see Fig. 14.2) with a fairly low melting point (115°C). It does not dissolve in water but will dissolve in solvents such as carbon disulphide or methylbenzene (toluene) (see Fig. 14.3).

Sulphur is found in metal ores such as zinc blende (ZnS) and copper pyrites ($CuFeS_2$), but it also occurs as the free element in sulphur beds in Poland, Iraq, USSR and USA. The sulphur beds are generally 100–200 metres below ground level. Between the sulphur deposits and the surface are layers of clay and sand and so a special method has been developed to extract the sulphur. It is called the **Frasch process.**

Fig. 14.2   Roll sulphur

Fig. 14.3(a)   Sulphur will not dissolve in water

Fig. 14.3(b)   Sulphur produces a pale yellow solution when dissolved in carbon disulphide or methylbenzene

The Frasch process

A 20 cm diameter steel pipe is sunk into the deposits. Two smaller diameter pipes are put down inside this first pipe to form a set of three concentric pipes (see Fig. 14.4). Superheated water at 170°C, at high pressure, is now pumped down the outer pipe. Sulphur melts at 115°C and so it becomes liquid. Hot air, at high pressure, is now forced down the centre pipe and this forces the molten sulphur up the remaining pipe. The heat from the outer and inner pipes keeps the sulphur molten on its journey to the surface. The molten sulphur is then stored in collecting tanks. The sulphur obtained by this process is already 99% pure. Some of the sulphur is cooled and solidified; the remainder is kept molten and sold in liquid form (see Fig. 14.5).

Fig. 14.5   Solid grains of sulphur after processing

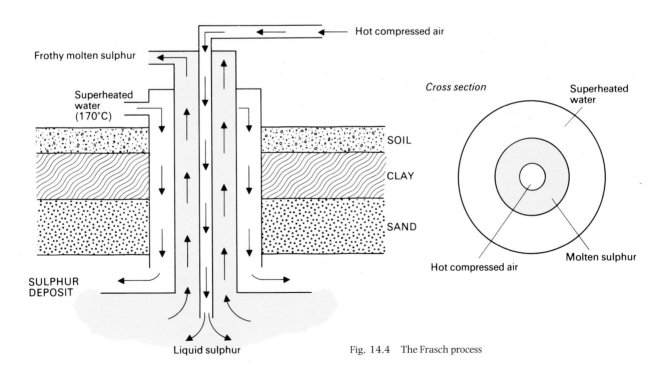

Fig. 14.4   The Frasch process

What is sulphur used for? Large quantities of sulphur are used to make sulphuric acid which in turn is used to make a variety of useful materials (see page 202). Sulphur is also used to **vulcanize** rubber (see Fig. 14.6). Rubber which has been vulcanized is harder and more elastic. Some sulphur is also used in fireworks and matches (see Fig. 14.1 and 14.6).

(b)   Matches contain some sulphur

(a) H_2SO_4

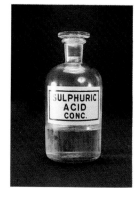

(c)   Tapping a rubber tree. The rubber will be vulcanized using sulphur

Fig. 14.6   Some uses of sulphur

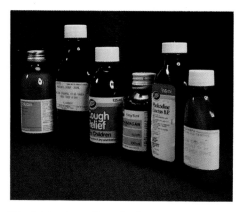

(d)   Sulphur is used to make drugs

Allotropes of sulphur

Solid sulphur exists as molecules. These molecules each contain eight sulphur atoms joined together by covalent bonds. The atoms are arranged as shown in Fig. 14.7.

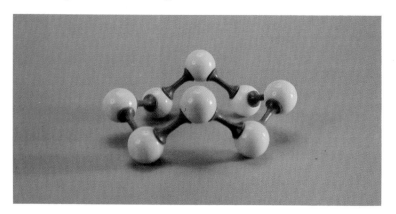

Fig. 14.7(a)   A molecular model of the sulphur 'molecule'

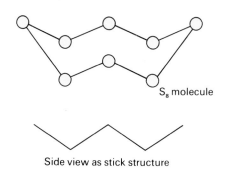

S_8 molecule

Side view as stick structure

Fig. 14.7(b)   Sulphur exists as S_8 molecules

Like carbon, sulphur has allotropes. Its main allotropes are called **rhombic sulphur** and **monoclinic sulphur**.

Rhombic sulphur

The sulphur we use in the laboratory is rhombic sulphur. Rhombic sulphur is the most stable allotrope of sulphur below $96\,°C$. In rhombic sulphur the S_8 molecules are packed as shown in Fig. 14.8. When we repeat this sort of pattern with a very large number of S_8 units then a crystal of rhombic sulphur forms (see Fig. 14.9).

This type of sulphur is formed whenever a solution of sulphur is allowed to evaporate below $96\,°C$. If a saturated solution of sulphur in methylbenzene is left to crystallize very slowly at room temperature, crystals of rhombic sulphur form (see Fig. 14.10).

Fig. 14.8   In rhombic sulphur the S_8 units pack like this

Fig. 14.9   A crystal of rhombic sulphur

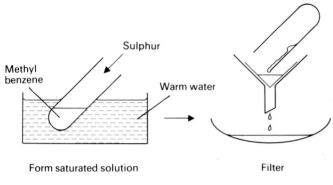

Methyl benzene   Sulphur   Warm water

Crystals of rhombic sulphur

Form saturated solution   Filter   Evaporate slowly

Fig. 14.10   Making rhombic sulphur

Monoclinic sulphur

Above $96\,°C$ monoclinic sulphur is the more stable form. In monoclinic sulphur the S_8 units are packed as shown in Fig. 14.11. By repeating this pattern a crystal of monoclinic sulphur forms (see Fig. 14.12).

Monoclinic sulphur is formed by heating sulphur until it just melts. If this molten sulphur is then poured into a filter paper as shown in Fig. 14.13 and allowed to cool, a crust will form on the surface. If the filter paper is now opened then needle-like crystals will be seen growing down from the crust. If monoclinic sulphur is left at room temperature then it very slowly changes to rhombic sulphur.

$$\text{monoclinic sulphur} \xrightarrow[96\,°C]{\text{below}} \text{rhombic sulphur}$$

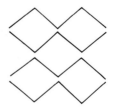

Fig. 14.11   In monoclinic sulphur the S_8 units pack like this

Fig. 14.12   A crystal of monoclinic sulphur

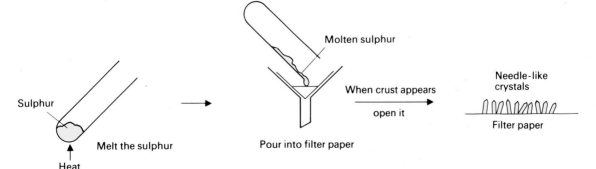

Sulphur   Molten sulphur   Needle-like crystals

Melt the sulphur   When crust appears, open it

Heat   Pour into filter paper   Filter paper

Fig. 14.13   Making monoclinic sulphur

Plastic sulphur

This is *not* an allotrope of sulphur. This type of sulphur is produced by heating sulphur to its boiling point of $444\,°C$ and pouring the hot running liquid into a beaker of cold water (see Fig. 14.14).

Plastic sulphur is so named because it is 'plastic', i.e. it has elastic properties. When sulphur is heated to this very high temperature the S_8 rings open and then break up into pairs of sulphur atoms (see Fig. 14.15). When the liquid is suddenly cooled the rings do not have time to form. Long tangled chains of sulphur atoms form instead. This is plastic sulphur. It is rubbery and will stretch. Plastic sulphur will slowly change to rhombic sulphur at room temperature.

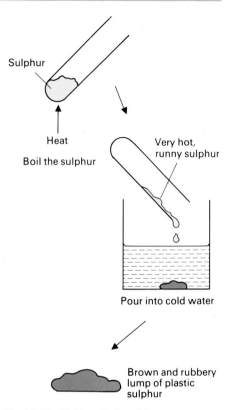

Fig. 14.14   Making plastic sulphur

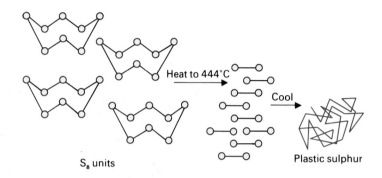

Fig. 14.15   The S_8 units break up when heated strongly

Some other properties of sulphur

Sulphur is in group VI of the periodic table. This is the same group as oxygen. It is less reactive than oxygen, however, it will still react with both metals and non-metals. For example, it will react with metals like iron forming iron(II) sulphide.

$$\text{iron} + \text{sulphur} \xrightarrow{\text{heat}} \text{iron sulphide}$$

$$\text{Fe}_{(s)} + \text{S}_{(s)} \longrightarrow \text{FeS}_{(s)}$$

It will also burn in oxygen with a blue flame producing sulphur dioxide.

$$\text{sulphur} + \text{oxygen} \xrightarrow{\text{heat}} \text{sulphur dioxide}$$

$$\text{S}_{(s)} + \text{O}_{2(g)} \longrightarrow \text{SO}_{2(g)}$$

Sulphur dioxide (SO_2)

This is a colourless gas with a choking smell. It is denser than air and is present as a pollutant gas (see Chapter 12, page 173). It is prepared in the laboratory, in apparatus like that shown in Fig. 14.17, by the reaction of a sulphite, such as sodium sulphite, with dilute hydrochloric acid.

$$\text{sodium sulphite} + \text{dilute hydrochloric acid} \longrightarrow \text{sulphur dioxide} + \text{water} + \text{sodium chloride}$$

$$\text{Na}_2\text{SO}_{3(s)} + 2\text{HCl}_{(aq)} \longrightarrow \text{SO}_{2(g)} + \text{H}_2\text{O}_{(l)} + 2\text{NaCl}_{(aq)}$$

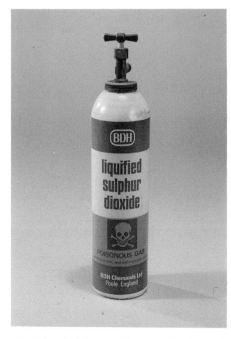

Fig. 14.16   Sulphur dioxide can be liquefied and stored in pressurized cylinders

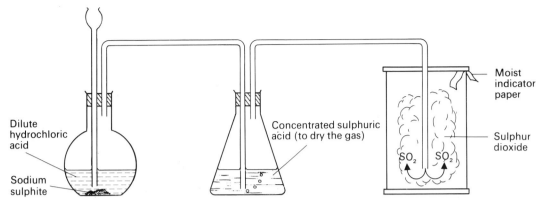

Fig. 14.17   Apparatus for making sulphur dioxide

Some properties of sulphur dioxide

Sulphur dioxide is very soluble in water. It is so soluble it will undergo the fountain experiment (see Chapter 13, page 184). As a non-metallic oxide, it dissolves in water to produce an acidic solution of sulphurous acid.

sulphur dioxide + water $\rightleftharpoons$ sulphurous acid

$$SO_{2(g)} \quad + H_2O_{(l)} \rightleftharpoons \quad H_2SO_{3(aq)}$$

This acid is not very stable and easily decomposes back to water and sulphur dioxide.

The high solubility of the gas means that it dissolves easily in rainwater producing an acid solution which attacks both metal and stone (see Fig. 14.18). It is also very harmful to plants and animals.

Since sulphur dioxide is acidic, it reacts with alkalis. Thus, when it is bubbled through solutions of alkali, such as sodium hydroxide, salts called sulphites are formed.

sodium hydroxide + sulphur dioxide $\longrightarrow$ sodium sulphite + water

$$2NaOH_{(aq)} \quad + \quad SO_{2(aq)} \quad \longrightarrow \quad Na_2SO_{3(aq)} \quad + H_2O_{(l)}$$

Sodium sulphite is a metal sulphite. It is a salt of sulphurous acid.

Sulphur dioxide will act as a reducing agent. For example, it will reduce acidified purple potassium manganate(VII) solution to a colourless solution of manganese(II) sulphate (see Fig. 14.19(a)). It will also reduce orange acidified potassium dichromate(VI) to a green solution of chromium(III) sulphate (see Fig. 14.19(b)). These two reactions are often used as tests for the gas.

Fig. 14.18   Acid rain has eroded the statue

Fig. 14.19(a)   Acidified potassium manganate(VII) is reduced by sulphur dioxide

Fig. 14.19(b)   Acidified potassium dichromate(VI) is reduced by sulphur dioxide

Sulphur dioxide will also act as an oxidizing agent. If a burning splint is plunged into a gas jar of sulphur dioxide it will go out. However, if a piece of strongly burning magnesium is plunged into a gas jar of this gas it continues to burn with a spluttering flame. A white powder (magnesium oxide) and a yellow deposit of sulphur are produced (see Fig. 14.20).

$$\text{magnesium} + \text{sulphur dioxide} \longrightarrow \text{magnesium oxide} + \text{sulphur}$$

$$2Mg_{(s)} \quad + \quad SO_{2(g)} \quad \longrightarrow \quad 2MgO_{(s)} \quad + \quad S_{(s)}$$

Uses of sulphur dioxide

Sulphur dioxide solution is used as a bleaching agent for wool and wood pulp in paper-making. Sulphur dioxide is also used as a preservative for jam and fruit. However, its most important use is in the manufacture of sulphuric acid.

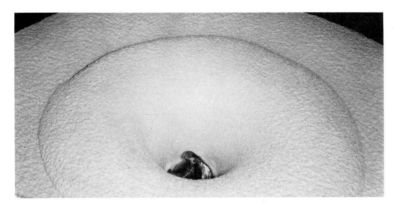

Fig. 14.20   Magnesium oxide and sulphur—the result of burning magnesium in sulphur dioxide

Fig. 14.21   Bleaching woodpulp slurry

Sulphuric acid (H_2SO_4)

Sulphuric acid is a chemical of major industrial importance. It is difficult to imagine life without sulphuric acid since it is used at some stage in the manufacture of a vast array of materials. For example, it is used to make fibres, chemicals, paints, detergents, fertilizers and dyes (see Table 14.1 and Figs 14.22–24). It is not surprising, therefore, that many millions of tonnes of this substance are made in Britain each year.

Fig. 14.22   15.7% of H_2SO_4 is used to make paints and pigments

Fig. 14.23   11.7% of H_2SO_4 is used to make soaps and detergents

Fig. 14.24   30.4% of H_2SO_4 is used to make fertilizers

Manufacture of sulphuric acid

The modern process for manufacturing sulphuric acid is known as the **Contact process** (see Fig. 14.25). The Contact process makes use of the following reversible reaction.

sulphur dioxide + oxygen $\rightleftharpoons$ sulphur(VI) oxide (sulphur trioxide)

$$2SO_{2(g)} \quad + \quad O_{2(g)} \rightleftharpoons \quad 2SO_{3(g)}$$

The sulphur dioxide for this process comes from two main sources. The first of these involves the heating of a metal sulphide ore such as zinc blende (ZnS) in air.

zinc sulphide + oxygen $\xrightarrow{\text{heat}}$ zinc oxide + sulphur dioxide

$$2ZnS_{(s)} \quad + \quad 3O_{2(g)} \longrightarrow \quad 2ZnO_{(s)} + \quad 2SO_{2(g)}$$

The process by which the majority of the sulphur dioxide is produced is that of burning sulphur in air. Air is used as the source of oxygen.

sulphur + oxygen $\longrightarrow$ sulphur dioxide

$$S_{(s)} \quad + \quad O_{2(g)} \longrightarrow \quad SO_{2(g)}$$

The sulphur dioxide and oxygen are then cleaned, dried and heated to a temperature of between 400–550°C. The hot gas mixture is fed into the reaction chamber where it is passed over a catalyst of vanadium(V) oxide (V_2O_5). The gas mixture leaving the reaction vessel contains about 98% sulphur(VI) oxide.

At this point the gases are cooled. If the sulphur(VI) oxide were dissolved directly in water to produce sulphuric acid much heat and 'misting' would occur. These misty acid fumes are difficult to deal with so the sulphur(VI) oxide is dissolved in concentrated sulphuric acid (98%) to give **oleum**, which is a thick, fuming, oily liquid. The oleum is then added to sufficient water to react with the dissolved sulphur(VI) oxide.

sulphur(VI) oxide + water $\longrightarrow$ sulphuric acid

$$SO_{3(g)} \quad + H_2O_{(l)} \longrightarrow \quad H_2SO_{4(l)}$$

The result is 98% sulphuric acid, 2% water.

UK usage of H_2SO_4	
Fertilizers/Agricultural	30.4%
Chemicals	16.4%
Paints/Pigments	15.7%
Detergents/Soaps	11.7%
Natural/Man made fibres	9.4%
Metallurgy	2.3%
Dyestuffs/Intermediates	2.0%
Oil/Petrol	1.0%
Miscellaneous	11.1%

Table 14.1

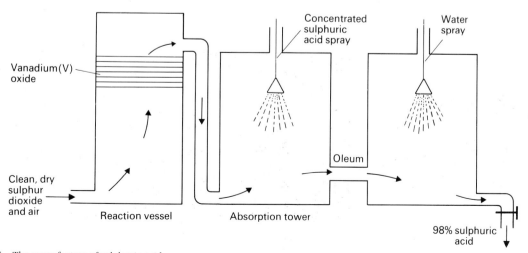

Fig. 14.25   The manufacture of sulphuric acid

Fig. 14.26   A contact process plant

As in other industrial processes, it is possible to reduce the cost of running such a large and complex plant. For example, the production of sulphur(VI) oxide is very exothermic. The heat given out may be utilized to increase the temperature of the incoming gases to the reaction vessel.

The present Contact process releases small quantities of sulphur dioxide into the air. This means that the process is not as 'clean' as the manufacturers would like. However, research continues to try to reduce the amount of released sulphur dioxide. The only other waste materials are the spent catalysts and warm water.

Dilute sulphuric acid

Dilute sulphuric acid will affect indicators turning both blue litmus and pH paper red. Dilute sulphuric acid will also react with bases such as sodium hydroxide or zinc oxide to form a salt and water.

$$\text{sodium hydroxide} + \text{dilute sulphuric acid} \longrightarrow \text{sodium sulphate} + \text{water}$$

$$2NaOH_{(aq)} + H_2SO_{4(aq)} \longrightarrow Na_2SO_{4(aq)} + 2H_2O_{(l)}$$

$$\text{zinc oxide} + \text{dilute sulphuric acid} \longrightarrow \text{zinc sulphate} + \text{water}$$

$$ZnO_{(s)} + H_2SO_{4(aq)} \longrightarrow ZnSO_{4(aq)} + H_2O_{(l)}$$

With many metals it produces the metal sulphate and hydrogen. For example, magnesium reacts to form magnesium sulphate and hydrogen.

$$\text{magnesium} + \text{dilute sulphuric acid} \longrightarrow \text{magnesium sulphate} + \text{hydrogen}$$

$$Mg_{(s)} + H_2SO_{4(aq)} \longrightarrow MgSO_{4(aq)} + H_{2(g)}$$

Sulphates
Sulphates are salts of sulphuric acid. They usually dissolve in water. The exceptions are calcium, lead and barium sulphates.

Calcium sulphate is used as 'plaster of Paris' to set broken bones. Magnesium sulphate is used as a purgative, ammonium sulphate is used as a fertilizer and barium sulphate is used in X-ray analysis.

To test for a sulphate a few drops of barium chloride solution and dilute hydrochloric acid are added to a dilute solution of the suspected sulphate. If a sulphate is present a white precipitate of barium sulphate is formed (see Fig. 14.27).

Fig. 14.27   A positive test for a sulphate

Concentrated sulphuric acid

In this form sulphuric acid will remove water from a variety of substances—it is a powerful dehydrating agent. For example, if a few drops of concentrated sulphuric acid are added to hydrated copper(II) sulphate then slowly the deep blue colour disappears (see Fig. 14.28).

$$\text{copper(II) sulphate pentahydrate} \xrightarrow{-\text{water}} \text{anhydrous copper(II) sulphate}$$

$$\underset{\text{blue}}{CuSO_4 \cdot 5H_2O_{(s)}} \xrightarrow{-5H_2O} \underset{\text{white}}{CuSO_{4(s)}}$$

It will also dehydrate cane sugar. Cane sugar, or sucrose, is a carbohydrate and the concentrated acid removes the oxygen and hydrogen as water. A black deposit of carbon is left (see Fig. 14.29(c)).

$$\text{sugar} \xrightarrow{-\text{water}} \text{carbon}$$

$$C_{12}H_{22}O_{11} \xrightarrow{-11H_2O} 12C$$

Many gases are also dried by passing them through concentrated sulphuric acid. One exception is ammonia gas—it is alkaline and cannot be dried in this way.

Concentrated sulphuric acid will also react as a powerful oxidizing agent. For example, when heated with metals such as copper it will oxidize them to copper ions and form copper(II) sulphate.

$$\text{copper} + \text{concentrated sulphuric acid} \xrightarrow{\text{heat}} \text{copper(II) sulphate} + \text{water} + \text{sulphur dioxide}$$

$$Cu_{(s)} + 2H_2SO_{4(l)} \longrightarrow CuSO_{4(aq)} + 2H_2O_{(l)} + SO_{2(g)}$$

This reaction is often used as an alternative method for making sulphur dioxide in the laboratory.

An interesting property of concentrated sulphuric acid is that it can be used to produce nitric acid and hydrochloric acid. (Both these acids are more volatile than concentrated sulphuric acid.)

If concentrated sulphuric acid is added to a metal chloride, such as sodium chloride, then hydrogen chloride gas is produced (see Chapter 15, page 212).

$$\text{sodium chloride} + \text{concentrated sulphuric acid} \longrightarrow \text{sodium hydrogen sulphate} + \text{hydrogen chloride}$$

$$NaCl_{(s)} + H_2SO_{4(l)} \longrightarrow NaHSO_{4(s)} + HCl_{(g)}$$

If the hydrogen chloride is dissolved in water then dilute hydrochloric acid is produced.

If concentrated sulphuric acid is heated with a metal nitrate such as sodium nitrate, then nitric acid vapour is produced.

$$\text{sodium nitrate} + \text{concentrated sulphuric acid} \xrightarrow{\text{heat}} \text{sodium hydrogen sulphate} + \text{nitric acid}$$

$$NaNO_{3(s)} + H_2SO_{4(l)} \longrightarrow NaHSO_{4(s)} + HNO_{3(g)}$$

Neither of these methods would be suitable for making these acids on the large scale.

Fig. 14.28   Effect of concentrated sulphuric acid on hydrated copper(II) sulphate

(a)   (b)

(c)

Fig. 14.29   Concentrated sulphuric acid removes the elements of water from cane sugar leaving a black deposit of carbon

———— QUESTIONS ————

1 Sulphur has an atomic number of 16, and it is represented as

$$^{32}_{16}S$$

a) How many electrons are there in a sulphur atom?

b) How many neutrons are there in a sulphur atom?

c) How many electrons will there be in the outer shell (energy level) of this atom?

d) To which group of the periodic table does sulphur belong?

e) Write down the names of two other elements found in the same group as sulphur.

f) Write down the symbol of the ion sulphur will form on its own.

g) Give one example of a metal and a non-metal with which sulphur will react. Also, write word equations and balanced chemical equations for the reaction which takes place between sulphur and the chosen element.

h) Describe with the aid of a diagram the extraction of sulphur by the Frasch process.

i) Give two large-scale uses of sulphur.

2 The diagram below shows the apparatus which could be used to prepare a sample of dry sulphur dioxide.

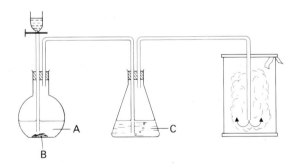

a) Name the chemicals labelled A, B, and C.

b) What is the function of liquid C?

c) Write a word equation and a balanced chemical equation for the preparation of sulphur dioxide.

d) Name the solution produced when sulphur dioxide dissolves in water.

e) Sulphur dioxide is very soluble in water. Describe an experiment which would show this property.

f) Sulphur dioxide is said to be an atmospheric pollutant. Mention two undesirable consequences of the pollution of the atmosphere by this gas.

g) Give one example in each case of sulphur dioxide as

i) a reducing agent;

ii) an oxidizing agent.

h) Give two large-scale uses of sulphur dioxide.

3

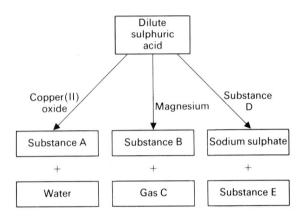

a) Name and give the symbol or formula of :

i) substances A, B, D, and E;

ii) gas C.

b) Write a word equation and a balanced chemical equation for the reactions in which substances A, B and E are formed.

c) Give a chemical test to confirm the identity of gas C.

d) i) Sodium sulphate is a 'normal salt'. What does this term mean?

ii) Give a chemical test which could be used to show that an unknown substance was a soluble sulphate.

e) Give one use for each of the following sulphates: magnesium sulphate, calcium sulphate, ammonium sulphate.

4 a) Concentrated sulphuric acid will react with hydrated copper(II) sulphate, with copper metal and with sugar. For each of these reactions:

i) write a word equation and a balanced chemical equation;

ii) state whether the acid is behaving as an *oxidizing agent* or a *dehydrating agent*.

b) Complete the following chemical equation:

$$NaCl_{(s)} + H_2SO_{4(l)} \longrightarrow NaHSO_{4(s)} + \text{gas A}$$

i) What is gas A? Write down its chemical formula.

ii) Name all the other chemical reagents in the equation.

iii) Gas A will dissolve quite readily in water to produce an acidic solution B. Name solution B.

c) Concentrated sulphuric acid will react with metal nitrates to produce another important mineral acid, C.
  i) Name acid C.
  ii) Name a suitable nitrate from which acid C can be made.

5 a) When powdered sulphur is added to an organic solvent, e.g. dimethylbenzene and the mixture warmed to $140\,^{\circ}C$, the sulphur dissolves. Crystals of sulphur form when the solution is slowly cooled to $100\,^{\circ}C$.
  i) Name the type of sulphur crystals formed. (1)
  ii) Describe the shape of the sulphur crystals. (1)

b) When the crystals obtained from the dimethylbenzene are kept at room temperature for some time, another crystalline form of sulphur is produced.
  i) Name the type of crystals formed at room temperature. (1)
  ii) Describe the shape of the crystals. (1)

c) Name the property of sulphur illustrated by the experiments in parts (a) and (b). (1)

d) When a stream of dry air is passed over burning sulphur, a colourless gas is produced. The gas condenses to form a liquid which boils at $-9\,^{\circ}C$ at atmospheric pressure.
  i) Name the gas formed. (1)
  ii) Write a symbol equation for the reaction forming the gas. (1)
  iii) How must the pressure on the substance be changed to keep it liquid at $20\,^{\circ}C$ (room temperature)? (1)
  iv) The colourless liquid has no reaction with dry indicator paper but gives an acidic reaction with moist indicator paper. Explain these observations. (2)

(JMB/WMEB 1982)

6 a) Sulphuric acid is manufactured by the Contact process. A mixture of sulphur dioxide and excess air, preheated to $450\,^{\circ}C$, is passed over a catalyst.
  i) State how the sulphur dioxide is made and give an equation for the reaction.
  ii) Write the equation for the reaction of sulphur dioxide with air.
  iii) Name a suitable catalyst for this reaction.
  iv) The product of this reaction does react directly with water forming sulphuric acid, but the method is impractical because an acid mist forms. Describe the modern indirect method of converting the product of the reaction between sulphur dioxide and air to sulphuric acid. (8)

b) In 1843 von Liebig said:

'You will perceive that it is no exaggeration to say we may fairly judge of the commercial prosperity of a country from the amount of sulphuric acid it consumes.'

This statement is still true today. Over four million tonnes of the acid are used every year in the UK.
  i) The most important use is for making fertilizers. State how one named fertilizer could be made from sulphuric acid.
  ii) State two other industrial uses of sulphuric acid. (4)

c) Sulphur dioxide is an acidic gas and is also an industrial pollutant.
  i) Why do you think that buildings made of limestone (calcium carbonate) eventually start to crumble if sulphur dioxide is present in the atmosphere?
  ii) Give one test for sulphur dioxide. (5)

(AEB 1982)

7 Rhombic (α) sulphur and monoclinic (β) sulphur are allotropes.
a) Explain what is meant by allotropes.
b) Which allotrope of sulphur is the stable form at room temperature?
c) Name one other element which has allotropes and give their names. (6)

(Cambridge 1983)

CHLORINE AND HYDROGEN CHLORIDE

Fig. 15.1   These soldiers in World War I were waiting for a chlorine gas attack

Chlorine

Chlorine is a pale yellow-green gas, which is denser than air. It has a choking smell and in even small quantities it can be of considerable harm to people and animals. It was this property along with its high density which caused it to be used as a poisonous gas in the trenches during the First World War 1914–18.

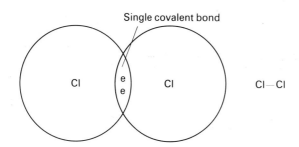

Fig. 15.2   The chlorine molecule

Fig. 15.3   Chlorine gas

Fig. 15.4(a)   Chlorine is used to make PVC

Fig. 15.4(b)   The weedkillers and pesticides on this shelf contain chlorine

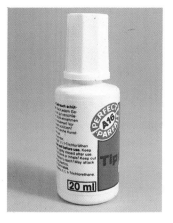

Fig. 15.4(c)   The solvent here is trichloroethane

In spite of its dangerous nature, chlorine is a very useful substance (see Fig. 15.4). The UK produces about 2 million tonnes annually, the USA over five times as much. It is a major industrial chemical being used not only in the extraction of metals such as titanium, but also in the manufacture of plastics, such as PVC, and solvents, such as trichloroethane. It is also used to make weedkillers and pesticides, as well as bleaches. Another major use is in the purification of drinking water (see Fig. 15.5).

Chlorine is a very reactive gas and consequently is not found as the 'free' element in the air. It is found mostly in nature combined with the element sodium. It is obtained from its 'ore' by the electrolysis of either molten sodium chloride (see Chapter 8, page 98) or the concentrated solution known as brine (see Chapter 6, page 69).

Preparation of chlorine in the laboratory

Chlorine is usually made by slowly dripping concentrated hydrochloric acid onto potassium manganate(VII) as shown in Fig. 15.6. In this preparation potassium manganate(VII), an oxidizing agent, is used to remove the hydrogen from concentrated hydrochloric acid.

Fig. 15.5   Chlorine is used to sterilize drinking water

$$\text{concentrated hydrochloric acid} + \text{potassium manganate(VII)} \text{(oxidizing agent)} \longrightarrow \text{chlorine} + \text{water}$$

$$2HCl_{(l)} + \underset{\text{from oxidizing agent}}{[O]} \longrightarrow Cl_{2(g)} + H_2O_{(l)}$$

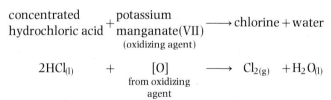

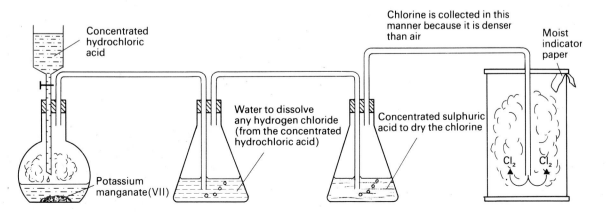

Fig. 15.6   Apparatus used to make chlorine

Some properties of chlorine

Chlorine is slightly soluble in water. The solution is known as chlorine water. It is a colourless solution with a tinge of green. Chlorine water is a mixture of two acids hydrochloric acid and chloric(I) acid (hypochlorous acid).

chlorine + water $\rightleftharpoons$ hydrochloric acid + chloric(I) acid

$$Cl_{2(g)} + H_2O_{(l)} \rightleftharpoons HCl_{(aq)} + HOCl_{(aq)}$$

If left in sunlight, chloric(I) acid slowly decomposes producing hydrochloric acid and releasing oxygen gas.

chloric(I) acid $\xrightarrow{\text{sunlight}}$ hydrochloric acid + oxygen

$$2HOCl_{(aq)} \longrightarrow 2HCl_{(aq)} + O_{2(g)}$$

Chloric(I) acid can therefore act as an oxidizing agent. It will oxidize other substances by giving oxygen to them. In this way chloric(I) acid (in chlorine water) acts as a bleach. Many dyes can be oxidized to colourless compounds by this solution (see Fig. 15.7).

Note, however, that most commercially available bleaches are not simply 'chlorine water'. They contain the hypochlorite of sodium, or calcium, formed by reacting chlorine with the appropriate alkali. They also sometimes contain an additive such as sodium phosphate, $Na_3PO_4 \cdot 11H_2O$. These bleaches, therefore, are *alkaline*. So-called 'liquid bleach' has a pH of about 11. In referring to the pH of a bleaching solution, it is therefore essential to make clear whether such a solution is simple 'chlorine water' (acidic) or a commercially available bleach (alkaline). A specific pH (or pH range) may be helpful.

The bleaching property of chlorine water is used as a test for chlorine gas. Damp blue litmus paper is introduced into a gas jar of chlorine. The chlorine dissolves in the water present on the indicator paper. Initially the indicator is turned red by the presence of hydrochloric acid. The chloric(I) acid present then removes the colour by acting as a bleach.

Chlorine is a very reactive non-metal. It will react with all metals including gold. For example, if aluminium is heated in a stream of dry chlorine then white fumes of aluminium chloride are produced. Since aluminium chloride reacts with water it must be collected as shown in Fig. 15.9.

Fig. 15.7   Chlorine water acts as a bleach

Fig. 15.8   Test for chlorine gas

aluminium + chlorine $\xrightarrow{\text{heat}}$ aluminium chloride

$$2Al_{(s)} + 3Cl_{2(g)} \longrightarrow 2AlCl_{3(s)}$$

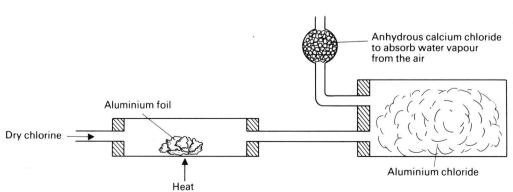

Fig. 15.9   When dry chlorine is passed over heated aluminium foil, aluminium chloride is formed

Other metal chlorides such as iron(III) chloride, can be synthesized in a similar manner.

$$\text{iron} + \text{chlorine} \xrightarrow{\text{heat}} \text{iron(III) chloride}$$

$$2Fe_{(s)} + 3Cl_{2(g)} \longrightarrow 2FeCl_{3(s)}$$

Chlorine will also react with non-metals. For example, hydrogen will burn in chlorine producing hydrogen chloride gas.

$$\text{hydrogen} + \text{chlorine} \longrightarrow \text{hydrogen chloride}$$

$$H_{2(g)} + Cl_{2(g)} \longrightarrow 2HCl_{(g)}$$

This is the essential reaction behind the manufacture of hydrochloric acid.

Displacement reactions

Chlorine is a member of group 7, the family of elements known as the halogens (see Chapter 3, page 38). Other members include bromine and iodine. Each halogen will displace those below it in the group. For example, if chlorine (as chlorine water) is added to a solution of potassium iodide then the solution will turn brown (see Fig. 15.10). This is due to the iodide ions present being displaced, from solution, by the more reactive halogen.

$$\text{chlorine} + \text{potassium iodide} \longrightarrow \text{potassium chloride} + \text{iodine}$$

$$Cl_{2(aq)} + 2KI_{(aq)} \longrightarrow 2KCl_{(aq)} + I_{2(aq)}$$

This shows that chlorine is a very good oxidizing agent. It causes the iodide ions (I^-) to lose electrons (and hence be oxidized) and hence become iodine molecules (I_2). The better an oxidizing agent it is the more reactive the halogen is.

Hydrogen chloride (HCl)

You have just seen that hydrogen can be burnt in chlorine. This is the method used in industry to produce hydrogen chloride. The hydrogen chloride gas, so produced, is then used to produce hydrochloric acid. This is done by passing the gas into an absorption tower where it is dissolved in water.

$$\text{hydrogen chloride gas} \xrightarrow{\text{water}} \text{hydrochloric acid}$$

$$HCl_{(g)} \xrightarrow{\text{water}} HCl_{(aq)}$$

It is an acidic solution because $H^+(aq)$ ions are formed when the gas dissolves in water

$$HCl_{(aq)} \longrightarrow H^+_{(aq)} + Cl^-_{(aq)}$$

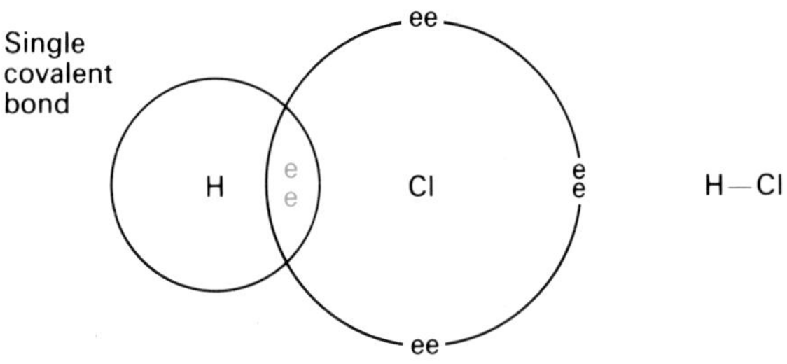

Fig. 15.10   The displacement of iodine by chlorine

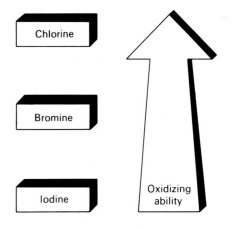

Fig. 15.11   Chlorine is the best oxidizing agent

Single covalent bond

H — Cl

Fig. 15.12   The hydrogen chloride molecule

Preparation in the laboratory

Hydrogen chloride is a colourless gas which produces 'fumes' in moist air. It has a choking smell. It is denser than air and when prepared by adding concentrated sulphuric acid to sodium chloride it is collected as shown in Fig. 15.13.

sodium chloride $+$ concentrated sulphuric acid $\longrightarrow$ sodium hydrogen sulphate $+$ hydrogen chloride

$$NaCl_{(s)} + H_2SO_{4(l)} \longrightarrow NaHSO_{4(s)} + HCl_{(g)}$$

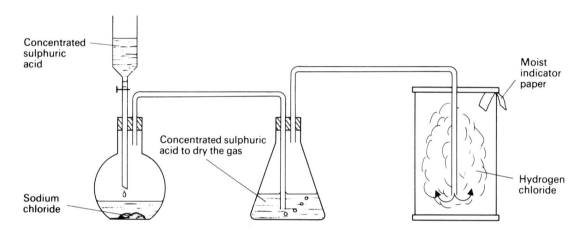

Fig. 15.13   Apparatus used for making hydrogen chloride

Some properties of hydrogen chloride

When hydrogen chloride gas reacts with ammonia, white fumes of ammonium chloride can be seen (Chapter 13, Fig. 13.12).

ammonia $+$ hydrogen chloride $\longrightarrow$ ammonium chloride

$$NH_{3(g)} + HCl_{(g)} \longrightarrow NH_4Cl_{(s)}$$

If dry hydrogen chloride gas is passed over heated iron wire then the wire becomes coated with a green solid—iron(II) chloride.

iron $+$ hydrogen chloride $\longrightarrow$ iron(II) chloride $+$ hydrogen

$$Fe_{(s)} + 2HCl_{(g)} \longrightarrow FeCl_{2(s)} + H_{2(g)}$$

Hydrogen chloride is also a very soluble gas. It will undergo the fountain experiment (see Chapter 13, page 184). The solution formed in the flask is acidic—hydrochloric acid.

Hydrochloric acid

Hydrochloric acid is a typical strong acid. It will affect indicators, turning both blue litmus and pH paper red. It will react with metals producing a salt and hydrogen. For example, magnesium reacts quite vigorously with the dilute acid producing magnesium chloride and hydrogen.

magnesium $+$ dilute hydrochloric acid $\longrightarrow$ magnesium chloride $+$ hydrogen

$$Mg_{(s)} + 2HCl_{(aq)} \longrightarrow MgCl_{2(aq)} + H_{2(g)}$$

Hydrochloric acid will also react with bases to form a salt (metal chloride) and water. For example, it will react with an alkali such as sodium hydroxide forming sodium chloride and water.

$$\text{sodium hydroxide} + \text{dilute hydrochloric acid} \longrightarrow \text{sodium chloride} + \text{water}$$

$$NaOH_{(aq)} + HCl_{(aq)} \longrightarrow NaCl_{(aq)} + H_2O_{(l)}$$

It will react with copper(II) oxide forming copper(II) chloride and water.

$$\text{copper(II) oxide} + \text{dilute hydrochloric acid} \longrightarrow \text{copper(II) chloride} + \text{water}$$

$$CuO_{(s)} + 2HCl_{(aq)} \longrightarrow CuCl_{2(aq)} + H_2O_{(l)}$$

Hydrochloric acid will react with carbonates forming a salt, water and carbon dioxide. For example, it will react with calcium carbonate forming calcium chloride, water and carbon dioxide.

$$\text{calcium carbonate} + \text{dilute hydrochloric acid} \longrightarrow \text{calcium chloride} + \text{water} + \text{carbon dioxide}$$

$$CaCO_{3(s)} + 2HCl_{(aq)} \longrightarrow CaCl_{2(aq)} + H_2O_{(l)} + CO_{2(g)}$$

Uses of hydrochloric acid

Large amounts of the acid are used to make vinyl chloride, the monomer for PVC, and for preparing metal surfaces before electroplating or galvanizing. The acid is also used in the manufacture of dyes and drugs where acidic conditions may be required (see Fig. 15.14).

Fig. 15.14   The shelving inside this fridge door is made of PVC which required hydrochloric acid in its manufacture

Chlorides

These are the salts of hydrochloric acid. They usually dissolve in water. The exceptions are lead and silver chloride. However, lead(II) chloride whilst being almost insoluble in cold water dissolves in hot water.

To test for a chloride, a few drops of silver nitrate solution are added to a dilute solution of the suspected chloride (acidified with a little dilute nitric acid). If a chloride is present, a white precipitate of silver chloride is formed (see Fig. 15.15). If left to stand the precipitate goes a little grey.

Fig. 15.15   A positive test for a chloride

As you will see from Fig. 15.16 common salt is a very important and useful chloride.

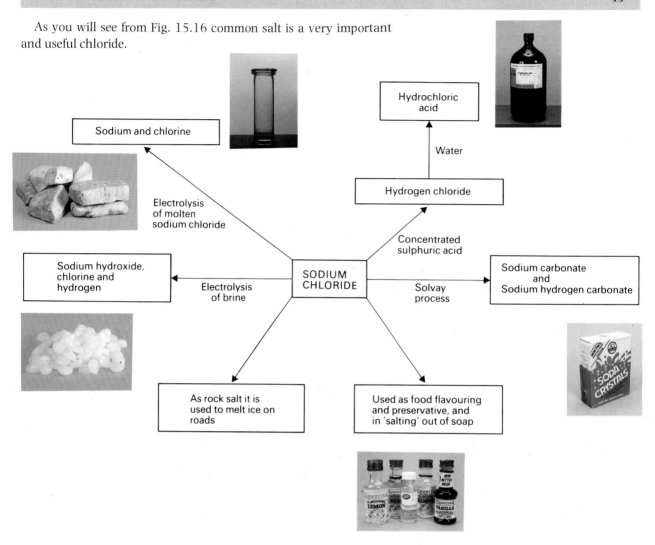

Fig. 15.16   Uses of sodium chloride

1 The diagram below shows apparatus which could be used to prepare a sample of dry chlorine in the laboratory.

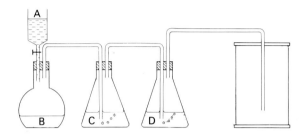

a) Name and write the formula of the chemicals labelled as A, B, C, and D.

b) What is the function of the liquids C and D?

c) Why would it be advisable to carry out this experiment in a fume cupboard?

d) Give a reason why chlorine is collected as shown above.

e) Give two reasons why chlorine is classified as a non-metal.

f) Chlorine when passed over heated iron wool reacts quite vigorously.
  i) Name the product of this reaction and state its colour.
  ii) Write a balanced chemical equation for this reaction.

g) Give two large-scale uses of chlorine.

2 The apparatus shown below can be used to prepare dry hydrogen chloride gas.

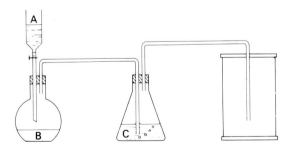

a) Name the chemicals labelled A, B, and C.

b) What is the function of the liquid C?

c) Name the solution produced when hydrogen chloride is dissolved in water.

d) If hydrogen chloride is passed over hot iron wool a green solid D is formed and flammable gas E is produced.

i) Name the solid D and the gas E.

ii) Give a word equation and a balanced chemical equation for this reaction.

iii) Draw a diagram to show how the reaction may be carried out and a sample of gas E collected.

3 The gas hydrogen chloride, HCl, is very soluble in water. Its solution in water is known as hydrochloric acid, HCl(aq). Hydrochloric acid may be made in the laboratory using the apparatus shown below, but a mistake has been made in the diagram.

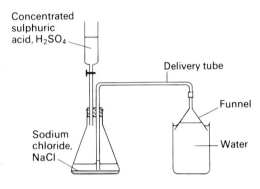

a) Explain the mistake made in drawing the diagram *or* re-sketch the incorrectly drawn part of the diagram. (1)

b) i) The end of the delivery tube is fitted with an inverted funnel. Describe, with reasons, what would probably happen if the experiment was attempted with plain glass tubing dipping into the water, instead of the inverted funnel. (2)

ii) By referring to the level of the water in the funnel, explain how the presence of the funnel prevents the occurrence you have described in (b)(i). (3)

iii) What is the name of the *type* of process you have described in (b)(ii)? (1)

c) Write an equation for the reaction between sodium chloride and concentrated sulphuric acid to produce hydrogen chloride. Include the states of reactants and products in your answer. (2)

d) Name the product(s) formed when the following substances react with dilute hydrochloric acid.
  i) Magnesium metal.
  ii) Copper(II) oxide. (4)

e) There are many examples in nature of gases which are dissolved in liquids being of vital importance to living things. Select *two* such examples and for each:
  i) name the gas and the liquid and
  ii) briefly explain the importance of the solution.   (6)
(AEB 1983)

4 By showing the outermost electron shells only, show the bonding in:
a) a molecule of chlorine(Cl_2);

b) a molecule of hydrogen chloride(HCl);
State the type of bonding found in *both* molecules.

5 You have been given three white powders. You are told that one of these is a chloride. How would you test the powders to find out which this was?

6 a) Which metallic chloride is soluble in hot water but insoluble in cold water?
  b) Name one other insoluble chloride.
  c) Name three useful substances obtained from sodium chloride and give a use for each.

RATES OF CHEMICAL REACTIONS

The rate or speed of a chemical reaction is a measure of how fast the reaction takes place. The photographs in Fig. 16.1 show a series of common slow and fast reactions. The two on the left are examples of slow reactions. Both ripening and rusting take place over a long period of time—days or even weeks and months. The other two examples are of fast reactions. The chemicals inside a firework burn and react very rapidly, and explosions take place very quickly. Fast reactions are often over in seconds or fractions of a second—sometimes in much less than the time it takes to blink your eyes.

Fig. 16.1 Which of the chemical reactions shown above are slow and which are fast?

Fig. 16.2   A night view of a large petrochemicals complex

As the chemical industry has expanded and processes have become more complex, scientists have looked for ways to control the speed at which chemical reactions take place. They have discovered that there are four main ways in which you can change the rate of a chemical reaction.

Change the concentration

When pieces of magnesium are placed in a boiling tube containing hydrochloric acid, bubbles of hydrogen are seen as the magnesium dissolves and magnesium chloride is formed.

$$\text{magnesium} + \frac{\text{hydrochloric}}{\text{acid}} \longrightarrow \frac{\text{magnesium}}{\text{chloride}} + \text{hydrogen}$$

$$Mg_{(s)} \quad + \quad 2HCl_{(aq)} \quad \longrightarrow \quad MgCl_{2(aq)} \quad + \quad H_{2(g)}$$

If the acid used is very dilute then only a few bubbles of hydrogen are seen (see Fig. 16.3(a)). If more concentrated acid is now poured onto a similar quantity of magnesium two things happen:
1 more bubbles of hydrogen are seen (Fig. 16.3(b));
2 the reaction stops after a shorter period of time.
From these observations it can be said that increasing the concentration of a substance will increase the rate at which it reacts.

(a)   (b)

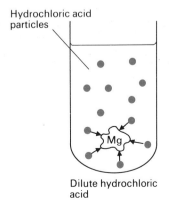

Fig. 16.3   Magnesium reacting with (a) dilute acid and (b) more concentrated acid. The concentrated acid produces more bubbles of hydrogen

Hydrochloric acid particles

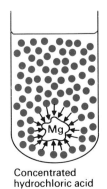

Dilute hydrochloric acid

Concentrated hydrochloric acid

Fig. 16.4   The more concentrated the acid the faster the reaction

How can we explain these observations? If the reaction between magnesium and acid is to take place, the magnesium and the ions in the solution must come into contact. On page 5, you learned that the particles in a solution move about. If the concentration of the acid is increased, the number of ions moving about in the solution will increase and there will therefore be an increase in the number of collisions with the magnesium. However, not all of these collisions will lead to a chemical reaction since some of the particles will not have enough energy to react. Nonetheless, the more often that particles with enough energy collide, the more the chemical reaction will take place. This means that the rate of a chemical reaction will increase if the concentration of reactants is increased. If the concentration of reactants is decreased, the rate of the chemical reaction will decrease.

Fig. 16.5(a)   Many people, many collisions

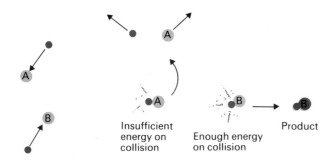

Fig. 16.6   If there is enough energy on collision, a reaction takes place

Fig. 16.5(b)   Few people, few collisions

Change the surface area of a reactant

In the previous section the reaction we discussed involved a solid, magnesium. In this case the reaction can only take place at the surface of the metal. If in this reaction we now use many smaller pieces of magnesium the reaction will happen faster (see Fig. 16.7). What have we done to cause the reaction to speed up?

Fig. 16.8 shows a piece of magnesium, as well as the same piece cut up into many smaller pieces. Eventually a powder is produced. By cutting it up you have increased the amount of surface which is available for the acid to react with. The reaction would be even faster if powdered magnesium were used.

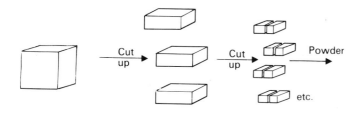

Fig. 16.8   A powder has a large surface area

Fig. 16.7   If a piece of magnesium is cut up, the many small pieces will have a larger total surface area and so the magnesium will react more rapidly with the acid

Change the temperature

We can alter the rate of a reaction by increasing or decreasing the temperature at which the reaction takes place. For example, if in our previous experiment the dilute hydrochloric acid were heated from room temperature to 60°C before it was poured onto the magnesium ribbon then a faster rate of reaction would be obtained.

Why should this occur? When we increase the temperature we increase the energy of the particles. These particles will now move faster. So the particles of hydrochloric acid will collide more often with the magnesium. Also because they have more energy these particles will be more likely to produce a chemical reaction. It is usually found, therefore, that if the temperature at which a reaction takes place is increased then the rate of the reaction will increase.

Measuring the rate of a reaction

If we wish to measure the rate of a reaction then we must measure the rate at which one or more of the products of the reaction is being formed. In the reaction we have used as our example one of the products is a gas—hydrogen. This reaction can be studied using the apparatus shown in Fig. 16.9.

When the flask is tilted, the ignition tube falls over. The magnesium ribbon is then covered by the hydrochloric acid, the reaction begins and hydrogen is formed. The volume of hydrogen produced is measured on the gas syringe at half-minute intervals. Some sample results from an experiment of this kind are shown in Table 16.1. The data from Table 16.1 are plotted in Fig. 16.10.

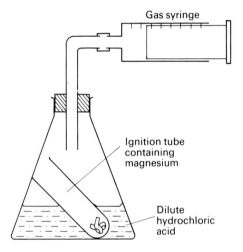

Fig. 16.9   Apparatus used for measuring the volume of hydrogen released

Time/minutes	0	0.5	1	1.5	2	2.5	3	3.5	4	4.5	5
Total volume of hydrogen/cm³	0	10	18	24	28	31	33	34	35	35	35

Table 16.1

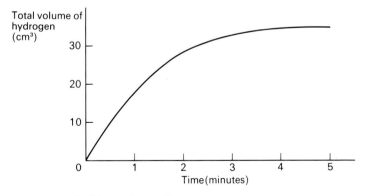

Fig. 16.10   Graph of the results in Table 16.1

Looking more closely at the results in Table 16.1 you will notice that in the first minute, 18 cm³ of hydrogen were produced, while in the second minute only 10 cm³ of hydrogen were produced (28 cm³–18 cm³). The amount of hydrogen produced in the third minute is even less—5 cm³. Eventually after 4 minutes no more hydrogen is produced. The reaction has stopped.

Now look at the graph plotted in Fig. 16.10. The curve is at its steepest in the first minute. The reaction rate is fastest in this first minute. The curve then gets less steep as less hydrogen is produced. The reaction is slowing down. Eventually the curve flattens. The reaction has stopped.

The reaction slows down because the concentration of the reactants is getting less. This in turn slows the reaction down. Eventually when all of one of the reactants has been used up in the reaction, the reaction stops.

Figure 16.11 shows the graphs produced when:
1 the concentration of acid is increased;
2 the particle size of the magnesium is reduced;
3 the temperature is increased.

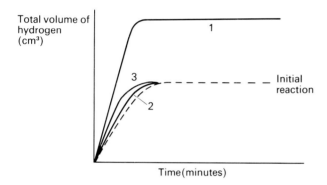

Fig. 16.11   Graphs of results for the reaction between magnesium and hydrochloric acid under various conditions

Using a catalyst

A **catalyst** is a substance which can alter the rate of a reaction, without being chemically changed at the end of the reaction. Catalysts will usually speed up a chemical reaction although there are catalysts, called **inhibitors**, which slow down chemical reactions.

Hydrogen peroxide decomposes very slowly to produce water and oxygen. In the presence of manganese(IV) oxide, the reaction is much faster. It is a catalyst for the decomposition of hydrogen peroxide.

$$\text{hydrogen peroxide} \xrightarrow{\text{manganese(IV) oxide}} \text{water} + \text{oxygen}$$

$$2H_2O_{2(aq)} \longrightarrow 2H_2O_{(l)} + O_{2(g)}$$

At the beginning of the reaction the manganese(IV) oxide is a black powder. At the end of the reaction it is still a black powder.

Catalysts are used extensively in the chemical industry. For example, vanadium(V) oxide is used in the production of sulphur(VI) oxide (used to make sulphuric acid) by the Contact process (see Chapter 14, page 203). Finely divided iron is used as the catalyst in the production of ammonia in the Haber process (see Chapter 13, page 187) and platinum is used in the conversion of ammonia into nitric acid (see Chapter 13, page 189). Biological catalysts (enzymes) are used in the production of beer (see Chapter 11, page 160).

QUESTIONS

1 a) Which of the following reaction mixtures will produce carbon dioxide more rapidly at a given temperature:
   i) dilute hydrochloric acid + marble chips;
   ii) dilute hydrochloric acid + powdered marble?
   b) Explain your answer to (a).
   c) Give two other ways in which the speed of this reaction can be altered.

2 a) Hydrogen peroxide solution decomposes slowly to oxygen and water. If manganese(IV) oxide is added to the hydrogen peroxide, what change in the rate of oxygen production is seen?
   b) In the reaction described in (a) manganese(IV) oxide acts as a _____.
   c) The results given in Table 1 were obtained using hydrogen peroxide solution and two metal oxides.
      i) Which oxide is faster at decomposing hydrogen peroxide?
      ii) Suggest the time that it would take to produce $100 \, cm^3$ of oxygen if 4 g of oxide A were added to the hydrogen peroxide solution at 20°C.
      iii) Does the mass of oxide added have any significant effect on the volume of oxygen?
      iv) What volume of oxygen would you expect to be produced if 3 g of oxide A were added to $75 \, cm^3$ of the hydrogen peroxide solution at 20°C?
      v) Give one other way, apart from temperature increase shown for oxide A, which would decrease the time needed to produce $100 \, cm^3$ of oxygen.
      vi) Write a word equation for the decomposition of hydrogen peroxide.
      vii) Write a balanced chemical equation for the decomposition of hydrogen peroxide.

3 Sketch a graph with fully labelled axes to show the rate of production of carbon dioxide when an excess of dilute hydrochloric acid is added to some calcium carbonate. The reaction lasts 60 s and produces $30 \, cm^3$ of gas.

4 a) Why are catalysts frequently used in industrial processes?
   b) Name the catalyst used in:
      i) the Haber process for manufacturing ammonia;
      ii) the Contact process for manufacturing sulphuric acid.
   c) Give one example of a laboratory experiment in which a catalyst is used.
   d) Name an important process in which a 'biological catalyst' is used.
   e) What is a biological catalyst called?

5 An excess of calcium carbonate, in the form of clean marble chippings, was added to dilute hydrochloric acid in a conical flask. A plug of cotton wool was placed in the neck of the flask and the flask was weighed at regular intervals for five minutes. The results are shown in Table 2.
   a) Why did the mass of the flask and its contents decrease? (1)
   b) Write an equation for the reaction. (1)
   c) Plot the results of the experiment on a piece of graph paper and draw the graph. (2)
   d) Why was the plug of cotton wool used? (1)
   e) i) How does the rate of reaction change during the experiment? (1)
      ii) Why does the rate change in this way? (1)
   (JMB 1984)

	Mass of oxide added to $25 \, cm^3$ of hydrogen peroxide solution (g)	Temperature at which reaction took place (°C)	Time for $100 \, cm^3$ of oxygen to be evolved (s)	Total volume of oxygen evolved (cm^3)
Oxide A	3	20	12	500
	2	20	25	498
	1	20	38	502
	1	30	19	501
Oxide B	3	20	10	499
	2	20	21	501
	1	20	32	502

Table 1

Time (mins)	Loss in mass (g)
0.00	0.00
0.50	0.33
1.00	0.56
1.50	0.74
2.00	0.87
2.50	0.94
3.00	1.00
3.50	1.03
4.00	1.06
4.50	1.07
5.00	1.08

Table 2

Time (mins)	Volume (cm^3)
5	18
10	27
15	36
30	53
50	67
75	79
100	84
115	86
120	86
150	86

Table 3

6

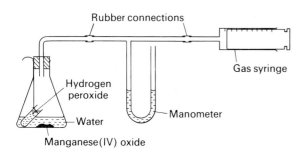

In the presence of the catalyst manganese(IV) oxide, hydrogen peroxide decomposes according to the equation

$$2H_2O_2 = 2H_2O + O_2.$$

The rate of evolution of oxygen can be investigated using the above apparatus.

a) In an experiment, $30 \, cm^3$ of water and $0.5 \, g$ of manganese(IV) oxide were placed in the left-hand flask, and $5 \, cm^3$ of hydrogen peroxide were suspended in the test tube. The flask was tilted so that the reactants mixed completely, and the volume of oxygen evolved was measured in the gas syringe at various time intervals. The results were as shown in Table 3.

i) Plot a graph of volume of oxygen (y-axis) against time (x-axis), and label it A.
ii) From the graph, determine the total volume of gas evolved after 40 minutes.
iii) Why were readings taken more often in the early part of the experiment?
iv) Why were the readings stopped after 150 minutes?
v) What is the purpose of the manometer? (9)

b) In a second experiment, $60 \, cm^3$ of water and $0.5 \, g$ manganese(IV) oxide were placed in the flask and $5 \, cm^3$ of the same concentration of hydrogen peroxide were placed in the test tube. The experimental procedure was repeated as in (a).
On the same graph and same axes sketch a second curve to show how the collected volume of oxygen would vary with time. Label this curve B. (2)

c) Calculate the mass of hydrogen peroxide needed to yield $86 \, cm^3$ of oxygen at standard temperature and pressure. (4)
(O & C 1984)

223

7 An experimental procedure was designed to investigate the rate of reaction between zinc and aqueous sulphuric acid under various conditions.

In experiment A, an excess of granulated zinc was reacted with a known volume of aqueous sulphuric acid at 20°C.

In experiment B, the reactants and temperature were the same as in experiment A but this time a few drops of aqueous copper(II) sulphate were added.

The results were as shown in Table 4.

a) i) Draw a labelled diagram of an apparatus which could be used to perform this experiment, and write an equation for the reaction. (4)

ii) Name the gas evolved and describe one chemical test which would identify it. (2)

b) State briefly how the results of the two experiments differ, and suggest *one* reason for the difference. (2)

c) Explain briefly why the volume of gas evolved during each one minute time interval decreases as the reaction proceeds. (2)

d) State what would happen to: (i) the initial rate of reaction, and (ii) the final volume of gas if each of the following changes in the conditions were made in separate experiments:

Time	Volume of gas evolved in experiment A (cm^3)	Volume of gas evolved in experiment B (cm^3)
0	0	0
1	20	24
2	37	44
3	50	63
4	60	74
5	67	74
6	72	74
7	74	74
8	74	74

Table 4

I) the temperature of the reactants was increased to 30°C.

II) the concentration of the acid was doubled but the volume of acid remained constant.

III) powdered zinc was used instead of granulated zinc. (6)

(AEB 1983)

FUELS

Fig. 17.1 This power station uses coal to produce electrical energy

A fuel is a substance which can be conveniently used as a source of energy, usually heat. It is often found that light energy is produced at the same time. Most fuels will liberate this heat energy when burnt in air (see Fig. 17.2). This happens during a process known as **combustion**.

The most widely used fuels today are natural gas, coal and oil. These fuels are known as **fossil fuels**. This is because they are formed from dead animals and plants which have become fossilized over millions of years. All these fuels contain the elements carbon and hydrogen. A general chemical reaction may be written to represent the burning of these fuels.

Fig. 17.2 Combustion is an exothermic reaction!

fossil fuel + oxygen $\longrightarrow$ carbon dioxide + water + energy

An example of such a reaction would be:

methane + oxygen $\longrightarrow$ carbon dioxide + water + energy

$$CH_{4(g)} + 2O_{2(g)} \longrightarrow CO_{2(g)} + 2H_2O_{(g)}$$

The energy released from burning methane is used to keep us warm, to heat water and cook food (see Fig. 17.3).

Fuels in large quantities are used in producing electricity. The fuel is burned to heat water to produce steam (see Fig. 17.4). The steam is used to drive large turbines in power stations. This turbine, in conjunction with a generator, produces electricity which goes into the **national grid**. Through this national system the electricity is distributed to wherever it is needed.

Fig. 17.3   This gas fire is burning methane

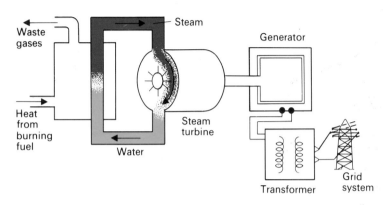

Fig. 17.4   The way a fuel is used to produce electricity

Formation of fossil fuels

Coal

Most of the coal used in the UK was formed from forests and vegetation which grew over 200 million years ago. At this time great forests of trees and giant ferns flourished on this planet (see Fig. 17.5). This vegetation grew quickly, died and fell to rot in the swampy ground. New plants grew up and the whole cycle repeated itself many, many times. The swampy land then sank slowly and the forests became covered by sand and mud. As the weight of material above the vegetable matter increased, changes began to take place. First of all the vegetation layer decayed in the presence of bacteria, to form peat. Over millions of years as the layers were pushed deeper and deeper and the pressure and temperature increased, the conversion to coal took place.

Fig. 17.5   Fossilized fern in a lump of coal

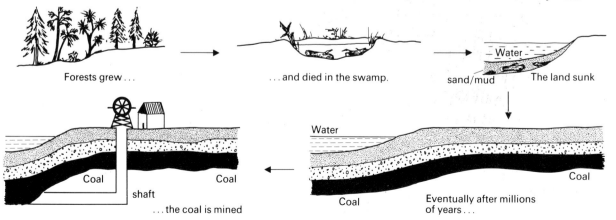

Fig. 17.6   Coal was formed over millions of years

Different types of coal were produced at different pressures. The harder coal, which has a higher carbon content, was produced at greater depth. This coal is known as **anthracite** and it contains about 90% carbon. In the UK, this type of coal is mined mainly in South Wales. The softer coals are **lignite** and **bituminous coal** which contain about 40% and 60% carbon respectively. These are mined in many areas of the UK including the Nottingham and Yorkshire coalfields.

Fig. 17.7   A modern coal mine

Fig. 17.8   A coal-cutting shearer in action

Oil and gas

Crude oil and gas were formed over millions of years from the remains of marine animals and plants that sank to the bottom of lakes and seas. This material became covered in mud which thickened with time. As the thickness of the mud layers built up, high temperatures and pressures were created. The conditions were just right for the decay of the marine creatures in the presence of bacteria, to form oil and gas. As rock layers, which had developed above this material, buckled and split, the oil and gas were trapped in porous rocks like sandstone and stopped from rising further by hard non-porous or 'cap' rock (see Fig. 17.10).

Fig. 17.9   Natural gas being 'flared off' on an oil production platform in the Forties oilfield in the North Sea

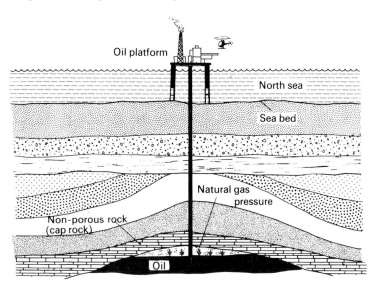

Fig. 17.10   Oil and natural gas are trapped under non-porous rock

Fuels from fossil fuels

Oil is used to produce other useful fuels such as petrol, diesel and paraffin. These substances are separated from oil by fractional distillation (see Chapter 11, page 146). Coal is also used to produce another fuel—coke. This is generally used as a smokeless fuel. It is obtained from coal by a process called **destructive distillation**.

Destructive distillation of coal

In this process, coal is heated in the absence of air at temperatures ranging from 600–1200°C. When this is done a very complex mixture of substances is produced and a solid residue of coke is left (see Fig. 17.11). Different types of coal produce different types of coke. Coke for steel making is made from hard bituminous coal whilst other types of coke are sold for household use.

The other main products obtained from the destructive distillation of coal are:

1 Coal gas. This is a mixture of the gases carbon monoxide, methane and hydrogen (50%) and has now been almost completely replaced by natural gas for domestic consumption.

2 Ammoniacal liquor. This contains ammonia from which the fertilizer ammonium sulphate can be made.

3 Coal tar. There are over 2000 chemicals present in this tarry residue, including: phenol (used for plastics, disinfectants, drugs, dyes), pyridine (used in weed killers) and naphthalene (which is used for firelighters and moth balls). Tar for road surfaces is also obtained from this residue.

Fig. 17.11 Destructive distillation of coal takes place in a coke oven like that shown here

Fig. 17.12 Chemicals from coal tar have been used in the manufacture of all these items

(a)

(b)

(c)

(d)

The destructive distillation of coal can be illustrated in the laboratory using the apparatus shown in Fig. 17.13.

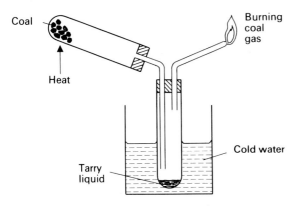

Fig. 17.13   Apparatus used for carrying out the destructive distillation of coal

The energy crisis

Because we live in a world in which there is an ever-increasing demand for energy, we are using up our resources of these fossil fuels at a tremendous rate. Table 17.1 shows how long our present supplies of fossil fuels are expected to last.

Uranium is a **nuclear fuel**. This type of fuel does not burn like fossil fuels and it provides an alternative source of energy to fossil fuels.

Uranium nuclei are unstable. When the nucleus of an unstable atom splits up (**nuclear fission**) large amounts of heat energy are released (see Fig. 17.14). This energy is harnessed in the nuclear reactor which is at the centre of a nuclear power station (see Fig. 17.15). The main problem associated with a power station based upon nuclear fission is that the reactor produces highly radioactive waste materials which cannot be disposed of easily and are difficult to store. Accidents at a small number of nuclear power stations have also led to some concern about their safety, although the nuclear power industry is subject to strict controls and its safety record is good.

Fossil fuel	Date it is expected to run out
Coal	Beyond 2250
Gas	2030
Oil	2050

Table 17.1   How long our fossil fuels will last

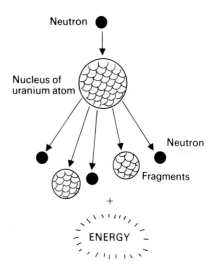

Fig. 17.14   The nuclei of unstable uranium atoms split up like this

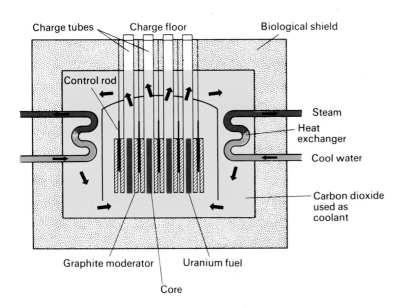

Fig. 17.15   In a reactor at a nuclear power station the fission process cannot be allowed to get out of control as it does in an atomic bomb. The control rods can be pushed into different positions so absorbing some of the neutrons and slowing down the reaction. In this way the energy released from the reaction is obtained in a more controlled way over a longer period of time

The extent to which it is either necessary or economical to use nuclear power to generate electricity, rather than rely upon the fossil fuels of coal, oil or gas, is also a matter of debate.

Other sources of energy

Some other sources of energy which are *renewable* and which could be feasible to use in the UK are as follows.

1 Hydro-electric power. HEP has been generated in Wales and Scotland for some time. It is very useful because it can be quickly used to supplement the national grid at times of high demand. It is also possible to use cheap off-peak electricity to pump water back into the high-level dam.

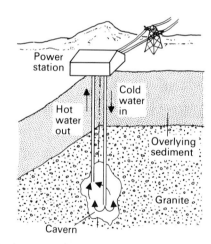

Fig. 17.16   This hydro-electric power station has been screened with trees as it is sited in an area of great scenic beauty (Loch Lomondside, Scotland)

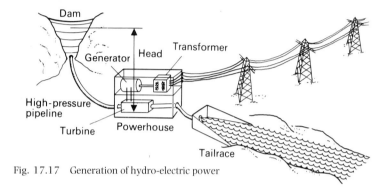

Fig. 17.17   Generation of hydro-electric power

2 Geothermal energy. Heat is extracted from hot rocks which are far below ground level. Some geothermal energy is being obtained from rocks in Cornwall at the present time (see Fig. 17.18).

3 Wave power. In this method, movement (kinetic) energy is taken out of moving waves using the Salter's Duck (see Fig. 17.19).

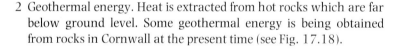

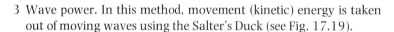

Fig. 17.19   Generation of electricity by wave power

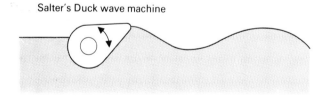

Fig. 17.18   Geothermal—getting energy from hot rocks

4 Tidal power. This method uses the flow of water through a turbine of the type shown in Fig. 17.20.

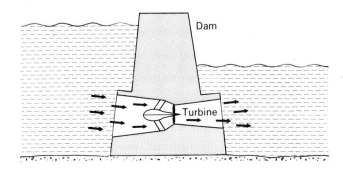

Fig. 17.20   Tidal power—the ebb and flow of the tides drive the turbine

5 Solar power. This method uses the sun's heat energy absorbed onto a black painted collector plate (see Fig. 17.21).

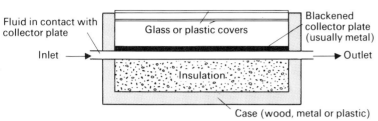

Fig. 17.21(a)   A simple solar energy panel

Fig. 17.21(b)   This house is using some solar energy panels

6 Wind power. This method uses the kinetic energy of the wind to turn generators to produce electricity (Fig. 17.22).

The perfect fuel

The perfect fuel should be:
1 cheap and available in large quantities;
2 safe to store and transport;
3 capable of releasing large amounts of energy;
4 easily burned (in a controlled way) without producing substances which would cause pollution.

It is fair to say that scientists have not yet found the perfect fuel!

Chemical energy

At the present time the world gets most of its useful energy from the burning of fuels. During these chemical reactions heat is given out. They are **exothermic reactions**. Many other chemical reactions also are exothermic. For example, if calcium reacts with water (see Fig. 17.23) or magnesium reacts with acid (see Fig. 16.3) the reaction mixtures get quite hot.

There are some other reactions which absorb energy from the surroundings. In these cases the temperature of the reaction mixture falls. They are called **endothermic reactions**. For example, the formation of nitrogen monoxide gas from its elements is an endothermic reaction.

The energy produced or absorbed in chemical reactions is usually measured in joules (or kilojoules). About 4.18 joules are needed to raise the temperature of one gram of water through 1 °C. The energy changes which take place during chemical reactions can be shown on an **energy level diagram**.

Fig. 17.22   This 24 metre-high wind turbine is capable of generating up to 200 kilowatts of electricity

Fig. 17.23   When calcium is added to water it first sinks and then as it reacts producing hydrogen it floats to the surface. It is a very exothermic reaction

Fig. 17.24   In exothermic reactions the test tubes get hot!

Figure 17.25 shows the energy level diagram for an exothermic reaction. In this type of reaction energy is released to the surroundings. The energy of the reactants must be greater than the energy of the substances produced. The energy is usually stored in the chemical bonds. So in an exothermic reaction less energy is required to form new bonds than to break existing bonds. This extra or surplus energy is given out to the surroundings.

This stored energy is called the **enthalpy** and given the symbol H. The change in energy in going from reactants to products is called the **change in enthalpy** and shown as ΔH. For an exothermic reaction ΔH is given a negative sign and shown as $-\Delta H$. This is to show that the chemicals are losing energy to the surroundings. (Fig. 17.25 becomes Fig. 17.26.)

Some examples of exothermic reactions with their ΔH values are:

1 methane (natural gas) burning in air:

methane + oxygen ⟶ carbon dioxide + water + energy

$$CH_{4(g)} + 2O_{2(g)} \longrightarrow CO_{2(g)} + 2H_2O_{(g)} \quad \Delta H = -890\,kJ$$

2 hydrochloric acid neutralized by sodium hydroxide:

dilute hydrochloric acid + sodium hydroxide ⟶ sodium chloride + water + energy

$$HCl_{(aq)} + NaOH_{(aq)} \longrightarrow NaCl_{(aq)} + H_2O_{(l)} \quad \Delta H = -57\,kJ$$

Figure 17.27 shows the energy level diagram for an endothermic reaction. In this type of reaction energy is absorbed from the surroundings. The energy of the products must be greater than the energy of the reactants.

In an endothermic reaction more energy is required to break the bonds of the reactants than is liberated when the new bonds are formed in the products. So energy has to be absorbed from the surroundings to make up for the shortage of energy. For endothermic reactions ΔH is given a positive sign and is shown as $+\Delta H$. This is to show that the chemicals are gaining energy from the surroundings.

Some examples of endothermic reactions are:

1 the formation of nitrogen monoxide:

nitrogen + oxygen ⟶ nitrogen monoxide

$$N_{2(g)} + O_{2(g)} \longrightarrow 2NO_{(g)} \quad \Delta H = +184\,kJ$$

2 the formation of hydrogen iodide:

hydrogen + iodine ⇌ hydrogen iodide

$$H_{2(g)} + I_{2(g)} \rightleftharpoons 2HI_{(g)} \quad \Delta H = +52\,kJ$$

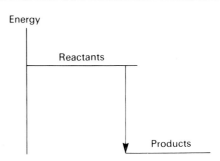

Fig. 17.25   Energy level diagram for an exothermic reaction

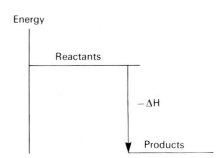

Fig. 17.26   Energy level diagram for an exothermic reaction showing the (−) enthalpy change

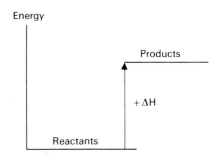

Fig. 17.27   Energy level diagram for an endothermic diagram showing the (+) enthalpy change

Dissolving

When ammonium nitrate dissolves in water the temperature falls. It is an endothermic process. However, when concentrated sulphuric acid is added very slowly to water the temperature goes up quite a lot. It is a highly exothermic reaction.

Change of state

Ice melts to produce liquid water (see Fig. 17.28). For this to happen the ice must absorb energy from its surroundings. The energy is used to break down the forces between the water molecules in the ice. This energy is called the **enthalpy of fusion** and is given the symbol ΔH_{fusion}.

When liquid water is changed into steam the energy used to break down the forces between the water molecules is called the **enthalpy of vaporization**. It is given the symbol ΔH_{vap}.

Fig. 17.29 shows the energy level diagrams for these two changes of state.

Fig. 17.28(a)   Ice absorbs heat . . .

Fig. 17.28(b)   . . . and melts to become liquid water

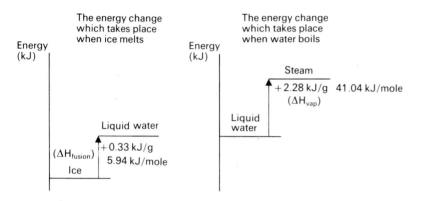

Fig. 17.29   Energy level diagrams for ice melting and water boiling

Chemical cells and batteries

A simple cell

A simple cell is produced when pieces of zinc and copper are placed in a beaker of dilute sulphuric acid and connected as shown in Fig. 17.31. For the bulb to light there must have been a flow of electrons around the circuit. How are these electrons produced? The zinc electrode dissolves in the dilute sulphuric acid producing zinc ions and releasing 2 electrons per atom.

$$zinc \longrightarrow zinc\ ions + electrons$$

$$Zn_{(s)} \longrightarrow Zn^{2+}_{(aq)} + 2e^-$$

Fig. 17.30   In these cells electricity is produced from chemical processes

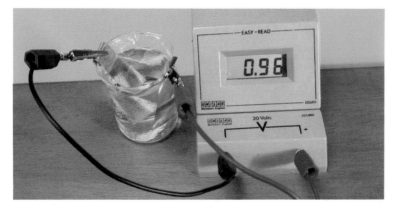

Fig. 17.31(a)   A simple copper–zinc cell

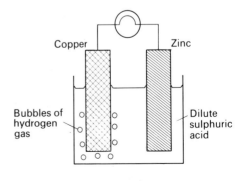

Fig. 17.31(b)   Hydrogen is released at the copper electrode

An electric current is a flow of electrons. The electrons produced at the zinc electrode flow around the circuit through the bulb (see Fig. 17.32). The bulb glows. The electrons arrive at the copper electrode where hydrogen ions, from the acid solution, collect them. The hydrogen atoms, so produced, combine to produce hydrogen gas molecules.

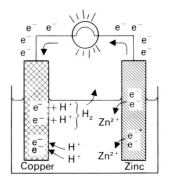

Fig. 17.32   The electrons flow from the zinc to the copper

hydrogen ion + electron $\longrightarrow$ hydrogen atom

$$H^+_{(aq)} \quad + \quad e^- \quad \longrightarrow \quad H$$

then,

two hydrogen atoms $\longrightarrow$ hydrogen molecule

$$2H \quad \longrightarrow \quad H_{2(g)}$$

If the zinc is replaced by a more reactive metal such as magnesium then the bulb glows more brightly. This happens because the magnesium reacts more rapidly than the zinc and so releases the electrons sooner. A less reactive metal such as iron in place of zinc produces a very dim light indeed.

This type of cell does not operate too well because there is a build-up of hydrogen around the copper electrode. This build-up is called **polarization**. This polarization hinders the flow of the electric current. Also the cell gets warm. This is because not all the energy in this cell is turned into electricity.

Fuel cells

Scientists have found a much more efficient way of changing chemical energy into electrical energy. This is done in the **fuel cell**. In this type of cell there is a continuous supply of electricity from the controlled reaction between, for example, hydrogen and oxygen. Fuel cells produce no pollution since the only product is water. They have already been used extensively in space rockets as well as to power special types of car. There is a lot of research being carried out at the present time to adapt these fuel cells and devise others for use in the home.

─────────────────────────────── QUESTIONS ───────────────────────────────

1 a) State what a 'fuel' is.
   b) What are the essential properties of a good fuel?
   c) Name:
      i) a liquid fuel;
      ii) a solid fuel;
      iii) a gaseous fuel.
   d) Write a word equation and a balanced chemical equation for the burning of a named gaseous fuel.

2 a) Describe how coal was formed.
   b) i) What is the name of the smokeless fuel produced from coal?
      ii) Smokeless fuel is produced by the 'destructive distillation' of coal. Below is a diagram showing some of the products of this process along with some of their uses. Some of the information is missing.
         I) Name the products A and B.
         II) Give one use of coke.
         III) Give two uses of product B.
      iii) How is the 'destructive distillation' of coal carried out in the laboratory?

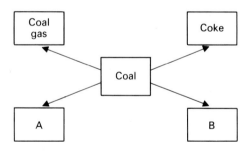

3 There are a growing number of people in the UK who are against the use of nuclear energy for the generation of electricity. What are your views on this matter?
   Using information from newspaper and magazine articles as well as other sources, discuss the advantages and disadvantages of nuclear energy being used in this way.

4 Imagine you are living in the year 2150 A.D. In no more than 150 words write a short account of what your life is like. In your account refer to the following questions:
   a) Will the oil fractions still be used as fuels?
   b) Will coal still be in plentiful supply?
   c) Will any alternative sources of energy be extensively used to heat and light your homes as well as power industry?
   d) Will you have a car and, if so, what fuel will you be using in it?

5 Complete the following sentences:
   a) Nuclear power could be dangerous because . . .
   b) Solar panels use . . .
   c) Hydroelectric power is very useful because . . .
   d) In the future coal may have to be used to make substances now obtained from oil because . . .

6 Water is formed and energy is released when hydrogen combines with oxygen.
   a) Write the equation, including the state symbols, for this reaction.
   b) In this reaction the covalent bonds in the molecules of hydrogen and oxygen are broken.
      i) Is the bond breaking process exothermic or endothermic?
      ii) What bonds are formed in the reaction?
   c) State three forms in which energy may be released.
   (Cambridge 1982)

7 a) State whether the following processes are exothermic or endothermic:
      i) the breaking of a covalent bond;
      ii) the formation of a covalent bond.   (2)
   b) In the formation of hydrogen chloride from hydrogen and chlorine

$$H_2 + Cl_2 = 2HCl$$

      i) Which bonds are broken?   (1)
      ii) Which bonds are formed?   (1)
   c) In the photochlorination of methane

$$CH_4 + Cl_2 = CH_3Cl + HCl$$

      i) Which bonds are broken?   (1)
      ii) Which bonds are made?   (1)
   (OLE 1983)

8 A public enquiry is to be held into the building of a nuclear power station not far from the home of your Uncle George. Uncle George is a vigorous but fair-minded defender of citizens' rights, and he feels that his lack of background knowledge ('Never had a science lesson at school; can't say I missed it much.') will limit his understanding of the arguments. He has therefore asked you to brief him under the headings:
   a) Safety record and chances of a major disaster.   (5)
   b) Dangers of radiation during normal working.   (5)
   c) Problems of waste disposal.   (5)
   d) Do we need nuclear power?   (5)
   (O & C 1984)

9 Read the passage below and then answer the questions which follow.

Hydrogen as a fuel

With the world's fossil fuel resources rapidly dwindling, considerable research is being directed towards finding a replacement for them. One such fuel is hydrogen, despite the
5 difficulties associated with its manufacture from water, potentially its major source. The main problem of its economical extraction is associated with the strength of the hydrogen/oxygen bonds, which require about 460 kJ
10 mol^{-1} to break them.

Apart from its manufacture, there are also many problems attached to the use of hydrogen. How can it be transported safely? Can it be used in modern engines without causing
15 too many re-design problems? Are the hazards associated with its use acceptable? On the credit side, it has much to commend it. Its combustion product, when it is burnt with pure oxygen, is virtually pollution free; al-
20 though if it were mixed with air and used in internal combustion engines in the same way as conventional fuel, this mixture would still produce oxides of nitrogen. Furthermore, because of its much faster burning rate, a dif-
25 ferent carburettor system would be needed. One way of overcoming this problem would be to use the gas in fuel cells which, unlike petrol, are able to generate electricity very efficiently. However, with present-day technol-
30 ogy, fuel cells are unable to cope with the relatively large amount of power needed to drive a vehicle.

As an aircraft fuel, mass for mass, hydrogen is able to deliver about three times as much
35 energy as kerosene. This would reduce the problem of having to dump fuel if an aircraft were to turn back after take-off. On the other hand, the volume needed to store the fuel is greater than the corresponding volume needed
40 for kerosene, mainly on account of its different state.

Liquefaction may be the answer, but then the maintenance of a very low temperature is a serious problem. However, in spite of all the
45 difficulties associated with its use, the future prospects of hydrogen are encouraging, and, if the main obstacle to its extraction can be overcome, it has great potential as a replacement for fossil fuels.

a) What factor makes the extraction of hydrogen from water a particularly difficult problem? (1)

b) How much energy is needed to separate all the atoms in one mole of water? (1)

c) i) Why is the combustion product 'virtually pollution free'? (lines 18–19)
    ii) What pollutants could still be produced if hydrogen were used as a fuel in an internal combustion engine?
    iii) Explain briefly how these pollutants would be formed.
    iv) What other property of hydrogen presents a problem when hydrogen is used in internal combustion engines?
    v) What advantage would a hydrogen-driven fuel cell have over petrol as an energy source for motor vehicles?
    vi) What prevents a fuel cell being used in present day vehicles? (6)

d) i) What particular property of hydrogen gives it an advantage over conventional aircraft fuels?
    ii) Why would the use of hydrogen as a fuel reduce the wastage in the event of a fault developing soon after take-off? (2)

(JMB 1983)

10   *Either*

In April 1979 an accident occurred at a water-cooled nuclear power station at Three Mile Island, Pennsylvania. A leak in the water coolant system led to overheating of the reactor core, and a large bubble of hydrogen formed inside the reactor. There was a risk that, as a result of the overheating, radioactive fuel might melt and escape, or the gas bubble might explode and scatter radioactive materials over a wide area. Eventually the reactor was made safe, but not before a certain amount of radioactive gas had been released into the atmosphere, and some ground contamination had occurred.

a) This incident has been used to support the arguments of those who oppose the use of nuclear energy. What further details would you wish to know before making a judgment? (4)

b) Supporters of nuclear energy claim that there is no practical alternative, despite the risks. Why do they make this claim? (4)

c) Some people oppose nuclear energy because they think that a reactor can explode 'like an atom bomb'. Explain briefly why this is impossible. (4)

d) What disadvantages, other than the possibility of accident, are inevitably attached to the use of nuclear energy? (4)

e) What advantages do fast reactors have over thermal reactors? (4)

or

Explain the various ways in which the Sun is the primary source of our energy. (20)
(O & C 1982)

11 Table 1 gives figures for fuel consumption for different sectors in the UK in 1976 and is based on the Digest of United Kingdom Energy Statistics 1976. (Figures are in thousands of tonnes of coal equivalent.)

a) Which two sectors between them accounted for nearly half of the UK's fuel consumption?

b) Which type of fuel supplied about a quarter of our total needs?

c) Which sectors used solid fuel for more than half of their requirements? Why did solid fuel particularly suit their needs?

d) Which sectors used more electricity than solid fuel? Suggest a reason for this, for each sector separately.

e) Which sector depended on liquid fuel for the highest proportion of its requirements? Why was this so?

f) Which sectors other than the one you have named in your answer to (e) used liquid fuel for over half their requirements?

g) Which sector used more gas than electricity and liquid fuel put together?

h) Did any type of fuel contribute as much as all the others put together? Which figures will you have considered if you used the simplest way of answering this question? (20)
(O & C 1982)

12 a) What limits the usefulness of peat as fuel for a conventional power station? (3)

b) Hydro-electric schemes contribute about 2% of our electricity supply; why do we not have ten times as many? (3)

c) Why do we not get all our energy from the tides? (3)

d) If energy is obtained from the waves by 'Salter's Ducks' or similar devices, how will that energy be stored and transported? (3)

e) Why cannot Worcestershire's electricity be supplied by a hundred large windmills on the Malvern Hills? (3)

f) If Skylab could be run on four sails of solar cells, why do we not heat a semi-detached house in the same way? (3)

g) I told Aunt Georgina that I heated my cottage by burning wood. 'I will give you a tip,' she replied. 'Wet it before you put it on the fire. You will find that it takes much longer to burn.' Is this true, and is it good advice? (2)
(O & C 1981)

Sector	Solid fuel	Gas	Liquid fuel	Electricity	Total
Agriculture	60	—	2 213	489	2 762
Iron and steel	11 100	3 220	5 210	1 572	21 102
Food	1 007	1 711	4 077	923	7 718
Cement	2 523	442	326	271	3 562
Engineering and chemicals	2 726	13 930	11 482	4 994	33 132
All other trade and industry	3 307	5 023	13 782	3 220	25 332
Transport	84	—	50 134	390	50 608
Domestic	15 968	24 652	5 711	11 562	57 893
Public services	2 165	2 734	6 961	1 894	13 754
Miscellaneous	489	3 319	4 521	3 968	12 297
Total	39 429	55 031	104 417	29 283	228 160

Table 1. (The Miscellaneous sector is included only to produce correct totals. It should not be given as the answer to any of the questions above.)

13 a) Alcohols are organic compounds which have a general formula $C_nH_{2n+1}OH$, where n is the number of carbon atoms present in one molecule. Alcohols burn completely in oxygen forming carbon dioxide and water.

Table 2 gives the molar heat of combustion of a number of alcohols, i.e. the heat given out when one mole of an alcohol is completely burned in oxygen.

Alcohol	Number of carbon atoms in one molecule	Formula	Heat of combustion kJ mol^{-1}
methanol	1	CH_3OH	730
ethanol	2	C_2H_5OH	1370
propanol	3		2020
butanol	4	C_4H_9OH	2650
pentanol	5		

Table 2

i) Write down the formula of propanol. (1)
ii) Balance and complete the following equation to represent the complete combustion of ethanol in oxygen. (2)

$$C_2H_5OH + \underline{\hspace{1cm}} O_2 \longrightarrow \underline{\hspace{1cm}} CO_2$$
$$+ \underline{\hspace{1cm}} H_2O; \Delta H = \underline{\hspace{1cm}} kJ$$

iii) Complete the energy level diagram to show the energy changes taking place during this reaction. (1)

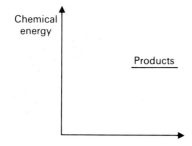

iv) Plot a graph on the axes provided of the molar heat of combustion of the alcohols against the number of carbon atoms in one molecule. (1)

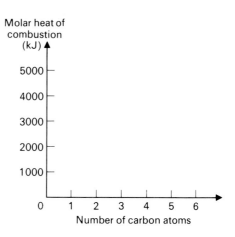

v) Use the graph to determine the molar heat of combustion of pentanol. (1)
vi) State the number of carbon atoms and hydrogen atoms in one molecule of the alcohol which has a molar heat of combustion of 3900 kJ mol^{-1}. (2)

b) Alcohols are used as fuels as one alternative to fossil fuels.
i) State one property of alcohols which makes them useful as fuels. (1)
ii) Why is it important to discover sources of energy as an alternative to the use of fossil fuels? (1)

(NEA 1985)

CALCULATIONS IN CHEMISTRY

Fig. 18.1   Eggs are measured in dozens. Atoms, ions and molecules are measured in moles!

Atoms, ions and molecules are very tiny particles. It is not possible to measure out a dozen or even a gross (144) of them. Scientists instead weigh a very large number called a **mole**. A mole is

$$600\ 000\ 000\ 000\ 000\ 000\ 000\ 000$$

(or 6×10^{23}) atoms, ions or molecules. This number (6×10^{23}) is known as **Avogadro's number**.

Fig. 18.2(a)   A mole of magnesium

Calculating moles

Atoms
The R.A.M. of magnesium is 24. In 24 g of magnesium it is found that there are 6×10^{23} atoms. Therefore, 24 g of magnesium is a mole of magnesium atoms.

The R.A.M. of carbon is 12. In 12 g of carbon it is found that there are 6×10^{23} atoms. Therefore, 12 g of carbon is 1 mole of carbon atoms.

The masses of material which represent 1 mole of magnesium and 1 mole of carbon are shown in Fig. 18.2.

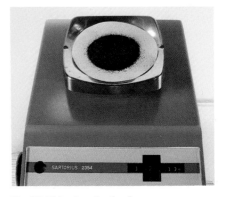

Fig. 18.2(b)   A mole of carbon

Compounds

The relative formula mass of water is:

Formula	H_2O	
Atoms present	$(2 \times H)$	$(1 \times O)$
R.A.M.s	(2×1)	(1×16)

Relative formula mass $= 2 + 16 = 18$.

In 18 g of water it is found that there are 6×10^{23} molecules. Therefore, 18 g of water is one mole of water molecules.

The relative formula mass of sodium chloride is:

Formula	NaCl	
Atoms present	$(1 \times Na)$	$(1 \times Cl)$
R.A.M.s	(1×23)	(1×35.5)

Relative formula mass $= 23 + 35.5 = 58.5$.

In 58.5 g of sodium chloride it is found that there are 6×10^{23} sodium ions and 6×10^{23} chloride ions. Therefore, 58.5 g of sodium chloride is 1 mole of sodium ions plus 1 mole of chloride ions.

The masses of material which represent 1 mole of water and sodium chloride are shown in Fig. 18.3.

In summary, 1 mole of a substance contains 6×10^{23} particles and the mass of this number of particles is found by weighing out the R.A.M. or formula mass in grams.

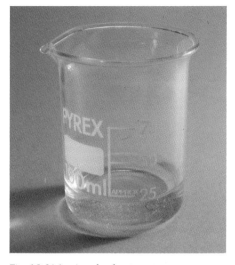

Fig. 18.3(a)   A mole of water

Fig. 18.3(b)   A mole of sodium chloride

Some calculations

1 Calculate the mass of 1 mole of neon atoms.

Symbol	Ne
R.A.M.	20

Mass of 1 mole $= 20$ g.

2 Calculate the mass of 1 mole of hydrogen molecules (*remember* hydrogen is diatomic).

Formula	H_2
Relative formula mass	$(2 \times 1) = 2$

Mass of 1 mole $= 2$ g.

3 Calculate the mass of 1 mole of copper(II) oxide.

Formula	CuO
Relative formula mass	$(1 \times 64) + (1 \times 16) = 80$

Mass of 1 mole $= 80$ g.

4 Calculate the mass of 1 mole of ammonia.

Formula	NH_3
Relative formula mass	$(1 \times 14) + (3 \times 1) = 17$

Mass of 1 mole $= 17$ g.

5 Calculate the mass of 0.5 mole of butane.

Formula	C_4H_{10}
Relative formula mass	$(4 \times 12) + (10 \times 1) = 58$

Mass of 1 mole $= 58$ g.

Hence mass of 0.5 mole $= \dfrac{58}{2} = 29$ g.

6 Calculate the mass of 0.25 mole of bromine.

    Formula Br_2
    Relative formula mass $(2 \times 80) = 160$

    Mass of 1 mole $= 160$ g.

    Hence mass of 0.25 moles $= \dfrac{160}{4} = 40$ g.

7 Calculate the number of moles of magnesium oxide in 20 g of that substance.

    Formula   MgO
    Relative formula mass $(1 \times 24) + (1 \times 16) = 40$

    Mass of 1 mole $= 40$ g.

    Hence 20 g $= \dfrac{20}{40}$ moles $= 0.5$ mole.

8 Calculate the number of moles of calcium oxide in 168 g of that substance.

    Formula   CaO
    Relative formula mass $(1 \times 40) + (1 \times 16) = 56$

    Mass of 1 mole $= 56$ g.

    Hence 168 g $= \dfrac{168}{56}$ moles $= 3$ moles.

Remember:

Mass of substance = mass of 1 mole × number of moles of substance

$$\text{Number of moles of substance} = \frac{\text{mass of substance}}{\text{mass of 1 mole}}$$

Moles and formulae

Empirical formula

The formula of a substance tells you the type and number of atoms present. For example, hydrogen peroxide has the formula H_2O_2. This tells you that: 1 molecule of H_2O_2 contains 2 atoms of hydrogen combined with 2 atoms of oxygen.

If we now refer to moles: 1 mole of hydrogen peroxide molecules contains 2 moles of hydrogen atoms combined with 2 moles of oxygen atoms.

Or in grams: $(2 \times 1) + (2 \times 16) = 34$ g of hydrogen peroxide contains $(2 \times 1) = 2$ g of hydrogen combined with $(2 \times 16) = 32$ g of oxygen.

You can use these ideas to calculate what is called the **empirical formula** of a compound, that is, the simplest ratio of atoms present.

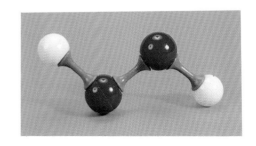

Fig. 18.4   A hydrogen peroxide molecule

Examples

1 0.4 g of calcium reacts with 0.16 g of oxygen to form calcium oxide. What is the empirical formula of calcium oxide?

	Ca	O
Atoms present	Ca	O
Masses	0.4 g	0.16 g
Moles	$\dfrac{0.4}{40} = 0.01$	$\dfrac{0.16}{16} = 0.01$

Simplest ratio of moles   1 : 1

Simplest possible formula is CaO.

2 0.24 g of magnesium react with 0.71 g of chlorine to form magnesium chloride. What is its empirical formula?

	Mg	Cl
Atoms present	Mg	Cl
Masses	0.24 g	0.71 g
Moles	$\dfrac{0.24}{24} = 0.01$	$\dfrac{0.71}{35.5} = 0.02$

Simplest ratio of moles   1 : 2

Simplest possible formula is $MgCl_2$.

Molecular formula

The actual formula of hydrogen peroxide is H_2O_2. This is called the **molecular formula** of the compound. In this formula the ratio of atoms present is 2H : 2O that is 2 : 2 or 1 : 1. As we have already seen, the simplest ratio of 1 : 1 or HO is called the **empirical formula** of the compound. Table 18.1 shows the molecular and empirical formulae for a series of compounds.

You can work out the molecular formula of a compound if you know the empirical formula and its relative molecular mass. For example, the empirical formula of ethene is CH_2 and its relative molecular mass is 28. What is its molecular formula?

Compound	Molecular formula	Empirical formula
Ethane	C_2H_6	CH_3
Ethene	C_2H_4	CH_2
Benzene	C_6H_6	CH

Table 18.1

Empirical formula	CH_2
Relative molecular mass	28
Mass of empirical formula (CH_2)	14

Fig. 18.5(a)   The empirical formula of ethane is CH_3

Fig. 18.5(b)   The empirical formula of ethene is CH_2

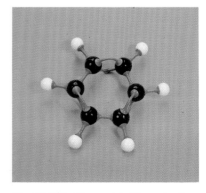

Fig. 18.5(c)   The empirical formula of benzene is CH

Therefore, the number of empirical formula units which make up the
molecule of ethene $= \dfrac{28}{14} = 2$.

$$\begin{aligned}
\text{The molecular formula} &= 2 \times \text{empirical formula} \\
&= 2 \times CH_2 \\
&= C_2H_4
\end{aligned}$$

The molecular formula of ethene is C_2H_4.

Moles and equations

Let us consider the reaction between sulphur and oxygen.

$$\text{sulphur} + \text{oxygen} \longrightarrow \text{sulphur dioxide}$$

$$S_{(s)} + O_{2(g)} \longrightarrow SO_{2(g)}$$

This equation tells you that 1 atom of sulphur *reacts with* 1 molecule
of oxygen *producing* 1 molecule of sulphur dioxide. It also tells you
that 1 mole of sulphur atoms *reacts with* 1 mole of oxygen atoms
producing 1 mole of sulphur dioxide. Since we know the masses of a
mole of oxygen molecules, a mole of sulphur atoms and a mole of
sulphur dioxide molecules, we can replace the numbers of moles by
masses.

$$\text{R.A.M. of sulphur} = 32$$
$$\text{Therefore, 1 mole of S} = 32\,g$$

$$\text{R.A.M. of oxygen} = 16$$
$$\text{Therefore, 1 mole of O} = 32\,g$$

$$\text{Relative formula mass of sulphur dioxide} = 64$$
$$\text{Therefore, 1 mole of SO}_2 = 64\,g$$

Element	Relative atomic mass
H	1
C	12
N	14
O	16
F	19
Ne	20
Mg	24
Ca	40
Cu	64
Br	80

Table 18.2

i.e. 32 g of sulphur dioxide reacts with 32 g of oxygen to produce
64 g of sulphur dioxide.

The method used in the previous example can be shortened. For
example, hydrogen burns in chlorine to produce hydrogen chloride
gas (R.A.M.s are: H = 1, Cl = 35.5).

$$\text{hydrogen} + \text{chlorine} \longrightarrow \text{hydrogen chloride}$$

$$H_{2(g)} + Cl_{2(g)} \longrightarrow 2HCl_{(g)}$$

1 molecule of hydrogen + 1 molecule of chlorine $\longrightarrow$ 2 molecules of hydrogen chloride

$$1 \text{ mole} + 1 \text{ mole} \longrightarrow 2 \text{ moles}$$

$$(1 \times 2) = 2\,g + (2 \times 35.5) = 71\,g \longrightarrow [2 \times (1 + 35.5)] = 73\,g.$$

This tells you that 73 g of hydrogen chloride gas are formed when 2 g
of hydrogen reacts with 71 g of chlorine.

Calculating the mass of product formed in chemical reactions

You can now use this sort of calculation to work out the mass of
product formed.

243

Examples

1 How much magnesium oxide will be produced when 48 g of magnesium are burned in an excess of oxygen. (R.A.M.s are: Mg = 24, O = 16.)

$$\text{magnesium} + \text{oxygen} \longrightarrow \text{magnesium oxide}$$

$$2Mg_{(s)} \quad + \quad O_{2(g)} \quad \longrightarrow \quad 2MgO_{(s)}$$

$$2 \text{ moles} \quad + 1 \text{ mole} \longrightarrow \quad 2 \text{ moles}$$

$$(2 \times 24) = 48 \text{ g} + \frac{\text{excess}}{\text{oxygen}} \longrightarrow [2 \times (24 + 16)] = 80 \text{ g}$$

80 g of magnesium oxide are obtained when 48 g of magnesium are burned in excess oxygen.

2 How much sodium chloride would be produced when 23 g of sodium reacts with an excess of chlorine. (R.A.M.s are: Na = 23, Cl = 35.5.)

$$\text{sodium} + \text{chlorine} \longrightarrow \text{sodium chloride}$$

$$2Na_{(s)} + Cl_{2(g)} \longrightarrow \quad 2NaCl_{(s)}$$

$$2 \text{ moles} \quad + 1 \text{ mole} \longrightarrow \quad 2 \text{ moles}$$

$$(2 \times 23) = 46 \text{ g} + \frac{\text{excess}}{\text{chlorine}} \longrightarrow [2 \times (23 + 35.5)] = 117 \text{ g}.$$

$$1 \text{ g} \qquad \longrightarrow \qquad \frac{117}{46} \text{ g}$$

$$23 \text{ g} \qquad \longrightarrow \qquad \frac{117}{46} \times 23 = 58.5 \text{ g}$$

58.5 g of sodium chloride are obtained when 23 g of sodium react with excess chlorine.

Calculations of mass of reactants required to obtain a given mass of product

Examples

1 Calculate the mass of copper required to produce 160 g of copper(II) oxide when heated in an excess of oxygen. (R.A.M.s are: Cu = 64, O = 16.)

$$\text{copper} + \text{oxygen} \longrightarrow \text{copper(II) oxide}$$

$$2Cu_{(s)} + O_{2(g)} \quad \longrightarrow \quad 2CuO_{(s)}$$

$$2 \text{ moles} + 1 \text{ mole} \longrightarrow \quad 2 \text{ moles}$$

$$(2 \times 64) = 128 \text{ g} + \frac{\text{excess}}{\text{oxygen}} \longrightarrow [2 \times (64 + 16)] = 160 \text{ g}.$$

128 g of copper are required to form 160 g of copper(II) oxide.

2 Calculate the mass of zinc required to produce 81 g of zinc oxide when heated in a excess of oxygen. (R.A.M.s are: Zn = 65, O = 16.)

$$\text{zinc} + \text{oxygen} \longrightarrow \text{zinc oxide}$$

$$2Zn_{(s)} + O_{2(g)} \quad \longrightarrow \quad 2ZnO_{(s)}$$

Fig. 18.6   Magnesium oxide is formed when magnesium burns in the air

Fig. 18.7   Copper, when heated in oxygen, becomes copper(II) oxide

$$2 \text{ moles} + 1 \text{ mole} \longrightarrow 2 \text{ moles}$$

$$(2 \times 65) = 130 \, \text{g} + \begin{array}{c} \text{excess} \\ \text{oxygen} \end{array} \longrightarrow [2 \times (65 + 16)] = 162 \, \text{g}$$

$$\frac{130}{2} (= 65 \, \text{g}) \longrightarrow \frac{162}{2} (= 81 \, \text{g})$$

65 g of zinc are required to produce 81 g of zinc oxide.

Moles and volumes of gases

Some chemical reactions involve gases. In these cases you usually work in volumes. When doing this you use the fact that: *1 mole of any gas, at room temperature and pressure, occupies 24 litres* (24 000 cm³).

The examples below show you how to calculate volumes of gases from given data.

1 Calculate the volume of carbon dioxide produced when 10 g of calcium carbonate are decomposed by heating. (R.A.M.s are: Ca = 40, C = 12, O = 16.)

$$\text{calcium carbonate} \longrightarrow \text{calcium oxide} + \text{carbon dioxide}$$

$$CaCO_{3(s)} \longrightarrow CaO_{(s)} + CO_{2(g)}$$

$$1 \text{ mole} \longrightarrow 1 \text{ mole} + 1 \text{ mole}$$

$$\begin{array}{c} (1 \times 40) + (1 \times 12) + (3 \times 16) \\ = 100 \, \text{g} \end{array} \longrightarrow \begin{array}{c} (1 \times 40) + (1 \times 16) \\ = 56 \, \text{g} \end{array} + 24 \text{ litres}$$

There are 10 g of calcium carbonate which is 10/100 of that shown in the equation. Hence:

$$24 \times \frac{10}{100} = 2.4 \, \text{l of } CO_2 \text{ are produced.}$$

2.4 litres of carbon dioxide are produced when 10 g of calcium carbonate are decomposed by heating.

2 Calculate the volume of water vapour which would be produced if 6 litres of hydrogen were burned in excess oxygen. (R.A.M.s are: H = 1, O = 16.)

$$\text{hydrogen} + \text{oxygen} \longrightarrow \text{water}$$

$$2H_{2(g)} + O_{2(g)} \longrightarrow 2H_2O_{(g)}$$

$$2 \text{ moles} + 1 \text{ mole} \longrightarrow 2 \text{ moles}$$

$$(2 \times 24) = 48 \, \text{l} + \begin{array}{c} \text{excess} \\ \text{oxygen} \end{array} \longrightarrow (2 \times 24) = 48 \, \text{l}$$

There are 6 litres of hydrogen which is 6/48 of that shown in the equation. Hence:

$$48 \times \frac{6}{48} = 6 \, \text{l of water are produced.}$$

6 litres of water vapour are produced when 6 litres of hydrogen are burned in an excess of oxygen.

Moles and solutions

When 1 mole of a substance is dissolved in water and the solution made up to 1 litre ($1000\,cm^3$) a **1 molar** (or 1 M) solution is produced. For example, if 1 mole of sodium hydroxide (NaOH) is dissolved in water and made up to 1 litre then a 1 M solution of sodium hydroxide is produced. How many grams of NaOH would have to be dissolved to produce this 1 M solution? (R.A.M.s are: $Na = 23, O = 16, H = 1$)

$$\text{Formula} \qquad NaOH$$
$$\text{Mass of 1 mole} \qquad 23 + 16 + 1 = 40\,g$$

Hence $40\,g$ of sodium hydroxide are required to produce a 1 M solution.

The more moles present in a given solution the more concentrated the solution is. For example: a 2 M solution is more concentrated than a 1 M solution of the same substance and a 0.1 M solution is less concentrated than a 1 M solution of the same substance. When we write the concentration of solutions in this way we call it a **molarity**.

Using these ideas you can calculate the number of moles present in a given volume of solution.

$$\frac{\text{Number of moles}}{\text{present in a solution}} = \frac{\text{volume of solution }(cm^3)}{1000} \times \frac{\text{molarity of}}{\text{solution}}$$

1 How many moles of potassium sulphate are present in $250\,cm^3$ of its 2 M solution?

$$\text{Volume of solution} = 250\,cm^3$$
$$\text{Molarity} = 2\,M$$
$$\text{number of moles present in solution} = \frac{250}{1000} \times 2$$
$$= 0.5\,mole$$

2 How many moles of magnesium chloride are present in $500\,cm^3$ of its 0.1 M solution?

$$\text{Volume of solution} = 500\,cm^3$$
$$\text{Molarity} = 0.1\,M$$
$$\text{number of moles present in solution} = \frac{500}{1000} \times 0.01$$
$$= 0.005\,mole$$

You may wish to find the mass of substance in such solutions.

3 How many grams of sodium hydroxide (NaOH) are present in $100\,cm^3$ of its 0.1 M solution? (R.A.M.s are: $Na = 23, O = 16, H = 1$.)

$$\text{Volume of solution} = 100\,cm^3$$
$$\text{Molarity} = 0.1\,M$$
$$\text{number of moles present in solution} = \frac{100}{1000} \times 0.1$$
$$= 0.01\,mole$$

$$\text{Relative formula mass of NaOH} = 23 + 16 + 1 = 40$$
$$\text{Mass of 1 mole} = 40\,g$$
$$\text{Hence 0.01 mole is } 40 \times 0.01 = 0.4\,g$$

$0.4\,g$ of sodium hydroxide are in $100\,cm^3$ of its 0.1 M solution.

4 How many grams of potassium nitrate (KNO_3) are present in 500 cm³ of its 2 M solution? (R.A.M.s are: $K = 39, N = 14, O = 16$.)

$$\text{Number of moles present in solution} = \frac{500}{1000} \times 2$$

$$= 1 \text{ mole}$$

Relative formula mass of $KNO_3 = 39 + 14 + (3 \times 16) = 101$

Mass of 1 mole $= \underline{101 \text{ g}}$

101 g of potassium nitrate are present in 500 cm³ of its 2 M solution.

Moles and titrations

The technique of **titration** is used to find the concentration of a solution. This technique is often used in reactions between acids and alkalis.

In the laboratory the titration of hydrochloric acid with sodium hydroxide is normally carried out in the following way. Sodium hydroxide solution (25 cm³) is pipetted into a conical flask (Fig. 18.8). A few drops of phenolphthalein indicator are added. It is pink in alkali conditions and colourless in acid. Hydrochloric acid (0.1 M) is put into the burette (Fig. 18.9). It is filled up exactly to the zero mark using a filter funnel. The filter funnel is removed. The hydrochloric acid is added to the sodium hydroxide solution in small volumes (0.5 cm³ at a time). The contents of the flask are swirled after each addition of acid. The acid is added until the pink colour of the indicator *just* disappears. The final reading on the burette is recorded. This procedure is repeated until consistent results are obtained. Some sample results are shown below.

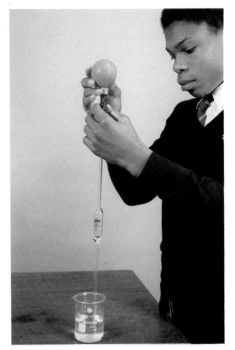

Fig. 18.8(a) Exactly 25 cm³ of sodium hydroxide is pipetted into the conical flask

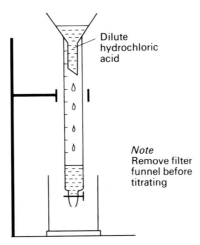

Dilute hydrochloric acid

Note Remove filter funnel before titrating

Fig. 18.9 Dilute acid is poured into the burette

Fig. 18.8(b) The titration is carried out with great care to ensure an accurate volume of acid is added

Volume of sodium hydroxide solution $= 25$ cm³

Average volume of 0.1 M hydrochloric acid added $= 20$ cm³

The neutralization reaction is:

hydrochloric acid + sodium hydroxide $\longrightarrow$ sodium chloride + water

$$HCl_{(aq)} + NaOH_{(aq)} \longrightarrow NaCl_{(aq)} + H_2O_{(l)}$$

You can find out the molarity of the sodium hydroxide solution used by substituting into the following mathematical equation:

$$\frac{M_1 \times V_1}{M_{\text{alkali}}} = \frac{M_2 \times V_2}{M_{\text{acid}}}$$

Where:

M_1 = molarity (concentration) of the alkali used
V_1 = volume of alkali used (cm^3)
M_{alkali} = number of moles of alkali shown in the chemical equation
M_2 = molarity (concentration) of the acid used
V_2 = volume of the acid used (cm^3)
M_{acid} = number of moles of acid shown in the chemical equation

In our example:

M_1 = unknown $M_2 = 0.1$
$V_1 = 25$ $V_2 = 20$
$M_{\text{alkali}} = 1$ $M_{\text{acid}} = 1$

Substituting in the equation:

$$\frac{M_1 \times 25}{1} = \frac{0.1 \times 20}{1}$$

rearranging:

$$M_1 = \frac{0.1 \times 20 \times 1}{1 \times 25}$$

$$M_1 = 0.08 \, M$$

The molarity of sodium hydroxide solution $= 0.08 \, M$.

If $30 \, cm^3$ of $0.1 \, M$ sulphuric acid just neutralized $25 \, cm^3$ of sodium hydroxide solution, what is the concentration of the sodium hydroxide solution?

sodium hydroxide + sulphuric acid $\longrightarrow$ sodium sulphate + water

$$2NaOH_{(aq)} \quad + \quad H_2SO_{4(aq)} \quad \longrightarrow \quad Na_2SO_{4(aq)} \quad + H_2O_{(l)}$$

M_1 = unknown $M_2 = 0.1$
$V_1 = 25$ $V_2 = 30$
$M_{\text{alkali}} = 2$ $M_{\text{acid}} = 1$

Substituting:

$$\frac{M_1 \times 25}{2} = \frac{0.1 \times 30}{1}$$

Rearranging:

$$M_1 = \frac{0.1 \times 30 \times 2}{25 \times 1}$$

$$= 0.24 \, M$$

The molarity of sodium hydroxide used is $0.24 \, M$.

——————————————————— QUESTIONS ———————————————————

1 Calculate the mass (in g) of 1 mole of:
  i) argon;
  ii) nitrogen molecules;
  iii) water;
  iv) calcium oxide.

2 Calculate the mass (in g) of 0.5 mole of:
  i) carbon dioxide;
  ii) zinc oxide;
  iii) ethane;
  iv) copper(II) nitrate.

3 a) 0.24 g of magnesium reacts with 0.38 g of fluorine to form magnesium fluoride. What is the empirical formula of magnesium fluoride?
  b) 0.28 g of silicon reacts with 0.32 g of oxygen to form silicon oxide. What is the empirical formula of silicon oxide?

4 Which member of the alkane family of hydrocarbons contains 75% by mass of carbon?

5 Show that glucose ($C_6H_{12}O_6$) and ethanoic acid (CH_3COOH) have the same empirical formula.

6 i) A hydrocarbon gas contains 80% by mass of carbon. Calculate the empirical formula of this gas.
  ii) The relative formula mass of the hydrocarbon is 30. What is the molecular formula?

7 a) Calculate the empirical formula of a hydrocarbon which contains 92.3% of carbon by mass.
  b) The relative molecular mass of the hydrocarbon is 78. What is its molecular formula?
(JMB 1977)

8 How much zinc oxide will be produced when 13 g of zinc are heated in an excess of oxygen?

9 How much calcium oxide will be produced when 10 g of calcium carbonate are decomposed by heat?

10 6.4 g of a stable allotrope of sulphur were burned completely in air. What mass of sulphur dioxide was formed?

11 Calculate the mass of calcium required to produce 11.2 g of calcium oxide.

12 Calculate the volume of carbon dioxide produced when 8.4 g of magnesium carbonate are decomposed by heating. (1 mole of any gas at room temperature and pressure occupies 24 litres.)

Element	Relative atomic mass
H	1
C	12
N	14
O	16
F	19
Na	23
Si	28
S	32
Cl	35.5
Ar	40
Ca	40
Cu	64
Zn	65

Table 1

13 Calculate the volume of oxygen produced when 6.8 g of hydrogen peroxide are decomposed. (1 mole of any gas at room temperature and pressure occupies 24 litres.)

14 How many moles of sodium chloride are present in 250 cm³ of its 4 M solution?

15 What fraction of a mole of sodium nitrate is present in 100 cm³ of its 0.1 M solution?

16 How many grams of sodium hydroxide are there in 250 cm³ of its 2 M solution?

17 How many grams of magnesium chloride are there in 200 cm³ of its 0.1 M solution?

18 30 cm³ of 0.2 M hydrochloric acid just neutralized 20 cm³ of a sodium hydroxide solution. What is the concentration of the sodium hydroxide solution used?

19 40 cm³ of 0.1 M sulphuric acid just neutralized 20 cm³ of a potassium hydroxide solution. What is the concentration of the potassium hydroxide solution?

20 When lead(IV) oxide is heated, a yellow solid and oxygen are formed. The equation for the reaction is:

$$2PbO_2 \longrightarrow 2PbO + O_2$$

(R.A.M.s are: $O = 16$, $Pb = 207$. The volume of 1 mole of any gas at room temperature and pressure is 24 litres.)

a) i) Name the type of reaction. (1)
   ii) Name the yellow solid. (1)
   iii) What is the relative formula mass of lead(IV) oxide? (1)
   iv) What is the mass in grams of 1 mole of oxygen molecules? (1)
   v) If 4.78 g of lead(IV) oxide is used in the experiment, calculate: the number of moles of oxygen molecules formed and the volume of oxygen formed at room temperature and pressure. (4)

b) i) Describe an experiment by which the yellow solid could be converted to lead. (2)
   ii) Write a symbol equation for this reaction. (2)

(JMB/WMEB 1980)

21 0.048 g of magnesium was reacted with excess dilute sulphuric acid at room temperature and pressure. The hydrogen given off was collected and its volume found to be 50 cm³.
The equation for the reaction is:

$$Mg + H_2SO_4 \longrightarrow MgSO_4 + H_2$$

a) Draw a diagram of an apparatus which could be used for the experiment. (3)
b) How many moles of magnesium were used in the experiment?
   (Relative atomic mass $Mg = 24$.) (2)
c) Using the equation given and your answer to (b), work out the number of moles of hydrogen (H_2) produced by 0.048 g of magnesium. (1)
d) Using your answer to (c), work out the volume of hydrogen which would be produced if 1 mole of magnesium reacted. (2)
e) Calculate the volume of 0.1 M sulphuric acid which would be needed to react exactly with the 0.048 g of magnesium. Show clearly all the steps in your calculation. (3)

(JMB/WMEB 1978)

22 The reaction taking place when carbon monoxide is passed over heated copper(II) oxide is represented by:

$$CO + CuO \longrightarrow CO_2 + Cu$$

a) Complete the sentence below by inserting words chosen from the following list:
   reduced, oxidized, reducing agent, oxidizing agent.

In the reaction the copper(II) oxide is_____ to copper and the carbon monoxide is the _____. (1)

b) Relative atomic masses $C = 12$, $O = 16$, $Cu = 64$. Molar volume of a gas is 24 litres at room temperature and pressure.
Complete the following:
1 mole of carbon monoxide reacts with _____ mole(s) of copper(II) oxide to produce _____ mole(s) of copper. (2)
∴ 24 litres of carbon monoxide at room temperature and pressure react with _____ g of copper(II) oxide to produce _____ g of copper. (2)
∴ _____ litres of carbon monoxide at room temperature and pressure react with 10 g of copper(II) oxide to produce _____ g of copper. (2)

(JMB/WMEB 1981)

23 In a titration of 25 cm³ 1.0 M sodium hydroxide solution against a solution of sulphuric acid, 20 cm³ of the acid was found just to neutralize the alkali completely.

a) Name a suitable indicator for the titration. (1)
b) State the colour change observed with this indicator. (2)
c) Write the equation for the reaction. (1)
d) Calculate the molarity of the acid solution. (2)
e) State the name of the salt formed during the reaction. (2)
f) State the name of a different salt which can be made from sodium hydroxide and sulphuric acid, and write the equation for this reaction. (2)
g) What volume of the same solution of sulphuric acid must be added to 25 cm³ 1.0 M sodium hydroxide in order to prepare this different salt? (1)
h) Describe one simple chemical test which you would use to differentiate between crystalline samples of the two salts named in (e) and (f). Give the result of the test with each salt. (3)

(JMB 1977)

24 a) When 1.5 g of a hydrocarbon were completely burned in oxygen, only carbon dioxide and water were formed. When the products were passed through a reagent which absorbed all the water vapour, it was found that 2.7 g of water had been formed.
(Relative atomic masses: $H = 1$, $C = 12$, $O = 16$. 1 mole of gas at room temperature and pressure occupies 24 000 cm³.)
   i) State what is meant by the term 'hydrocarbon'. (1)

ii) Calculate the mass of hydrogen present in 2.7 g of water. (2)

iii) What mass of carbon is present in 1.5 g of the hydrocarbon? (1)

iv) Calculate the empirical formula of the hydrocarbon. (2)

b) 0.125 g of the gaseous hydrocarbon occupy a volume of 100 cm³ at room temperature and pressure.

i) Calculate the relative molecular mass of the hydrocarbon. (2)

ii) Determine the molecular formula of the hydrocarbon. (2)

(JMB 1983)

25 Consider the following information about an imaginary new element named bodium, symbol Bo, which has recently been discovered.

'Bodium is a solid at room temperature but is easily cut with a knife to reveal a shiny surface which rapidly tarnishes. It reacts vigorously with water liberating a flammable gas and forming à solution with a high pH value. When bodium reacts with chlorine, it forms a white solid containing 29.5% by mass of chlorine. A_r(Bo) = 85.'

a) Calculate the empirical formula of bodium chloride. (3)

b) To which group in the periodic table should bodium be assigned? (1)

c) What type of bonding is likely to be present in bodium chloride? (1)

d) If concentrated aqueous bodium chloride was electrolysed, what would be the main products discharged at carbon electrodes? Write equations for the reactions which take place. (4)

e) Write an equation and name the products for the reaction between bodium and water. (2)

f) Write the formula for (i) bodium nitrate and (ii) bodium carbonate. For each of these compounds, state whether it would be expected to decompose at Bunsen burner temperature. Name any product(s) and write an equation for any reaction which occurs. (5)

(AEB 1983)

26 a) A hydrocarbon contains 82.8% carbon. Determine the empirical (i.e. simplest) formula for this compound. (5)

b) A rough estimation puts the relative molecular mass of this hydrocarbon between 50 and 60. What is the actual value? Explain your answer. (3)

(OLE 1983)

27 a) i) A compound containing sulphur and chlorine only contains 47.4% of sulphur by mass. Determine the empirical (i.e. the simplest) formula for this substance. (4)

ii) Given that the relative molecular mass of this compound is 135, what further information does this tell us about the molecules of this sulphur chloride? (2)

b) Sulphur dichloride dioxide (SO_2Cl_2) reacts with water to form sulphuric acid and hydrogen chloride only.

i) Write a balanced equation for this reaction. (2)

ii) How could you show that this reaction is *exothermic*? (2)

(OLE 1984)

APPENDIX 1
RADIOACTIVITY

Elements with an atomic number greater than 83 have unstable nuclei. The nuclei of these atoms split up with the emission of certain types of radiation. These isotopes are called **radioisotopes**. When this happens new elements are formed. Atoms whose nuclei do this are called **radioactive**.

One or more of three types of radiation may be emitted. They are named with the Greek letters alpha, beta and gamma (see Fig. A.2):

α-particle

β^--particle

γ-rays

Some of the properties of these emissions are shown in Table A.1.

Fig. A1   When an atomic bomb explodes a huge amount of energy is released as well as a deadly burst of radioactivity

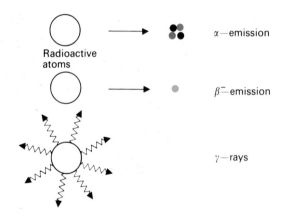

Fig. A2   Types of radiation

Radiation	Nature	Relative charge	Ability to penetrate	Effect on nucleus of atom when radiation emitted
α-particle	2 protons and 2 neutrons (written as $^4_2\alpha$)	$+2$	Stopped by a few sheets of paper	Mass number decreases by 4. Atomic number decreases by 2
β^--particle	Electron	-1	Stopped by a few mm of plastic	Mass number is unchanged but atomic number is increased by 1
γ-rays	Electromagnetic radiation with shorter wavelength than x-rays	0	Stopped by several cm of lead	No change to mass number or atomic number. However, nucleus does lose energy

Table A.1

Both β^--particles and γ-rays can easily pass through the skin and damage or even kill cells (see Fig. A3). This can cause illness and even death. α-particles are not as dangerous since they cannot penetrate the skin, however, they can be dangerous if they get inside the body.

The radiations are usually detected using an instrument called a **Geiger counter** (see Fig. A4). The radiations trigger electrical signals which are electronically counted.

Radioactive decay

When radioactive atoms split up and emit α- or β^--particles they are said to **decay**. The process is known as **radioactive decay**. During the process new elements are formed.

α-particles are usually emitted from heavier nuclei (high atomic number) which have too much mass to be stable. For example, radium-206 ($^{206}_{88}Ra$) emits α-particles. It is said to undergo α-decay. When it emits the α-particle ($^4_2\alpha$) the mass number of the atom decreases by 4 and the atomic number decreases by 2. Hence an atom is formed with a nucleus of mass number, $(206-4) = 202$, and atomic number $(88-2) = 86$. So the product of this change is $^{202}_{86}Rn$. This description can be simplified to:

$$^{206}_{88}Ra \longrightarrow {}^{202}_{86}Rn + {}^4_2\alpha$$

β^--particles are usually emitted from heavier nuclei which have too many neutrons compared with the number of protons. One neutron changes to a proton and an electron. The emitted electrons come from the nucleus.

$$\text{neutron} \longrightarrow \text{proton} + \text{electron}$$

The product then has one more proton than the starting isotope. For example, thorium-234 ($^{234}_{90}Th$) undergoes β^--decay:

$$^{234}_{90}Th \longrightarrow {}^{234}_{91}Pa + \beta^-$$

γ-rays usually accompany α- or β^--emission. Different atoms are not produced when γ-rays are emitted.

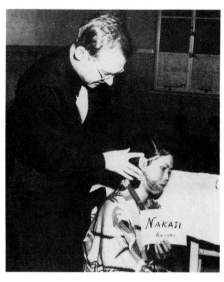

Fig. A3   A World War II victim with radiation burns

Fig. A4   A geiger counter measures amounts of radiation

Half-life

Radioactive isotopes decay at a particular rate. The **half-life** ($t_{1/2}$) of a radioactive isotope is the time taken for half its atoms to decay. Some radioactive isotopes have a very long half-life whilst others have a very short half-life. For example, the half-life of $^{14}_6C$ is about 6000 years whilst that for $^{214}_{84}Po$ is less than half a second.

Let us take a closer look at the half-life of $^{14}_6C$. In 6000 years half of the atoms will have decayed by β^--emission:

$$^{14}_6C \longrightarrow {}^{14}_7N + \beta^-$$

In another 6000 years half of the remainder will have decayed. We will now have a quarter of the original atoms left, and so on. If a Geiger counter is used to measure the radioactivity of $^{14}_6C$ samples then it would be found that the counts taken (per minute) decrease in a similar way (see Fig. A5).

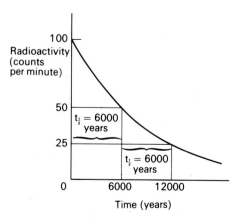

Fig. A5   A graph showing how the radioactivity of carbon-14 changes with time

Uses of radioactivity

Radioactive isotopes are used widely throughout industry and in the field of medicine (see Fig. A6).

1 Nuclear power stations—A tremendous amount of energy is released when uranium-235 decays. This is harnessed in a nuclear power station to produce electricity (see Chapter 17, page 229). In an atomic bomb the nuclear fission of uranium-235 proceeds at an uncontrolled rate resulting in a tremendous explosion (see Fig. A1).

2 Carbon dating—The most common isotope of carbon is $^{12}_{6}C$. However, there is another isotope which is radioactive—$^{14}_{6}C$. Small and constant quantities of this isotope are present in all living things. When the plant or animal dies no more $^{14}_{6}C$ is taken in and the proportion present undergoes radioactive decay. So by measuring the amount of $^{14}_{6}C$ left it is possible to determine the age of a sample such as that shown in Fig. A7.

Fig. A6   Because of a large increase in the use of radioactive isotopes in industry and medicine, radiation levels in their workers have to be constantly monitored. The blue lapel badge records any radioactivity that the wearer is exposed to

Fig. A7   Found at Lindow Moss, south of Manchester, the 'age' of this 'Bogman' was determined using carbon-14 dating. He died about 2000 years ago

3 Tracers—Leaks in oil or gas pipes or in ventilating systems can be detected by using radioactive material. Also, the activity of the thyroid gland can be monitored by use of radioactive iodine. When isotopes are used in this way they are termed **radioactive tracers**.

Radiation leaks and can be detected

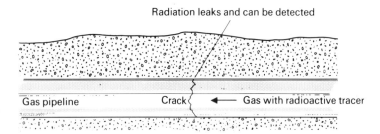

Gas pipeline   Crack   ◄—— Gas with radioactive tracer

Fig. A8   Using radioactivity to detect leaks in a pipeline

4 Nuclear fusion—There are some nuclei which can be made to fuse together. When this takes place there is usually a very large release of energy. This is the process which takes place in the Sun

(see Fig. A9) and it is also the process by which a hydrogen bomb works. Nuclear scientists are currently attempting to control the fusion process. If they succeed, the world will have a major new source of energy.

5 Medicine—The radiations from a cobalt-60 source can be harnessed to treat some cancers. Surgical instruments can also be sterilized by γ-radiation. (See Fig. A10.)

6 Industry—Radiation from radioactive isotopes can be used to monitor and control the filling of containers (see Fig. A11). A sudden decrease in the radiation reaching the detector in Fig. A11 means that the liquid has been filled up to the correct mark. The thickness of paper and plastic can be monitored in a similar way.

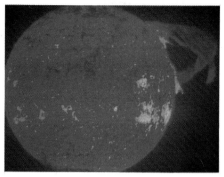

Fig. A9   Nuclear fusion takes place in the centre of the Sun

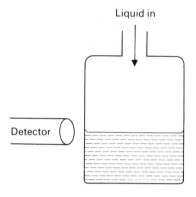

Fig. A11 The filling of containers can be monitored using radiation from radioactive isotopes

Fig. A10   One use of radioactive isotopes in medicine. Strips of iridium wire are being prepared prior to implantation in malignant tissue to kill tumour cells

—QUESTIONS—

1 The graph below shows how the radioactivity of a sample of a radioactive substance changes with time.

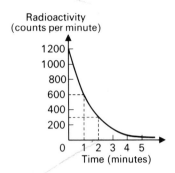

Radioactivity
(counts per minute)

a) What is the approximate half-life of the substance?
b) What instrument could be used to detect the radiations produced?
c) What is the count rate after 2 minutes?

2 a) Name a radioactive element which is used in nuclear power stations.
   b) Name the isotope of carbon used in carbon dating.
   c) How may radioisotopes be used as 'tracers'?
   d) Which radioactive isotope of cobalt is used in

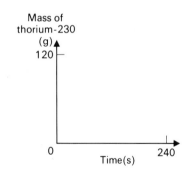

Mass of
thorium-230
(g)

Time(s)

   medicine to treat cancer?
   e) How may radioisotopes be used to control the filling of containers in industry?

3 On a piece of graph paper plot the decay of 120 g of thorium-230 (half-life 60 s) over 4 minutes. Use axes like those shown above.

4     $^{212}_{83}\text{Bi} \xrightarrow{\beta\text{-emission}} \text{Po} \xrightarrow{\alpha\text{-emission}} \text{Pb}$

The above scheme shows how the radioactive isotope of bismuth, $^{212}_{83}\text{Bi}$, changes first to polonium, Po, and finally to lead, Pb.
a) Explain what is meant by (i) β-emission and (ii) α-emission.
b) State the *atomic number* and *mass number* of (i) polonium, and (ii) lead, in the scheme.
c) State what is meant by the *half-life* of a radioactive element.   (5)
(WJEC 1983)

5 a) For the named emissions which occur in radioactivity, give:

	α (alpha)	β (beta)
i) the masses,	_____	_____
ii) the charges,	_____	_____

   b) i) For the three stages of the radioactive decay of the isotope of radium, of mass number 228, enter in the appropriate spaces the *atomic numbers, mass numbers* and *types of radiations emitted* (α or β).

   $^{228}\text{Ra} \longrightarrow \, ^{228}_{89}\text{Ac} \longrightarrow \text{Th} \longrightarrow \, ^{224}\text{Ra}$

      ii) Give the composition of the nuclei of the two isotopes of radium.   (6)
(WJEC 1982)

6 a) Name the *two* types of particle present in the nucleus of a carbon atom.   (2)
   b) State the relationship between the numbers of these particles and
      i) the atomic number of an atom;   (1)
      ii) the mass number of an atom.   (1)
   c) State *two* similarities between different isotopes of the same element.   (2)
   d) A radioactive isotope of carbon is a β-emitter. The decay process is represented by the nuclear reaction:

   $$^{14}_{6}\text{C} \longrightarrow \, ^{A}_{Z}\text{X} + \, ^{0}_{-1}\text{e}$$

      i) Write down the value of A.   (1)
      ii) Write down the value of Z.   (1)
(AEB 1984)

APPENDIX 2 THE ELEMENTS

The atomic masses are relative to carbon-12 ($^{12}C = 12.00$).
The values in brackets represent the most stable known isotopes.

Element	Symbol	Atomic number	Relative atomic mass	Approximate atomic mass	Element	Symbol	Atomic number	Relative atomic mass	Approximate atomic mass
Actinium	Ac	89	(227)	227	Mercury	Hg	80	200.59	201
Aluminium	Al	13	26.9815	27	Molybdenum	Mo	42	95.94	96
Americium	Am	95	(243)	243	Neodymium	Nd	60	144.24	144
Antimony	Sb	51	121.75	122	Neon	Ne	10	20.179	20
Argon	Ar	18	39.948	40	Neptunium	Np	93	(237)	237
Arsenic	As	33	74.9216	75	Nickel	Ni	28	58.71	59
Astatine	At	85	(210)	210	Niobium	Nb	41	92.906	93
Barium	Ba	56	137.34	137	Nitrogen	N	7	14.0067	14
Berkelium	Bk	97	(249)	249	Nobelium	No	102	(253)	253
Beryllium	Be	4	9.0122	9	Osmium	Os	76	190.2	190
Bismuth	Bi	83	208.980	209	Oxygen	O	8	15.9994	16
Boron	B	5	10.811	11	Palladium	Pd	46	106.4	106
Bromine	Br	35	79.909	80	Phosphorus	P	15	30.9738	31
Cadmium	Cd	48	112.40	112	Platinum	Pt	78	195.09	195
Caesium	Cs	55	132.905	133	Plutonium	Pu	94	(242)	242
Calcium	Ca	20	40.08	40	Polonium	Po	84	(210)	210
Californium	Cf	98	(251)	251	Potassium	K	19	39.102	39
Carbon	C	6	12.01115	12	Praseodymium	Pr	59	140.907	141
Cerium	Ce	58	140.12	140	Promethium	Pm	61	(147)	147
Chlorine	Cl	17	35.453	35.5	Protoactinium	Pa	91	(231)	231
Chromium	Cr	24	51.996	52	Radium	Ra	88	(226)	226
Cobalt	Co	27	58.9332	59	Radon	Rn	86	(222)	222
Copper	Cu	29	63.54	64	Rhenium	Re	75	186.23	186
Curium	Cm	96	(247)	247	Rhodium	Rh	45	102.905	103
Dysprosium	Dy	66	162.50	162	Rubidium	Rb	37	85.47	85
Einsteinium	Es	99	(254)	254	Ruthenium	Ru	44	101.07	101
Erbium	Er	68	167.26	167	Samarium	Sm	62	150.35	150
Europium	Eu	63	151.96	152	Scandium	Sc	21	44.956	45
Fermium	Fm	100	(253)	253	Selenium	Se	34	78.96	79
Fluorine	F	9	18.9984	19	Silicon	Si	14	28.086	28
Francium	Fr	87	(223)	223	Silver	Ag	47	107.868	108
Gadolinium	Gd	64	157.25	157	Sodium	Na	11	22.9898	23
Gallium	Ga	31	69.72	70	Strontium	Sr	38	87.62	88
Germanium	Ge	32	72.59	73	Sulphur	S	16	32.064	32
Gold	Au	79	196.967	197	Tantalum	Ta	73	180.948	181
Hafnium	Hf	72	178.49	178.5	Technetium	Tc	43	(99)	99
Helium	He	2	4.0026	4	Tellurium	Te	52	127.60	128
Holmium	Ho	67	164.930	165	Terbium	Tb	65	158.924	159
Hydrogen	H	1	1.00797	1	Thallium	Tl	81	204.37	204
Indium	In	49	114.82	115	Thorium	Th	90	232.038	232
Iodine	I	53	126.9044	127	Thulium	Tm	69	168.934	169
Iridium	Ir	77	192.2	192	Tin	Sn	50	118.69	119
Iron	Fe	26	55.847	56	Titanium	Ti	22	47.90	48
Krypton	Kr	36	83.80	84	Tungsten	W	74	183.85	184
Lanthanum	La	57	138.91	139	Uranium	U	92	238.03	238
Lawrencium	Lw	103	(257)	257	Vanadium	V	23	50.942	51
Lead	Pb	82	207.19	207	Xenon	Xe	54	131.30	131
Lithium	Li	3	6.939	7	Ytterbium	Yb	70	173.04	173
Lutetium	Lu	71	174.97	175	Yttrium	Y	39	88.905	89
Magnesium	Mg	12	24.312	24	Zinc	Zn	30	65.37	65
Manganese	Mn	25	54.9380	55	Zirconium	Zr	40	91.22	91
Mendelevium	Md	101	(256)	256					

APPENDIX 3
THE PERIODIC TABLE

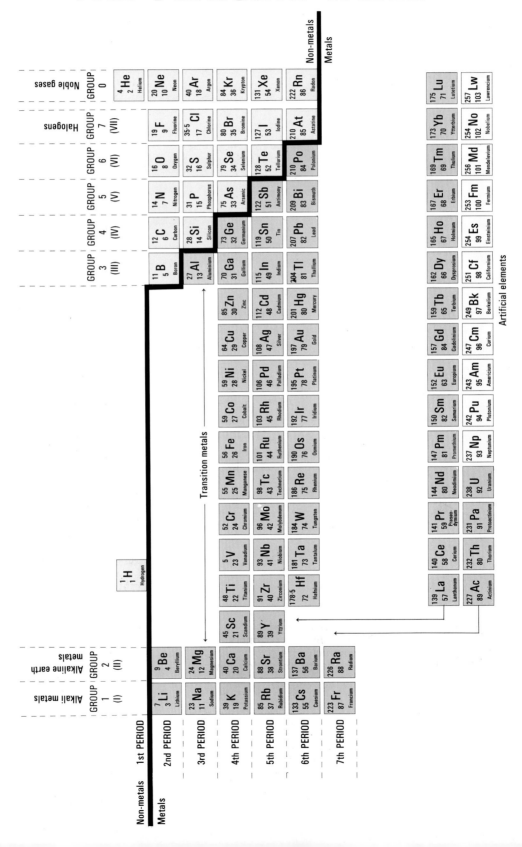

INDEX

The following examination boards kindly granted permission to reproduce questions from past examination papers:

University of Oxford Delegacy of Local Examinations
Joint Matriculation Board
Northern Examining Association (Associated Lancashire Schools Examining Board, Joint Matriculation Board, North Regional Examinations Board, North West Regional Examinations Board, Yorkshire and Humberside Regional Examinations Board)
Oxford and Cambridge Schools Examination Board
The Associated Examining Board
Southern Universities Joint Board
Welsh Joint Education Committee
University of Cambridge Local Examinations Syndicate